Dear General MacArthur

誓願書

今より四十餘年前　西洋の仏像の掛
物を今ふを家宝として庶人等を信仰する
ことして來ます
病をも治して來ます
如何ぞや其慈悲へもう少しや小検閲
右此願に

三重縣桑名郡天名村大字御願三四三
宮崎末蔵

明治十六年八月三十日　書年六十四才

Dear General MacArthur

Letters from the Japanese during the American Occupation

Sodei Rinjirō

Edited by JOHN JUNKERMAN

Translated by SHIZUE MATSUDA

Foreword by JOHN W. DOWER

ROWMAN & LITTLEFIELD PUBLISHERS, INC.
Lanham • Boulder • New York • Oxford

ROWMAN & LITTLEFIELD PUBLISHERS, INC.

Published in the United States of America
by Rowman & Littlefield Publishers, Inc.
4720 Boston Way, Lanham, Maryland 20706
www.rowmanlittlefield.com

12 Hid's Copse Road, Cumnor Hill, Oxford OX2 9JJ, England

Distributed by NATIONAL BOOK NETWORK

British Library Cataloguing-in-Publication Information Available

ISBN 0-7425-1115-4 (cloth only)

Printed in the United States of America

♾ ™ The paper used in this publication meets the minimum requirements of American National Standard for Information Sciences—Permanence of Paper for Printed Library Materials, ANSI/NISO Z39.48-1992.

CONTENTS

PHOTOGRAPHS

March 20th, 1950.

Sir,

I am Mitsue Sakuta, wife of Kiyoshi Sakuta, who was removed from Java to Japan and was sent to Sugamo Prison on the 29th of January, 1950.

At first I thought it was a dream but I could know it was true. I was greatly rejoiced at the news and I don't know how to express my rapture.

Many thanks for your and G. H. Q's kind intention to make my husband return.

He will surely live a life worthy living, thanking your kindness to give him a delight of restoration of life.

I pray a peaceful world will soon come!

Respectfully yours,

Mitsue Sakuta

To the Supreme Commander for the Allied Powers, General MacArthur

MITSUE SAKUTA
3-Ishikawa Kawamata-machi
Date-gun, Fukushima-ken

FOREWORD

Hail, the conquering hero! All peoples, all nations, do this. Myth, history, and public memory resonate with paeans to great generals and commanders. And almost invariably, the military leader whom a people idolize is one of their own. He is the putative creator of one's culture, the founder of one's state, the extender of one's imperial or national glory, the victor in foreign wars, the defender of one's native place. He is progenitor, father, protector. He is the culture, race, people writ large.

But what, then, are we to make of the Japanese response to General Douglas MacArthur after World War II that emerges so vividly in this fascinating book? MacArthur arrived in defeated Japan in August 1945 at the head of a huge American army of occupation and did not leave until over five years later. It would be an understatement to describe the reception he received as cordial. It was commonly adulatory and frequently bordered on the ecstatic. Here was a conquering hero hailed by the very people he had conquered.

It is difficult to think of anything comparable to this in the history of modern nations. In the wake of a defeat that shattered almost everything they had been indoctrinated to believe in, the Japanese turned the leader of yesterday's reviled enemy into the preeminent symbol of their deepest hopes and aspirations. Douglas MacArthur became a *Japanese* "culture hero" in ways his own American compatriots back home could never fully appreciate. In April 1951, when he was dismissed by President Truman for insubordination in his conduct of the war in Korea and simultaneously relieved of his command over occupied Japan, his Japanese admirers were thunderstruck. Crowds lined the streets of Tokyo to say farewell. Handmade signs read in English, "We love you, General MacArthur."

This is a remarkable episode in Japan's modern history. Indeed, it is more than that. It is a moment in Japanese-American relations that can be used to cast a searching light on historical memory and political consciousness in Japan today. And there is no better way to recreate all this than to listen to the Japanese voices of the time. This is what Professor Sodei has enabled us to do in this collection of intimate writings selected from the enormous number of letters Japanese wrote to General MacArthur and his staff during the long occupation that followed their lost war. This is a rare gem of a book. There is nothing else like it.

It is all too easy to belittle the positive Japanese response to General MacArthur with a smattering of popular psychology. Revering the country's new strongman, such arguments commonly go, was just old Japanese wine in a new bottle. The "herd mentality" of the Japanese predisposed them to acquiesce to authoritarian leaders. The "situation ethics" of the indigenous value system made it easy to esteem today what had been condemned only yesterday. "Popular consciousness" in Japan was but a weathervane, turning with whatever winds came in from on high. When the leadership commanded them to "die for the country," Japanese men, women, and even adolescents did so (unlike, we are apparently meant to assume, other peoples in other places). When the Japanese were told to "be good losers," they likewise did as they were told.

These are problematic notions, as we shall see, but we cannot just dismiss them out of hand. General MacArthur himself loved to ruminate on how understanding "the Oriental mind" was the key to promoting drastic reform in defeated Japan. As he explained it, Asian peoples, and the Japanese foremost among them, revered authority and could therefore be expected to go along with drastic changes dictated from above. The general was a thespian at heart; and with these Orientalist stage directions in mind, he threw himself into playing the role of a blue-eyed shogun or, indeed, into playing a more truly "imperial" role. When Japanese wrote letters praising him, they occasionally employed extravagant language that hitherto had been reserved for their own emperor. And MacArthur obviously relished such adoration.

Professor Sodei calls attention to these issues in his introduction, and rightly so. For if MacArthur's perceived mission in defeated Japan was to promote a transition to genuine democracy, this seemed an inherently contradictory way of doing so. From 1945 to 1949, MacArthur's command exercised formal censorship over the Japanese media, and until the end of the occupation the supreme commander and his overwhelmingly American staff were more impervious to criticism than the imperial Japanese military establishment had been even at the height of the war. Democracy under Shogun MacArthur, or Emperor Douglas, was democracy in a box. Once the occupation ended, the question was which would be the greater inheritance—the democratic legacy or the box itself.

There is a further dimension to the Japanese veneration of the conqueror that carries us into even more controversial areas—the issue of race. Imagine that the occupation of defeated Japan after World War II had been carried out not by the Americans but by the Chinese. Certainly the Chinese had earned the right to do this. Their war with Japan had lasted much longer, going back to 1937 (or, by another reckoning, to 1931). Their human losses were incalculably greater: around 15 million Chinese, possibly more, died in the war with Japan, compared with 100,000 U.S. combat deaths. The physical devastation they suffered as a consequence of Japan's aggression was incalculable. But could a Chinese conqueror, or any other non-Caucasian, have garnered the awe and adulation and plain respect that was accorded to MacArthur?

The answer is surely no. Here we enter a truly convoluted realm of psychohistory, tracing back in Japan's case to the mid-nineteenth century and the emergence of its volatile love/hate relationship with the more powerful "West." If we dwell on considerations such as this, embracing the alien conqueror after August 1945 becomes but the latest cycle in modern Japan's tumultuous engagement with the enticing and elusive chimera known as "Western civilization." MacArthur is transformed into the Great White Father. He becomes the white man as demigod.

The intimate letters Professor Sodei has so masterfully collected do not entirely repudiate such facile psychologizing. Rather, they reveal how thin and insufficient this is as a way of explaining Japanese hopes and dreams in the wake of shattering defeat. These intensely personal communications draw us into private worlds that the grand theories all but obliterate. They enable us to listen to *individuals* and, in the process, to appreciate the diversity of voices that found expression after Japan had surrendered unconditionally to the Allied Powers.

Prior to the defeat, ordinary Japanese did not and could not express their thoughts so openly. They did not inundate their prewar or wartime leaders with unsolicited letters, as they inundated MacArthur and his staff. They dared not speak freely about private aspirations (as opposed to public "duties") or praise "democracy" (a pejorative term in the ideological tracts of the war years, synonymous with "egoism," "materialism," and "decadence"). They were unable to express the despair they really felt when the notices of kin killed in battle arrived or when the war dragged on and on, clearly without hope of victory, or when the bombs came home and Japan's cities began to be systematically destroyed.

It is in this sense that these letters reveal a "psychology" of war and defeat *and starting over* that is more intricate, and more interesting, than theories about socialization for obedience or about collective feelings of cultural and racial inferiority. They lay bare the bone-deep war weariness that made so many postwar Japanese receptive to drastic change. They convey an almost visceral disgust with the incompetence of the ruling groups that had led the country into disaster, which goes far toward clarifying why it seemed appropriate to look *outside* for new leadership at the very highest level. And they express heartfelt, explicit appreciation for the early reformist policies associated with MacArthur's rule that helps illuminate why he was perceived as a conqueror who had brought genuinely beneficial "gifts from afar" to Japan. Here was a con-quering hero widely seen as not merely strong but also generous—and not just generous, but visionary.

The vision MacArthur articulated and personified found shorthand expression in a simple, compelling slogan. The victors defined their ob-jectives as bringing about the thoroughgoing "demilitarization and de-mocratization" of Japan. In Japanese parlance, the keywords became "peace" and "democracy." "Construct a nation of peace" (*Heiwa kokka kensetsu*) and "Construct a democratic nation" (*Minshushugi kokka kensetsu*) became by far the most popular slogans of the day, written out in schoolroom calligraphy lessons and discussed in local and community forums that involved virtually every sector of society. A third ubiquitous slogan, "Construct a nation of culture" (*Bunka kokka kensetsu*), really just reprised the other two: in these turbulent years, it went without saying that there could be no truly meaningful "culture"—for the Japanese or for anyone else—that did not encompass peace and de-mocracy.

Why should we take such sloganeering seriously? Were these not the same people who, indoctrinated and inspired by other rousing slogans, had just ravaged China and much of Asia?

These are valid questions that bring us back to the old situation ethics arguments. And it is precisely intimate, voluminous materials such as the letters to the supreme commander that enable us to assess the depth *and roots* of this popular engagement with the rhetoric of "peace" and "democracy." In my own reading of such materials—not only these letters but also the broader outpouring of writings and other forms of expression that flooded Japan in the wake of the war—I do not find the sentiments expressed superficial. Obviously, there are cranks and sycophants and special pleaders among the letter writers. There are dim bulbs as well as bright ones, and an embarrassing number of self-appointed informants, eager to condemn former officials and even their own neighbors. Unhappy and hateful letters are interspersed among more sanguine expressions of hope and gratitude. Praise of the occupa-tion is leavened with more than a few frank expressions of criticism. The range of individuals whom Professor Sodei has enabled us to listen in on is impressive, and what they have to say, as well as how they say it, is full of surprises. It is difficult to imagine any serious reader putting down these pages and thinking that he or she has merely encountered puppets voicing the puppeteer's words. There is no homogeneous "herd mentality" here.

On the contrary, the letters help us understand why the ideals of peace and democracy were not just catchphrases plucked from some voguish checklist of "Western ideas." Their attraction derived, first and foremost, from the prolonged and bitter war experience itself. Most Japanese did not give much thought to the misery they had inflicted on others. Like other peoples, they were obsessed and overwhelmed by their own suffering and victimization. Close to 3 million Japanese died in the war (out of a population of 70 million), and millions more were stranded overseas; some took years to return, and many never made it back at all. Sixty-six cities had been heavily bombed, culminating in the nuclear devastation of Hiroshima and Nagasaki. Illness, homelessness, and unemployment were rampant. War had savaged them; they cherished peace. Authoritarianism and outright police state repression had led them to follow irresponsible leaders into the very maw of disaster; "democracy" promised to enable them to take greater future control over their lives.

No Japanese leader, at war's end, offered any real vision for creating a new Japan out of the ruins of the old. It became MacArthur's destiny to do this, and he possessed the absolute authority to wed his words to action. Under MacArthur, the Japanese military was dissolved and a gamut of truly radical reforms was introduced by fiat, ranging from broad guarantees of civil liberties to land reform to revision of the structure and content of the educational system. As the Cold War intensified, U.S. occupation policy underwent a partial "reverse course" and shifted from reform to the reconstruction of Japan as an economic and military ally. To the very end, however, MacArthur continued to extol the social and political "revolution" the Japanese had embarked upon under his aegis.

Did these letters play any role in buoying his optimism concerning the thoroughgoing nature of this transformation? We can not say for sure, but it is difficult to think otherwise. Many of the letters we encounter here in *Dear General MacArthur* come from the general's personal files. They were carefully selected for his perusal by his staff, and they constitute one of the most intensely personalized ways by which he kept abreast of public opinion and evaluated the success of his mission. Most certainly, he read these communications carefully. And having read them, how could he not have been impressed?

The supreme commander was also held in esteem for reasons beyond his grand agenda per se. In our present-day world, where the Japanese have perfected the art of conspicuous consumption, for instance, it is all but impossible to picture Japan being on the verge of widespread starvation in 1945–1946. But it was, and serious food shortages continued to plague the country through 1949. MacArthur's authorization of massive relief shipments of basic foodstuffs helped avert disaster. At the same time, his image as a great humanitarian was enhanced by efforts to hasten repatriation of the millions of servicemen and civilians who were stranded overseas (a large percentage of letters focused on this issue). In such ways, the supreme commander's "benevolence" entered virtually every household in the most concrete manner imaginable.

In extolling "democracy," moreover, MacArthur was not promoting concepts alien to Japan. Japanese could—and did—turn to their own history for multiple examples of thwarted liberal or liberating traditions. They were able to point to concepts of repentance, conversion, rebirth, and egalitarianism in Buddhist teachings that dated back to the thirteenth century, for example, and to "rediscover" progressive notions of social justice even among writers of the late feudal period. The recurrent waves of peasant protest that swept over Japan between the seventeenth and mid-nineteenth centuries were evoked as a harbinger of genuine grassroots rebellion.

Moving on to "modern" times, both academics and political activists hastened to call attention to the "liberty and people's rights" movement of the 1870s and early 1880s, which had been effectively squelched by the oligarchic architects of the modern imperial state. They pointed to the rise of a labor movement after the turn of the century, and the flawed but still promising trends in parliamentary party politics that emerged around the same time. Socialism, communism, and feminism all had prewar roots in Japan. Such early twentieth-century developments, collectively referred to as the epoch of "Taishō democracy," had been aborted by the rise of militarism. Indeed, when hundreds of thousands of Japanese celebrated May Day in 1946, this was the seventeenth such annual celebration in Japanese history. The demonstrators—liberated by MacArthur's reformist edicts—were reviving an event that had been banned by the government in the mid-1930s.

In perhaps the most subtle of all permutations, MacArthur also offered the Japanese the possibility of a new nationalism wrapped in remnants of the old. When he told them—as he often did—that they might redeem their country's good name by becoming a beacon of "peace and democracy" that other nations could admire and emulate in the future, he was appealing directly to national pride. Here was a proud people shamed, reviled, brought to their knees, momentarily dispossessed even of sovereignty—and their conqueror was telling them they could turn all this into moral victory by undergoing *and institutionalizing* genuine conversion. Such a nation, MacArthur was promising, could look forward to a secure, honorable future in the global arena from which it was presently ostracized.

This was the compelling vision of a "new" nationalism. The old nationalism in which MacArthur wrapped this entailed not merely retention of the imperial system, but also the exoneration of Emperor Hirohito (who had reigned since 1926) from any taint of war responsibility, thus enabling him to remain on the throne. We may question the wisdom of this policy today, especially from the perspective of Japan's continuing difficulty in coming to terms with its war responsibility. Be that as it may, it unquestionably eased MacArthur's task and—as letters here attest—further burnished his image as a conqueror who respected the wishes of those whom he had conquered.

All of this came together in the famous "MacArthur constitution." This hybrid new national charter—this new "imperial democracy"—was drafted in MacArthur's headquarters in early 1946 and promulgated later that year after extensive discussion and moderate revision in the parliament. It came into effect the following year. Popular sovereignty was established—making all Japanese "citizens" for the very first time, rather than "subjects" of the emperor as had been the case under the old constitution. The emperor was designated "symbol of the State and of the unity of the people"—rather than "sacred and inviolable," as previously. Both the constitution's preamble and its "no war" provision (Article 9) renounced the right of the state to resort to belligerency—thus giving the "MacArthur constitution" an equally famous tandem sobriquet: the "peace constitution." Beyond this, article after article encoded strong guarantees of human and civil rights—in striking contrast to the old constitution's emphasis on the authority of the state and corresponding duties of the emperor's acquiescent subjects.

Many conservative Japanese did not welcome the general's reformist ardor, of course, and the centrist and right-wing politicians who have governed Japan since the 1950s have long bemoaned the "alien" origins of their national charter. These are the influential individuals, we can be quite certain, who did *not* write eulogistic letters to the conqueror in their younger days. It is a measure of the grassroots strength and resiliency of the early postwar dreams of "peace and democracy," however, that a half century later, as Japan entered the twenty-first century, not a word of the "MacArthur constitution" had been changed. And even when revision does take place, as will eventually happen, debate and discussion will still be defined by these ideals. They are now taken for granted as being an integral part of the political culture.

The letters, postcards, and petitions that Japanese in all walks of life sent to MacArthur and his staff now reside in archival collections in the United States. Years ago, I myself dipped into them. They are astonishing—and forbidding—to behold. As Professor Sodei notes, these communications number in the hundreds of thousands and take every conceivable form. Most are in Japanese, but many are in English. In the former case, they range from eloquent statements written in exquisite calligraphy on formal scrolled paper to earnest but roughly scribbled and articulated notes and postcards. Just to *decipher* this handwriting, let alone place it in proper context of style or allusion or class or gender or geographic locale, is a daunting challenge. Communications in English similarly run the board. Some are typed, others written in fluent cursive penmanship, others in labored handwriting, still others printed out in block letters. All levels of education are represented here, and all parts of the country. Rural as well as urban residents wrote to the conquerors, and seemingly as many women as men. Youngsters often did so, urged on by teachers and parents. Many of these communications, particularly those addressed directly to General MacArthur, were accompanied by gifts. The enumeration of these here in this book, just by itself, is remarkable.

Only someone with very special talents could make order out of this chaos. This is what Sodei Rinjirō has done, and there is no one better qualified to have taken on this challenge. Professor Sodei's prize-winning 1974 Japanese-language study of "MacArthur's two thousand days" (*Makkāsā no nisen nichi*) was a pioneering analysis of the occupation era transition from war to peace, and it established him as Japan's preeminent expert on the supreme commander. He has been one of the leading promoters of research on the occupation period ever since. In the process, he has come to personify one of the most precious (and fragile) legacies of the occupation—the transnational, intercultural, and interracial reciprocity that characterized the best of relations during this crucial time. Professor Sodei has been a generous friend and mentor to many foreign scholars, including myself—directing our attention to the most pertinent Japanese primary and secondary materials and showing us how to listen to Japanese voices at all levels.

To "listen to Japan" in this manner entails rethinking conventional notions of Japanese culture in profoundly subversive ways. It brings ordinary voices into the picture—and with this a cacophony of lively opinion that runs counter to the monolithic stereotype of a harmonious, consensual, "vertically oriented" society. It brings popular culture into the picture—and forces us to leaven the pristine abstractions that the apostles of "high" culture love to dwell on (such as Confucianism or "Bushidō" or flower arranging or "tea") with appreciation of a more disorderly arena of everyday thought and activity. To pay attention to *this* Japan is to encounter many cultures and subcultures and "traditions" indeed.

For those who do not read or speak Japanese, it is difficult if not impossible to enter this world. Making such voices more accessible outside

Japan is clearly one of the most difficult challenges that confronts scholars, journalists, and translators today. For now, we have *Dear General MacArthur*—and a great debt to Sodei Rinjirō for showing us what a rich, complicated, and contradictory human story waits to be further explored.

John W. Dower

ACKNOWLEDGMENTS

 I am indebted to many people for helping to make this book possible. Tsurumi Shunsuke helped arrange the first publication of these letters as serial installments in the journal *Shisō no kagaku;* Shibuya Teisuke, chairman of the Research Society for the Science of Thought, offered constant encouragement; and journal editor Haruta Chikakuni made thoughtful comments on each installment of the letters.

I offer my gratitude to Koseki Shōichi, now of Dokkyō University, for the selfless cooperation I received from him at the MacArthur Memorial and the National Records Center during the autumn of 1982. My research for the book would not have been possible without his assistance. I would also like to thank Izumi Shōichi, who spearheaded the effort to microfilm the letters and other materials as the former head of the Foreign Affairs Research Room in the National Diet Library's Research Department, as well as his successors, Hoshi Kenichi, Chiyo Masaaki, and Edamatsu Sakae. I am also obliged to Fujishiro Shunji (resident staff for the NDL project) and his wife, Manae (at the Library of Congress), for their diligent cooperation in Washington, and to the staff of the Contemporary Political History Materials Room at the National Diet Library, who made the microfilms available to me.

On the American side, I would like to offer my sincere gratitude to Lyman H. Hammond, Jr., director of the MacArthur Memorial; Edward J. Boone, Jr., archivist at the time I did my research; James W. Zobel, present archivist; and other staff members at the memorial. At the National Archives, I would first like to mention John E. Taylor, who helped me with the Emperor Hirohito file, and Hosoya Masahiro of the Center for American Studies at Dōshisha University, who provided me with copies of enlightening letters from that file during the serial publication of my research. With respect to comparative studies of the occupation of Germany, I would like to thank Robert Wolfe, the head of the Modern Military Branch of the National Archives, and the late John Mendelsohn. At the Washington National Records Center in Suitland, a place of fond memories, I take my hat off first to Sally Orton and then to Fred Pernell for his patience in supervising people who had little experience in copying Japanese material and coping with my often impatient requests. As to Frank Joseph Shulman, then curator of the East Asian Collection at McKeldin Library, University of Maryland, I am at a loss to find words to express my gratitude for his unstinting cooperation.

This book has received immense guidance from Hans H. Baerwald, under whom I studied at UCLA. With his experience as a member of the Government Section of GHQ and his later academic achievement, Professor Baerwald directed me to the study of the occupation of Japan. Discussions I had with Takemae Eiji and other members of the Japanese Association for the Study of the History of the Occupation (JASHO), chaired by Amakawa Akira, constantly broadened my perspective and elevated this book to a level I could not have attained alone.

I take this opportunity to offer thanks as well to my colleague Furukawa Terumi, who read and offered timely comments on the serialization of my research as soon as each issue appeared. I thank Kawahara Hiroshi of Waseda University, a senior colleague since my days at Waseda's graduate school, who briefed me on Kume Masao's theory of Japan as an American state, and bibliographic researcher Fukushima Jurō, who provided me with a copy of that essay. Professor Awaya Kentarō of Rikkyō University pointed me to the ATIS documents that reported the number of letters received by the occupation. And I cannot forget the goodwill of Hara Akira of Tokyo University, who put aside his own work to help me when, as usual, I faced the danger of running out of time when searching through material at the MacArthur Memorial.

For classifying the huge amount of material and making clean copies, I obtained the aid of Tajima Toshinobu, then a doctoral candidate at

Hōsei University. I also had help from Murakami Yumiko and Ōtsuka Yoko for draft translations into Japanese of some of the letters written in English.

This English edition would not have been possible if Shizue Matsuda had not volunteered to undertake the job of translating the letters, a task made more daunting by the wide variety of styles and inconsistent grammar of the original letters. She took early retirement from the University of Indiana library to devote herself to the work, which was truly a labor of love. In addition to contributing the foreword, my esteemed friend John W. Dower introduced the project to John Junkerman, who did a splendid job of editing the manuscript, the translations, and the illustrations for the book. Carol Gluck of Columbia University was generous in her praise for the original Japanese version and constantly encouraged me in producing the English edition. To these people, my many thanks are due. Finally, heartfelt thanks to my respected colleague and friend Mark Selden of Binghamton University, who arranged for the publication of this book and contributed a final edit, and to editor Susan McEachern at Rowman & Littlefield for her enthusiastic support of the book. Chrisona Schmidt copyedited the manuscript.

This book was born with the support of these many colleagues. Responsibility for the finished product, however, lies with me. I pray that the book has few errors and makes a real contribution to the world.

Finally, I wish to thank my wife, Takako, who watched over the development of this book. I still hope someday to respond to her usual chiding that I write a book entirely in my original words.

I dedicate this book to the late Tsukuda Jitsuo, the leading figure of the Occupation of Japan group of the Research Society for the Science of Thought. He went so far as to sacrifice his own professional fiction writing to lead us, but he fell along the way. My self-indulgence must have annoyed him in no small manner. Offering a single book to his memory can never atone for the past, but I believe, if he were still alive, he would smile at me through the thick lenses of his glasses, for he was like a strict but kind elder brother to me.

A NOTE ON JAPANESE NAMES

 Japanese names in the text follow the Japanese convention in which the family name precedes the given name,
with the following exceptions: the opposite (Western)
order is used for names that appeared in that order in
letters originally written in English, and for the names of Japanese (or
Japanese Americans) living outside of Japan (including the translator,
Shizue Matsuda) who choose to follow the Western convention.

To General MacArthur

Alight from his plane Bataan
    On the field at Atsugi,
Oh, how unassuming the figure of
    General MacArthur.

For the multitude of democratic education
    In the 1000 days of Occupation,
Respect and love the people of
    A new born Japan offer
To the Supreme Commander,
    General MacArthur.

                    From an Izu farmer

            Address: Mr. Masao Suzuki,
                      Akefushimi, Nakagawa-mura,
                      Kamo-gun,
                      Shizuoka Prefecture.

INTRODUCTION

 Two months after the Allied occupation of Japan began in the aftermath of World War II, the following letter arrived at General Headquarters (GHQ) in Tokyo, addressed to General Douglas MacArthur, the supreme commander for the Allied powers (SCAP).[1]

November 1, 1945

His Excellency General MacArthur:

The stationing of your troops in Japan and political reform are great things that are welcomed by all of the Japanese people.

I swear by the gods of heaven and earth my faith in and gratitude for the MacArthur administration. Japanese politicians are allies of the zaibatsu and their politics are dishonest, their politics are inhumane. In my humble opinion, you should introduce great reforms of Japanese politics, remake Japan's zaibatsu through and through, and return all property owned by the zaibatsu, without exception, to the government. I hope you would, in this manner, provide food for the unemployed. There is a great mold growing on Japanese politics today . . . [illegible] and there is a green growth upon it. The Shidehara cabinet [October 1945–May 1946] has likewise begun to grow mold. We the people, with freedom of speech, would cleanse the mold from the souls of the politicians. We hope thereby to arrive at a reborn, cultural Japan. With this in mind, I have organized the Greater Japan Loyalty Association, and I would like to request Your Excellency General MacArthur's efforts toward rebuilding the nation.

I sincerely apologize for interrupting your heavy military responsibilities, but I would ask you to take a look at two lengthy documents, an outline and a prospectus for the Greater Japan Loyalty Association. Thereupon, the unworthy Tsuchiya Gompei, founder of the Greater Japan Loyalty Association would like to pay his respects to Your Excellency General MacArthur. At that time I would like to discuss the state of affairs of Japan. I am, sir, a soldier of Your Excellency General MacArthur. Please do not ignore me; I truly want you to make use of me. I will explain everything when we meet.

Humbly,
Tsuchiya Gompei

The letter was in many ways typical of the 500,000 letters that were written to MacArthur and GHQ by Japanese citizens during the course of the occupation (1945–1952). The vast majority of this voluminous correspondence expressed unreserved support for the occupation and its goals, coupled with a thorough repudiation of the Japanese war effort and its military and political leaders. MacArthur himself was treated with extreme deference, and he was often addressed in a formal style of Japanese that had previously been reserved for the emperor. To many, he was the object of an adulation that sometimes bordered on deification. The above letter, for example, was accompanied by a series of poems, written in bold calligraphy on a scroll of paper, one of which read,

> *By the grace of godly General MacArthur, speech is free.*
> *Let us sing in freedom, over the green fields.*

At the same time, the letters often conveyed a surprising faith that MacArthur would take a benevolent interest in the thoughts and concerns of the Japanese people, that he would endorse and participate in their grand schemes and private endeavors, and that he would welcome their gifts and offers of hospitality. From all over Japan, men and women, old and young, everyone from farmers and housewives to former soldiers and members of the Communist Party unburdened themselves to their foreign ruler. They wrote to express gratitude for small favors, like the famous gifts of candy from GIs, and to ask for large favors, such as finding a soldier son stranded overseas. They sent complaints about taxes, warnings of political subversion, and invitations to share Japanese delicacies and dance programs. Some were penned in painstaking and broken English, others written with brushes dipped in blood. Often intense and intimate, the letters speak with telling detail of postwar life and the Japanese people's response to the extraordinary and far-reaching changes brought about by the end of the war and the occupation.

In the world's long history of military occupations, there has never been a people who corresponded with such intensity with their foreign rulers. Why did this phenomenon occur? To begin with, as devastating and traumatic as the Japanese defeat was, the end of the war represented a new beginning. This was also the case in Germany, and during the early stages of the Allied occupation there as well, a comparable outpouring of public correspondence greeted the victors.[2] In both Germany and Japan the occupying forces were identified as "liberation armies." The emotion of being freed from Nazism and Japanese militarism, including the discrediting of the former leadership, as well as relief at the end of a war whose final months were marked by massive destruction and civilian casualties, engendered feelings of affinity and trust toward the occupying forces. Thought control by the military and secret police had been pervasive under wartime regimes in which public criticism had been completely banned, and it was impossible for people to appeal directly to the ruling authorities. When this oppressive burden was lifted, people were suddenly free to express themselves, and many seized the opportunity.

These factors sparked a wave of letter writing in both countries, but the volume and intensity of the correspondence was much higher in Japan, and it continued throughout the occupation, whereas it quickly tapered off in Germany. This may be partially explained by the fact that this was not the first time the German people had experienced defeat and military occupation, while Japan was being occupied for the first time in its history. But more significantly, the different reactions of the Germans and the Japanese were shaped by the power and the personality of the military commanders of the occupations and the nature of the occupying regimes. MacArthur was the ultimate power in Japan, and he stimulated the impulse to write letters by playing the role of the enlightened monarch. In contrast, the occupation of Germany was divided among the United States, Great Britain, France, and the Soviet Union, and the commander of the American zone, General Lucius Clay, did not have a comparable scope of authority. Although he brought a certain dedication to his assigned task, Clay believed that occupation reforms could not go beyond the democratic institutions that existed in the United States, and he gave Germans little reason to be enthusiastic or excited by occupation policies.

MacArthur, on the other hand, believed that the democratic reform of Japan was a God-given mission and that he "had to be an economist, a political scientist, an engineer, a manufacturing executive, a teacher, and even a theologian of sorts."[3] The occupation

Photo I.1   General MacArthur talks to reporters upon his arrival at Atsugi airfield outside of Tokyo, August 30, 1945. Advance troops had secured the Japanese Navy Air Corps base just two days earlier. MacArthur's arrival marked the beginning of the Allied occupation. Source: U.S. Army

authorities in Japan embarked on a far-reaching program of reform that included the peace constitution, land reform, dissolution of the *zaibatsu*, and provisions ensuring women's equality that went far beyond those prevailing in the United States. MacArthur, as the compelling symbol of these widely popular reforms, was like a magnet that drew young and old to take up their pens with the feeling that surely he would listen to their concerns. Undoubtedly, MacArthur's personal charisma was also a contributing factor. Though he rarely addressed the Japanese people and almost never responded to their letters, he remained an electrifying presence—handsome and tall in stature, bold and confident in his manner. Crowds lined the streets outside his office at General Headquarters to catch a glimpse of the general as he arrived for work in the morning or departed for lunch at his residence in the American embassy. He filled the position of supreme commander with a remarkably personal aura, and it was to this image that the Japanese addressed their correspondence.

If the idea of addressing letters to the highest authorities was a fresh breeze in postwar Japan, it originated not with the occupation but with Japanese authorities on the eve of the occupation, resulting in a brief flood of letters addressed to the Japanese prime minister. These letters were written in response to an appeal issued by the first postwar prime minister, Prince Higashikuni Naruhiko. The appeal was released to the press on August 30, 1945, the very day that MacArthur arrived at the Atsugi airfield in the outskirts of Tokyo. It was featured in newspapers the following day, appearing as the lead story in the *Mainichi shimbun* in a six-column spread quoting the prime minister as saying, "I want to receive letters directly from you, my countrymen. They can be about anything, things that made you happy or sad, dissatisfactions or complaints. Letters about personal matters or public problems are fine. I want you to write the truth frankly. I want to hear directly from you, the general public, and to use your opinions to guide me in governing." To the left of this story was a headline, "Commander MacArthur Arrives," with a photograph of MacArthur shaking hands with General Robert Eichelberger, commander of the Eighth Army. All of the daily newspapers had similar layouts that day, treating the appeal for letters as the top story.

As early as September 4, the *Mainichi shimbun* carried a report that forty to fifty letters were being delivered daily, accompanied by a photo of Higashikuni reading letters spread on his desk and summaries of several letters complaining of hard living conditions. Hasegawa Takashi, a former newspaper editor on the staff of the cabinet secretariat, was given the job of sorting the letters and briefing the prime minister on their contents. He recalled that the flood of correspondence peaked at 1,371 in one day, and the daily briefings sometimes ran as long as three hours.[4]

According to the October 1 issue of the *Mainichi shimbun*, the letters included appeals for the early repatriation of sons and husbands held in prisoner of war camps, complaints about living conditions, concerns about low levels of educational achievement because of the war, and requests to lengthen the school year. It was as if the emotions of the people, suppressed throughout the war, had suddenly been uncorked. The headline of the *Mainichi* story read, "The People's Voice—Immediate Application in Policy," but only four days later the Higashikuni cabinet collapsed after the home minister, Yamazaki Iwao, announced that he intended to continue controls over ideological crimes. In response to Yamazaki's announcement, GHQ issued a series of human rights directives and announced the dismissal of the home minister and the abolition of the thought police. This prompted Higashikuni to submit his resignation, declaring, "I cannot govern under these circumstances." The noble idea of accepting letters from the people, a sharp departure from previous governmental practice, was not taken up by subsequent cabinets, and the flow of correspondence stopped.

But the idea of addressing letters to the highest authorities had been planted, and it soon reached SCAP. Initially GHQ did nothing to invite letters to MacArthur. They began arriving entirely unbidden in early September, and the pace of letter writing to MacArthur and GHQ grew rapidly after the fall of the Higashikuni cabinet. Although the correspondence to Higashikuni and to MacArthur was similarly rooted in the expression of long-suppressed emotions and the hope for change from on high, there was a much higher expectation that something might actually result from writing to MacArthur, as the following letter to the general suggested:

October 10, 1945

In Japan today, people are sending optimistic letters to the prime minister, but I know that this is meaningless. . . . Japan is now under Your Excellency's military control. No one in Japan has Your Excellency's political power. Your Excellency, you yourself should find out the people's true aspirations, through their letters and other means.

Nankai Senryū
Kumamoto City

GHQ did not miss the opportunity for public relations provided by the letters. The *Mainichi shimbun* ran a United Press wire story on October 15 with the headline, "Letters to General MacArthur: Punishment of War Criminals, Reform of the Ration System, Others—300 in Little over a Month." The bulk of the article was devoted to a list of 100 letters written in Japanese, which were classified by subject into twenty-one categories, from such topics as "antimilitarism, 28 letters" and "appreciation for the Allied occupation and General MacArthur, 25" to "support for the rapid democratization of Japan, 7" and "support for a lowering of alcohol consumption or prohibition, 2." It was clear from this article that the occupation authorities were diligently reading the letters from the public. The article encouraged people to believe that their opinions and requests would be heard if they wrote to MacArthur, and the flow increased until an average of several hundred letters were arriving every day, a pace that would continue for the duration of MacArthur's tenure as supreme commander.

The estimate of 500,000 letters sent to MacArthur and GHQ during the course of the occupation is derived from an Allied Translator and Interpreter Service (ATIS) report that placed the number of letters received between September 1946 and the end of 1950 at 438,831. No accounting of the letters received during the first full year of the occupation (through August 1946) has been found, but it is safe to estimate this number at more than 50,000. There is also no record of the letters received between January 1951 and MacArthur's dismissal in April of that year.

What did GHQ do with the letters? The occupation authorities not only read them but also prepared English summaries of all of the letters,

Photo I.2   Some letters were addressed simply to "Mr. MacArthur, Tokyo." As many as a thousand letters arrived daily at the peak of the correspondence. This photo taken by the Mainichi shimbun was dated August 3, 1948. Source: Mainichi Shimbunsha

and complete translations were made of the most important letters. One of the main duties of the ATIS, which was part of the Far East Command's Military Intelligence Section, was to read, analyze, and classify the letters. The occupation was an extension of the war, with the objective of winning the peace, and as such the letters provided a direct, unmediated source of information on the conditions, attitudes, hopes, and expectations of the occupied people.

According to occupation veterans who served in the ATIS,[6] MacArthur read every letter that was addressed to him personally. Working seven days a week, 365 days a year at his GHQ office in the Dai-Ichi Life Insurance Building in central Tokyo, a significant part of his intense work schedule must have been consumed by reading the letters. Copies of the letters that were passed on to MacArthur, along with letters addressed directly to GHQ, were routed according to their content to the appropriate section of the military administration, where they provided data for the development of occupation policies.

I have read approximately 10,000 of the letters. These include about 3,500 letters that are stored with the general's personal papers in the archives at the MacArthur Memorial in Norfolk, Virginia, arranged alphabetically by the name of the writer.[7] These letters are thought to be the ones that MacArthur valued most highly and kept with him until his death. The other major source for the letters is the National Archives II in College Park, Maryland. Six cartons of letters (the Letters from the Japanese file) are stored along with other GHQ/SCAP documents in the archives. I also discovered letters addressed to MacArthur in the files of the Civil Information and Education Section, the Government Section, and the Economic and Scientific Section at the archives. All of these have been microfilmed and are now available at the National Diet Library in Tokyo.

Not surprisingly, most of the letters kept among the general's personal papers at the MacArthur Memorial are quite laudatory, often extremely so. The latter collection of letters, at the National

Photo I.3   Children from the Taimei Elementary School in the Ginza line up in front of General Headquarters in the Dai-Ichi Building in Tokyo to sing "Happy Birthday" to General MacArthur on his seventieth birthday, January 26, 1950. Source: U.S. Army

Archives II, cannot be so easily characterized, but they appear to be fairly typical of the range of letters that Japanese addressed to the occupation forces. The contents are varied: While many praise MacArthur's administration, others are highly critical of the occupation and the behavior of Allied soldiers. Many support the purging of public officials and provide information about their wartime activities, but there were also many appeals to rescind purge orders against politicians and others whom the occupation authorities deemed significant figures in the war effort. While the large majority of the letters expressed support for the goals of the occupation, some of the letters (often sent anonymously) were sharply critical. These hostile letters provide some insight into the attitudes of critics and opponents of occupation policies, although it can be assumed that many such opponents never wrote to MacArthur.

Most of the letters included here were written directly to MacArthur by Japanese individuals. Wherever possible, I have included the entire letter. This volume is above all a record of the direct encounters that individual Japanese had with MacArthur as the absolute power figure. I wanted to listen to the breathing, so to speak, of the people who lived through the occupation. The letters were spontaneous and not written under coercion. Despite the fact that Japan had suffered a crushing military defeat, these letters were for the most part not voices of despair. Some were emotionally charged, but they only reflected the excitement of the times, the unfiltered voices of the Japanese people extracted from crisis and turmoil.

In culling the letters, I tried to select those in which the writer, in the course of communicating to MacArthur, reflected something of himself or herself in the mirror of history. Each of the letters, and each of the people who wrote them, is an individual. But as a group, the letters, addressed to the highest authority during the dramatic social and political upheaval of the occupation, reflect the spirit of the times. Regardless of how the writer felt toward MacArthur, these letters bear eloquent testimony to the character of the occupation, even as they illuminate the character of the Japanese people.

I first encountered these letters in the basement of the Washington National Records Center in Suitland, Maryland, where they were stored before being moved to the National Archives II in the mid-1990s. It was the spring of 1973. There were few researchers, and we were given free access to the material in the basement stacks. Research on the occupation of Japan was in its infancy.

Documents concerning the occupation were collected as GHQ/SCAP, Record Group 331. It was said that they totaled several tens of millions of pages. My colleague John W. Dower of the Massachusetts Institute of Technology once half-jokingly noted that a person who attempted to scale this mountain of material might not return alive.

The letters written to MacArthur were part of this mountain. I located this material through an excellent series about the occupation that was published in the weekly magazine *Shūkan shinchō*. Sally Orton, who was in charge of the stacks at the time, dismayed me by saying,

"You may take your time reading the material, but you are not allowed to make Xerox copies."

From the moment I spread the letters on a desk in the corner of the basement, I was captivated. Each letter brought back memories of my childhood, and I could feel the lifeblood, the frustrations, the sadness, the suffering, and the anger, but also the hopes and aspirations of a people under occupation. It was a spellbinding experience. I have pleasant memories of assiduously copying by hand whatever struck me as interesting among the letters I read.

Part of what I gathered at that time I included in a book on MacArthur that was published in 1974,[8] and the letters generated considerable interest among Japanese readers. I only used fragments of the letters in my book, but I kept thinking that someday I would revisit the letters and prepare a more complete version for publication. I was absorbed, however, by my research on MacArthur and the occupation in general, so this plan remained unfulfilled for many years.

I then encountered Nakagawa Sadamu, an editor at the Tokyo publishing house Ōtsuki Shoten. He told me that ever since reading my MacArthur book, he had dreamed of publishing a large compilation of the letters. I hesitated, considering the magnitude of the task, but I eventually gave in to his persistence. Having committed to many projects, however, I was unable to pull the book together, until it occurred to us to find a magazine that would be interesting in serializing the letters, which would both give the letters wider exposure and make the job more manageable for me. Tsurumi Shunsuke, my mentor for research on the occupation, took the initiative to have the series carried in the journal *Shisō no kagaku* (Science of thought), where it appeared in twelve issues between August 1983 and July 1984. The series was revised as a book, including newly discovered letters, and it was published in 1985, the fortieth anniversary of the end of the war.[9]

Throughout the writing process, my conscience was troubled by the question of publishing letters that were never intended for publication, regardless of what might be considered the official character of the letters and the historian's privilege. The letters, however, constitute important public statements of citizens of an occupied country to their ruler, and they are historical materials of the highest quality with few parallels in any society. The letters are, moreover, among the GHQ documents that have been made available to researchers. I convinced myself that it was my duty as a student of history to analyze these letters and make them available to the public. My intention was to follow the original letters faithfully, including names and addresses in most cases, so as to fully convey the powerful appeal of the materials themselves.

I sincerely hoped that those who wrote the letters, their families, and others concerned would appreciate their historical significance and not object to their publication. As it turned out, I have not received a single complaint from anyone whose letter was included in the book. If any felt chagrin at seeing their correspondence in print decades later, they may also have been aware that their letters constitute revealing historical documentation of that period.

That said, one cannot help but feel some embarrassment for the writers when reading some of the letters. After I submitted the manuscript for the book, I made a trip to Los Angeles, where I happened to meet a Nisei of Okinawan descent, who told me he had served in the ATIS and translated letters from the Japanese during the occupation. "I felt," he remarked, "that the Japanese were a small people, to write such letters to MacArthur." Perhaps with a sensitivity sharpened by the long history of discrimination by mainland Japanese toward Okinawans, he found it unseemly that many postwar Japanese had suddenly adopted an attitude of deference toward MacArthur and the Americans. Many of the letters are colored by an awe toward MacArthur and his authority that is tinged with subservience and obsequiousness.

Despite the fact that Japan remains subordinate in many ways to the United States in military and foreign affairs, it is hard for Japanese nowadays to imagine writing such letters. But if I had been an adult during the occupation, I might well have been one of those "small people." As I searched through the files of letters I was nagged by a curiosity, mixed with apprehension, that my late father, who was a village leader during the war, might have written to MacArthur. My heart skipped a beat when I discovered an unsigned letter from my hometown, Fudōdō-mura in Miyagi Prefecture, reporting on corrupt village administration. To my relief, the handwriting was not my father's. Nonetheless, I was made aware that throughout Japan during the occupation it was likely that someone in one's community, if not necessarily a close relative or neighbor, was writing to MacArthur.

The fact that half a million letters were sent to GHQ gives credence to this supposition. I was able to put my hands on so many letters that I could not actually read them all thoroughly before making a selection. Inevitably, I was swayed by my instincts and proclivities in selecting the letters that are included here, but I am confident that, in their totality, they present a fair picture of the Japanese during the occupation. In particular they provide a rare, unvarnished perspective on their fears and frustrations, their hopes and aspirations.

In preparing this English edition of the book, I have followed the approach adopted in the original version of presenting the letters with minimal editing. Where the letters were originally written in English (identified as such in the text or footnotes), all errors of grammar, spelling, and style are left intact. For those translated from the Japanese, we have tried to approximate the idiosyncrasies of expression and style that give the original letters their character and individuality. In fact, the wide variety of styles of the letters—from stiffly formal, sometimes archaic epistles to emotionally charged confessions and protests written in blood, from highly stylized and philosophical reflections to rambling, barely coherent outpourings of the heart—is one of the reasons that it has taken so many years to complete the English edition. I am nonetheless pleased to finally make these letters to MacArthur available in the language of the general.

1

COZYING UP TO THE VICTOR

CONGRATULATIONS

 One of the first letters to reach MacArthur was dated September 7, 1945, just five days after the instrument of surrender was signed on the deck of the USS *Missouri*. General Headquarters was still located at the Yokohama Customs Building, and the registered special delivery letter was addressed "c/o General Headquarters, Occupation Force, New Grand Hotel, Yokohama." The letter read as follows:[1]

Honorable Sir:

I raise three banzais to General MacArthur and extend my congratulations on the successful stationing of your country's troops.

I have been studying amateur name divination as a hobby for the past twenty years, and my divinations of famous people's fates have appeared in local newspapers and magazines.

After the beginning of the Greater East Asia War, when Japan quickly lost its edge in the war in the Pacific and suffered repeated defeat in a succession of battles, I realized that victory for Japan was impossible. Through the divination of the name "Amerika" [four Chinese characters that have traditionally been used to designate America in written Japanese] and the general's name, as explained below, I concluded that it would be absolutely impossible for the Japanese military and government to lead the people to victory in a final, decisive battle on the Japanese mainland. Since Japan has declared its unconditional surrender, I humbly believe that my divination was accurate.

I hereby take the liberty of offering the results of the divination of your country's and the general's honorable names, in place of a message of congratulations on the successful stationing of your troops. I would be most honored if you were to take some pleasure from this letter.

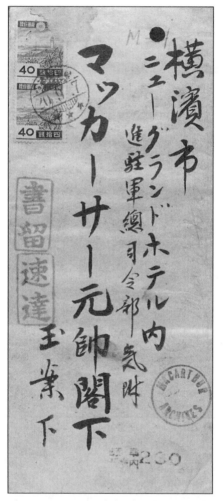

Photo 1.1   One of the first letters to be delivered to General MacArthur was sent by special delivery on September 7, 1945, addressed "To The Jade Desk of His Excellency, General of the Army MacArthur." Source: *MacArthur Memorial*

Divination

1. The character a in Amerika is the same as the a in Greater East Asia (Asia). The character me in Amerika is "rice," and the ancient name for Japan was "The Land of Bountiful Rice." The ri in Amerika is "increase," which means the rice will increase naturally. The ka in Amerika is "addition," which means the abundant annual harvest of rice will become larger. In essence, the meaning of the name "Amerika" is the same as Japan, and the name has a mystical connotation that America will come to Japan and rule Asia.

Just three weeks after the Japanese defeat, the writer of this letter was offering three cheers for MacArthur and congratulations to the American troops. He clearly hoped to forget the defeat as quickly as possible and find a way to rationalize the new order through the device of word play. A Japanese politician visiting Washington after the war engaged in similar word play, suggesting that "America is the country of rice, and Japan is the land of bountiful rice where rice is the main staple, so Japan and the United States can be friends," which caused his interpreters awful headaches. This letter is an early example of this conceit, while the "reading" that the United States is destined to come to Japan and rule Asia was a rudimentary expression of the concept of shared fate between the United States and Japan that later gained currency during the occupation. The foundation for this reading could not be more flimsy, but it reveals a will to internalize the heavy reality of the occupation by giving it the most favorable interpretation possible. The writer then turned to a reading of the name MacArthur:

2. To give a reading of the honorable name of General Makkāsā [MacArthur], I have transliterated it with the Japanese characters matsu (pine), ka (happiness), and sa (to assist). The pine tree traditionally has been treasured in Japan as the evergreen that never changes its color. The first three days of the new year are called matsu no uchi (days of pine), with fresh pine boughs decorating the doorways of houses throughout Japan. At wedding ceremonies and other celebrations and banquets, pine tree arrangements are always displayed or a painted scroll with pine trees is hung to celebrate the

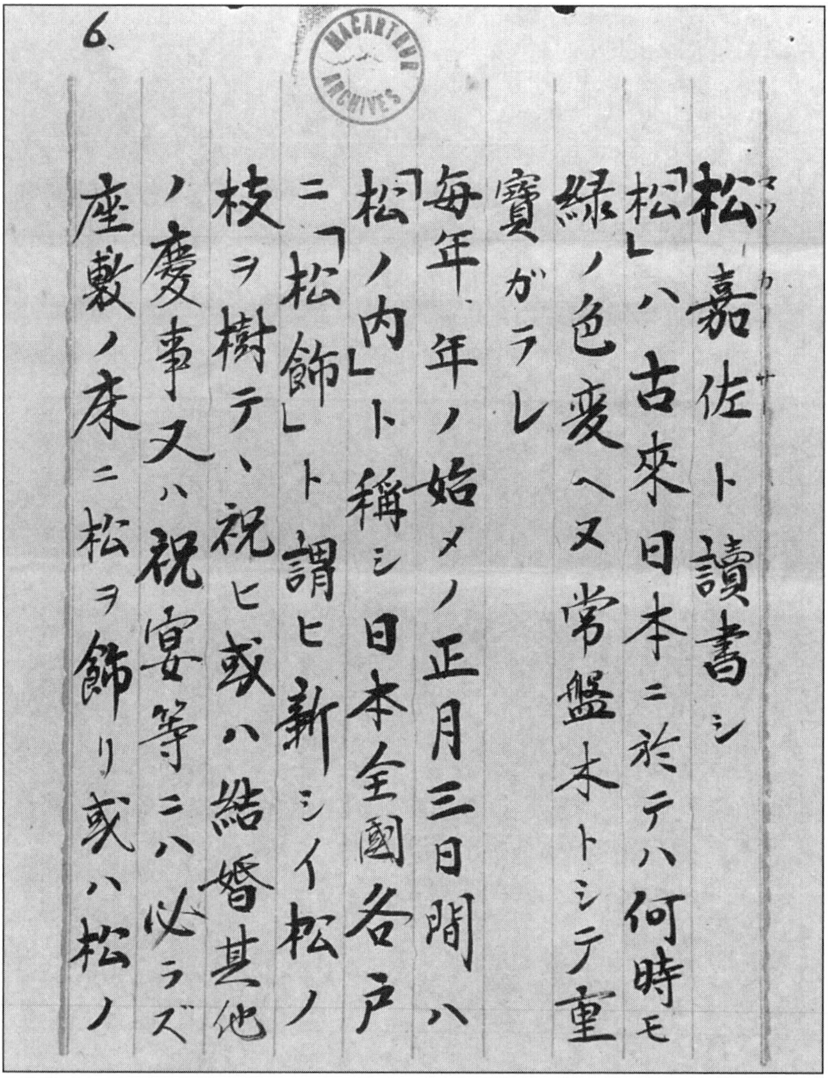

6、

「松」ハ「マツ」ト訓ヲ「カ」「サ」

「松」嘉佐ト讀書シ

「松」ハ古來日本ニ於テハ何時モ

緑ノ色変ヘヌ又常盤木トシテ重

寶ガラレ

毎年、年ノ始メノ正月三日間ハ

日本全國各戸ニ

松ノ内ト稱シ新シイ松ノ

二「松飾」ト謂ヒ

枝ヲ樹テ、祝ヒ或ハ結婚其他

ノ慶事又ハ祝宴等ニハ必ラズ

座敷ノ床ニ松ヲ飾リ或ハ松ノ

Photo 1.2   The writer bestowed upon MacArthur a fanciful, Japanese-style name that translates roughly as "the everlasting beauty of the glorious pine tree." Source: MacArthur Memorial

occasion. The character ka *is used in Japan for all celebrations and felicitations to mean "happiness." It is a most auspicious character. The character* sa *means to enhance the beautiful green of the pine and increase happiness. It is difficult to express, but the result is that the unchanging beauty of the pine will continue for a thousand and ten thousand years. The meaning of this divination is that General MacArthur will continue to rise in stature and position in the years to come.*

This letter parades beautiful words as an offering to the new ruler. The Japanese have always prided themselves on being able to flatter others by creating auspicious combinations of characters to match a needed pronunciation, though the absurdity of a forced pun has also been a favorite subject for the comic sketches of Rakugo, traditional Japanese storytelling. I have been unable to locate any characters used for written references to MacArthur during the war (his name was always transliterated using *katakana*), but in the hands of the writer of this letter, the general has been transformed from the butt of a wartime song ("Come on, Nimitz and MacArthur, you'll fall headfirst into hell") into a symbol of beauty to last ten thousand years. Was the writer among those singing "Come on, Nimitz and MacArthur" just months before Japan's defeat?

The letter continues, noting without explanation that the names of Japanese generals, including Tōjō Hideki and Yamashita Tomoyuki, indicated they were destined to fail, while Franklin Roosevelt's name suggested he would not fulfill his goals. The defeat of the Japanese generals and Roosevelt's death in office provided sufficient evidence to the writer that they were born under unlucky stars. *Post hoc, ergo propter hoc.* In short, the writer was simply using name divination as a means to flatter the American victors and the new ruler, MacArthur, and to open the way for the new order, the occupation. The last part of his letter reinforces this impression:

I humbly believe that if the people of the earth desire true happiness there must be world peace, and I am one who desires and loves world peace absolutely. America is the only country that can create world peace and civilization, and I praise the greatness of your country without cease. In closing,

Photo 1.3   The American fleet arrives in Japanese waters in late August in advance of the surrender ceremony that is to take place aboard the USS Missouri *on September 2, 1945. Mount Fuji provides the backdrop for this dramatic sunset. By the end of October, 400,000 troops were stationed throughout Japan. Source: U.S. Navy*

for the sake of world peace and the well-being of Japan, I pray to God for your good health.

Respectfully yours,
Ueno Bun'ichi
Speaker of the Gifu Prefectural Assembly

The entire letter was written in an impressive block style of calligraphy, and it is clear that the writer was a well-educated gentleman. Still, I cannot forget the shock I felt when I saw his title. An assembly speaker ranks with a prefectural governor in terms of regional prominence, and he undoubtedly played a central role in implementing national mobilization policies during the war. This is why I suspect he joined in singing "Come on, MacArthur." It is quite startling to see someone engage in such ostentatious rationalizing and self-promotion even before the Americans had assumed power in Japan. I am sure that he was not alone.

The salutation of the letter read, "To the tiger skin on which His Excellency General MacArthur sits." Traditionally, a tiger skin was considered a mat for a warrior of the highest rank. But the writer went even further, addressing the envelope, "To the Jade Desk of His Excellency, General of the Army MacArthur," an allusion to an emperor's desk. Could the writer have already understood the position MacArthur would assume in occupied Japan? Because, in fact, the supreme commander would reign above the emperor as a modern shogun.

MAKE JAPAN AN AMERICAN COLONY

MacArthur said of the Japanese, "They are like all Orientals. They have a tendency to adulate a winner, and to have the most supreme contempt for a loser."[2] No matter how much word play the speaker of the Gifu assembly engaged in, his letter amounted to abject flattery. And the Japanese did have contempt for the losers—themselves. When the nation's pride hit rock bottom with the defeat, people scorned themselves and turned to the American victors for help. The following letter is an example.[3]

February 18, 1946
The Honorable Representative of the United States MacArthur

Dear Sir:

It is with great reluctance that I write to ask you, for the sake of Japan's future and our descendants, to please make Japan a colony of the United States. I believe that no matter who becomes a minister, no matter who forms a government, our leaders will not think of the people, as all Japanese think only of themselves. During the war, the leaders deceived the people by telling them that Americans are terrible. American soldiers are kind. There were rumors that when American soldiers came, they would take our watches and money and everything else, so most Japanese hid all of their valuables.

Contrary to the rumors, they did nothing wrong. Because Japan was doing evil, they lied to us that Americans would go wild, but instead they are kinder than the Japanese. If I were young, I would like to go to the United States, but I am sixty-two so this is not possible. My eldest son, Tarō, twenty-three, is a former army doctor and second lieutenant who was reported missing two years ago as a member of the Mori 1353d Squadron in Burma. If he is so lucky as to return alive, I will bring him to see you. I want him to go to America, and I beg you to assist in making this happen. In March of last year, the newspaper reported that the whole army in Burma had been annihilated. An army doctor is a noncombatant, so if he was taken as a prisoner of war by Britain, he may still be alive. I am worried because he was taught by the Japanese state to fight to the death.

If the Japanese were kind, they could contribute to the world, even with their small stature, but whoever forms a government will not think about the Japanese people, they will only think about themselves. For the sake of all Japanese and our descendants, I believe that the future of Japan will be brighter under American control.

Shiomi Kitarō [seal]
Okayama City

As this letter suggests, the Japanese had formed an image of a postwar occupation on the basis of the Japanese military's savage occupation of China and other parts of Asia. Before the American troops landed, people hid their valuable possessions. Some cities and towns even ordered young girls to cut their hair, disguise themselves as men,

Photo 1.4   Children receive candy from soldiers in the U.S. Army's Eleventh Airborne Division, in front of a temporary post office erected in the ruins of the city of Yokohama, September 1945. The image of GIs passing out candy to Japanese children quickly became a symbol of the benevolence of the Allied occupation. Source: Mainichi Shimbunsha

and escape to the mountains. When the arriving soldiers did not commit the expected crimes, some, such as the writer of this letter, concluded that they had been deceived because the Japanese military had been committing those very crimes. (In fact, there were numerous incidents of looting and rape by American GIs in the early months of the occupation, but word of MacArthur's threat of stern punishment for misdeeds was widely disseminated; in any case, the writer of this letter had not heard of such misdeeds.) The perception of the American military changed quickly, and the United States soon became a country that held great appeal, even for this sixty-two-year-old man. His notion to have Japan adopted as an American dependency for the sake of Japan's future and the well-being of future generations is just as sincere as his parental concern for his son, missing in action in Burma.

The next letter was written at about the same time, six months after the end of the war. The writer was a rather well educated man of considerable social standing. He worshiped the victors and went on at great length to make his case that the only hope for bringing Japan back from the depths was through annexation by the United States. Few of the letters reveal so clearly this dependence on the victor, a psychology that was quite prevalent among Japanese of that time.[4]

February 15 [1946]
The Honorable General MacArthur
c/o His Secretary

Dear Sir:
Honorable general, whom I most admire, please forgive me, a person of low status, for directly and suddenly writing a letter to you, the hero of the world. Before sending this letter, I debated for a long time whether or not it was proper for me to send a letter to you, but I could not help myself, and despite my rudeness, I decided to send it. I apologize and ask you to please forgive me.

In 1924, after graduating from the political science and economics department of Waseda University's professional college, I spent three years running my family's sake brewery. Because of the depressed economic conditions, we were forced to close, and I served as the head of an industrial cooperative in my hometown for more than ten years. During this time I also served on the board of the Kyoto Prefecture Credit Union Federation. In 1938 I resigned all of my honorary positions and moved to Tokyo to work for a company, until last year when I evacuated to Shiga Prefecture because of the bombing. Since then I have been working on the reclamation of the old Yokkaichi airfield. I failed to mention earlier that Kyoto Prefecture is my legal residence.

The misguided military cliques led our innocent people into war and caused great difficulties for your country. No apology, no matter how sincere, can erase this. Also as a result, the Japanese people are experiencing indescribable suffering. At present, many have no place to live, there is not enough food to eat, and with the soaring cost of living, many are hovering at the edge of death. This is because the people were stupid and because they did not bravely resist the militarists, so they must reap what they have sown, but the people are in a truly pitiful state.

The writers of many of the letters to MacArthur go on at great length about their personal histories. This reflects a desire to confide in the general, and it may also have been an unconscious strategy to get closer to the man by baring their bosoms. Many of the letters also place the entire responsibility for the war on the militarists, the *zaibatsu*, and government bureaucrats, arguing that ordinary citizens were innocent victims, so this letter is a rare example of one who acknowledges the people's shared responsibility. But this, it turns out, was only the prologue. The body of the letter follows:

Ever since you entered Japan, the face of the country has been changing. Your leadership is truly godlike. Your vision penetrates every corner of Japanese society, and every one of your directives is superbly on target. We are all deeply grateful that your guidance is humanitarian, and that your directives are good government that Japanese politicians will never match. Embarrassingly, the Japanese people have belatedly come to understand that, in all matters, we are no match for your country. Now for the first time, through the occupation forces, the people of Japan have come to know how fine your country is, and we deeply regret provoking a reckless war against a country as great as yours. As our respect for your country increases steadily, we are convinced that yours is the only country to which Japan's future can be entrusted. The high esteem the Japanese have for you is unlike the formal respect they have for the emperor; it is admiration that truly comes from the heart, a devoted respect. This respect is growing deeper and deeper, and with it the feeling that only your country can rescue Japan from its destitution, only your country can help this miserable Japan prosper again as it once did. The Japanese people's confidence in your country leads us to entrust every aspect of Japan to your country and to depend upon your leadership. Trust in your country deepens by the day, and I now believe that there is no other way to reconstruction except to entrust everything to your country and to depend upon your sympathy.

As to the future of the emperor system, this is second or third in priority. I don't think it matters. I only hope that reconstruction can take place quickly and that our livelihood can be stabilized. What should be done to bring Japan back from the dead and bring the Japanese people happiness?

It is worth noting here the lack of concern the writer shows for the future of the emperor system. By the time this letter was written (as will be addressed in later chapters), the emperor had publicly declared that he was a human and not a god (the "declaration of humanity" of January 1946), and the debate over the emperor system had quieted considerably. Still, at a time when public opinion generally supported the maintenance of the emperor system, to be able to say so clearly that the future of the emperor was immaterial compared with economic recovery shows a certain sober clarity.

I have discussed this with people around me. They all feel that if possible and if difficult conditions allow, everything about Japan should be entrusted to your country, and we should rely on your country's wise, spiritual guidance. In other words, there is a fervent wish and desire that if it were possible for Japan and the United States to merge to save this drowning Japan, then everyone agrees the Japanese people would be exceedingly happy. This is an honest fact. Even if they do not say it in so many words, there is no doubt that all of the Japanese people believe in the bottom of their hearts that there is no way for Japan to return to prosperity except through United States–Japan union and reliance upon your country's guidance and mercy in all matters. This is true. I firmly believe that Japan can be saved only through annexation by your country. Am I mistaken in my thinking? The fact is that many present-day Japanese are beginning to think the same way. . . .

I fear that I may face your anger for presenting this kind of letter to you, but I harbor no intention of betraying my country in writing it. I am sincerely concerned for the country, and no matter how often I think it through, I believe there is no way to save Japan other than to have your country save Japan by agreeing to annex it. There is a theory that Japan's situation is similar to that of the Balkan Peninsula in Europe. Japan is truly like the Balkans of Europe. Not only will Japan be saved by uniting with your country and doing as it is ordered, but I believe that by doing so peace in the world will be maintained. If my thinking is unfortunately mistaken, please consider me a stupid person and forgive me.

However, I believe what I have written. Not only I, but many other Japanese are thinking like this, and the number who think this way is growing daily. This is a destiny Japan cannot avoid. In hindsight, what should have happened at the time of the Meiji Restoration [1868] has only been delayed until now.

The writer states that he has no intention of selling out his country, even though he advocates its union with the United States. He certainly cannot be labeled a "traitor," or someone who sells out to the enemy for personal gain, because the erstwhile enemy had become the victor and was now in a position of aiding Japan. It is more likely that this man, with his keen business sensibilities, concluded that the best path was to depend totally on the United States. At this point, his letter suddenly turns emotional and becomes a personal appeal to MacArthur:

Your Excellency! Please take pity on Japan. No, you have already forgiven Japan's crimes and are being merciful. Your Excellency! I beg you to save pitiful Japan from the roots up. No, there is no need to beseech you, you already intend to help Japan from the roots. Your goodwill is evident in the directives you issue every day. We Japanese people, who battled your country as our enemy until now, can find no words to express our gratitude for the compassionate guidance we are receiving today. This is only possible because of the extraordinary generosity that is your national character. It is embarrassing to say so, but I wonder what attitude Japan would have shown if the outcome of the war had been reversed. The thought makes me shudder. The Japanese are truly barbarians. We must repent and reform ourselves.

At present, I am living in the country where I evacuated from the devastation of Tokyo, impoverished, without means or clothing, just managing to stay alive day by day. I regret that there is nothing I can do, but if I had the power, I would forge myself into a member of the Diet and arouse public opinion by speaking my mind freely. All Japanese feel as I have described here, but they are too frightened to express themselves. Nowadays when I meet people, I discuss with them how to get Japan to rise from the ashes. They all agree with my plan for United States–Japan unification. I have been amazed to find that people have this opinion even before I talk with them. I cannot do anything because I do not have any resources, but if I had the means, I would bravely go forth, even in the face of death, to help Japan and bring the people peace, but alas, there is nothing I can do. However, even if I do not start such a movement, the idea of United States–Japan unification will likely spread naturally among the people in due time.

I apologize deeply for taking so much of your busy time with my long letter. Please forgive me for speaking out of place. I apologize earnestly.

Finally, let me say that the Japanese people are fortunate. They have been blessed beyond measure to be under the direction of a great people such as

Photo 1.5   November 1945: Contraband foodstuff is lined up for sale at a black market, providing a meager source of income for the jobless and homeless. In short order, racketeers began charging a concession fee to those selling goods. Source: *Mainichi Shimbunsha*

yours. The Japanese people have been enlightened by the well-mannered occupation forces. I doubt the Japanese people would have been as fortunate at the hands of another people instead of your country. We Japanese never imagined that, as guilty as Japan was, we would be saved.

Honorable sir, I beg of you, please continue to guide and help Japan. Only with the help of your people will the Japanese people find happiness and prosperity. I will continue to humbly appeal for unification of the United States and Japan.

In closing, I offer my heartfelt respect and gratitude to all of the members of the occupation forces.

With deep respect,
Yagi Chōsaburō

Thus the letter ends with the greatest praise for the new rulers and one last refrain of the United States–Japan unification chorus. An interesting postscript was appended: If the United States fails to aid Japan, "there will be no other recourse for Japan but to follow the path toward communism." I will return to such threats in later chapters, but suffice it to say that the comment revealed a striking level of calculation among the Japanese of the period. The three letters discussed here all display a loss of confidence because of the military defeat, and by endorsing the American colonization of Japan reveal a tendency to align with the victors in an effort to survive.

2

INVITATIONS

INVITATION TO A MASS RALLY

 There is a two-page letter in English that seems to have been written on an old typewriter with a dried-up ribbon. It is dated November 1945. The type is blurred, and the letter is difficult to read. "T. Fuse" is typed at the end of the letter, but the signature is nearly illegible. It was hard to believe that the letter was written by Fuse Tatsuji, a famous political lawyer with links to the Communist Party, until I saw his name listed as the spokesman for the organizers of "a mass rally to welcome the occupation forces" in the prospectus that was sent with the letter.

Before the war, Fuse and a colleague, Yamazaki Kesaya, were widely known as "socialist lawyers." Fuse began by serving as an attorney for the defendants in the 1918 Rice Riot, and he later defended Pak Yeol and Kaneko Fumiko, who were tried for high treason in 1923. During the following decade he led a team of defense lawyers in a succession of trials of Japan Communist Party members indicted under the Maintenance of Public Order Act. As a result of this legal work Fuse himself was prosecuted under the same law, his license was revoked, and he spent more than a year in Chiba Prison beginning in June 1939.

Japan's defeat in the war was thus greeted by Fuse as the arrival of liberation. When a group of political prisoners was released on October 10, 1945, Fuse gave the opening speech at the "people's rally to welcome the liberated freedom fighters," which was held at Aviation Hall in Tokyo that afternoon. It was only natural that Fuse would come up with a plan to give a heartfelt welcome to the occupation forces that had brought about the liberation. But this was not a simple matter. Fuse's letter begins by seeking MacArthur's understanding of how the rally is to be held. The letter has an old-fashioned feel to it, with numerous expressions that are characteristically Japanese:[1]

Office of Preparation for Welcome
Mass-meeting for Allied Forces
c/o Kyobunkan, 4-chome, Ginza
Kyobashi-ku [Tokyo]
Nov. 1945

Your Excellency General Douglas MacArthur,
Supreme Commander for Allied Troops,
etc, etc, etc.

Your Excellency, Being desirous of having an interview with Your Excellency on the matter undermentioned, I would be honored if Your Excellency would be good enough to indicate me on what date and time and at what place it would be convenient for Your Excellency to receive me.

1) To beseech Your Excellency's favourable understanding our sincerity implied in promotion of Welcome Mass-meeting for Allied Troops, particulars of which are mentioned in the printed matter enclosed herewith.

The use of "etc., etc., etc." after MacArthur's title is reminiscent of the musical *The King and I,* where the king of Siam humorously adds "et cetera, et cetera, et cetera" at the end of his lines. In this letter, it probably was used to indicate MacArthur's many other titles, such as general of the army and commander of the U.S. Far East Command. Fuse is not as humorous as the king of Siam, but still his letter has a quaint charm.

The prospectus for the rally—the enclosed "printed matter," in Japanese—went into some detail about why Fuse believed MacArthur and the occupation forces deserved to be welcomed with a mass rally. Here is the description of the purpose of the rally:

[The leaders of the occupation] have abolished the Special Thought Police that suppressed assemblies for the expression of public opinion and interfered with the freedom of thought and association that contribute to human culture.

They have dissolved Japan's military cliques and the bureaucracy, who in their haughty and aggressive dream of world conquest drove one hundred million Japanese into the war effort, squandering the precious lives and resources of the people, and resulting in the misery and calamity of defeat. They have liquidated Japan's zaibatsu that exploited the energies of the masses of workers and farmers and forced them into the duress of starvation. For the future of the Japanese people, they have brought the peaceful dawn of liberty, equality, and benevolence. They have ably assisted and conscientiously directed the Japanese in the building of a democratic nation. To express our deep respect for General MacArthur, commander of the occupation forces in Japan, and all of the leaders of the occupation forces, who in the eighty days of the occupation have decisively and effectively taken every opportunity to order the stubborn Japanese government to dismantle every ordinance and structure that oppresses the people, and to show our gratitude for their accomplishments, we will hold a mass rally to welcome the occupation forces.

The prospectus is written with difficult Chinese characters, but the enthusiasm that is coursing through Fuse's heart is quite evident. The writing has a pell-mell quality that seems breathless in its urgency. The letter is filled with anger toward the ruling class that dragged Japan into war, as well as unstinting gratitude toward the soldiers of the occupying army who defeated that military power. A similar note was struck in an "Appeal to the People" issued by Tokuda Kyūichi, Shiga Yoshio, and other members of the Communist Party leadership when they were released from Fuchū Prison after eighteen years of incarceration. Their statement read, "We express our deepest gratitude for the fact that the occupation of Japan by the Allied forces seeking to liberate the world from fascism and militarism has opened the path for a democratic revolution in Japan." This statement came to be known as the "liberation army declaration."

Though many Japanese welcomed the occupation army, it was widely believed that the occupation had established a nonfraternization policy that prohibited American soldiers from associating with the Japanese people. There is some dispute about this; in a contemporary account, John Gunther wrote that "fraternization was never forbidden in Japan and in fact there has been only one public pronouncement about it in the whole history of the occupation. This was an early order by [Eighth Army Commander] General Robert Eichelberger that there should be

Photo 2.1 Imprisoned leaders of the Japan Communist Party are greeted upon their release from Fuchū Prison on the morning of October 10, 1945. Source: Kyōdō News Service

no 'public display' of affection between Americans and Japanese."[2] In any case, Fuse believed there was such a policy, which he thought should be rescinded. His letter continued:

2) To solicit Your Excellency's kind considerations on removing by opportunity of the Welcome Meeting, a ban of exchange of courtesies between Allied troops and Japanese populace, as I believe firmly that it would be released in the near future, though it may be forbidden now, and that then men of the Allied Troops should easily enjoy hearty reception by our intelligent and cultured homes, being kept from faked so-called "Recreation and Amusement" schemed by Japanese Government.

The "recreation and amusement" centers mentioned here refer to the prostitution facilities, successor to the wartime "comfort woman" system for Japanese soldiers, established with the support of the Japanese government prior to the American occupation at the suggestion of former prime minister Prince Konoe Fumimaro. Nonfraternization policy or no, one wonders how many "intellectual and cultural families" could afford to welcome American soldiers into their bombed-out homes in the immediate postwar period. Perhaps it is enough to note Fuse's unbowed national pride in making this suggestion. His letter continues:

3) To ask Your Excellency's opinion as to date and time of the Mass-meeting to be held if Your Excellency would be good to grant it.

4) To entreat Your Excellency's instruction as to the members, as I expect more than one hundred, to be invited to the Meeting, so that I may dispatch invitations to the nominated.

Apparently Fuse was not confident that support for the rally would arise spontaneously, so he planned to get MacArthur to sign off on the plan first and then mobilize his key participants. The prospectus, issued in October, listed about seventy names as "prominent supporters," but Fuse wrote to MacArthur in November because he was having difficulty getting people to sign on as coorganizers of the rally. The list of supporters in the prospectus was made up of forty-one leading liberal intellectuals (including Fuse himself) and twenty-six regional representatives, who appear to be labor and peasant movement leaders from prefectures throughout Japan. The events these representatives would be expected to support were explained as follows:

[F]or Your Excellency's reference, our projects prepared for the Meeting are as followings.

a) At First Meeting Place, 5 to 10 deputies for populace are to give welcome speeches and outspoken reports on our country's conditions of today, the manuscripts of which be previously forwarded to Your Excellency's hand by the day before the Meeting.

b) Your Excellency's speech of impression on the above-mentioned reports and greeting to our populace are expected. About 150 civil guards will watch over the place.

According to the prospectus, Hibiya Hall in central Tokyo was planned for the first gathering; it was to be attended by "three thousand to five thousand representatives, selected by the organizers as reflecting public opinion." There was every possibility that some incident might occur if MacArthur were to participate in a public rally so soon after the surrender. Fuse proposed to have the grounds patrolled, not by soldiers of the occupation and not by Japanese police, but by civilian guards. This is another indication of Fuse's extraordinary belief in democracy. The program continues:

c) At Second Meeting Place, several welcome speeches are to be given by our promoters and also spontaneously by populace offering adoration and gratitude to Allied Troops.

The second gathering was to take place in the square in front of Hibiya Hall, and Fuse envisioned the mobilization of "tens of thousands of the ordinary public through reports in the news media." MacArthur's role at this gathering was not touched upon.

d) At Third Meeting Place (to be used only for bad weather), services carried on at First Meeting Place would be transferred to all the moving populace on spot by means of radio.

For the third venue, the central hall of Tokyo Station had been selected. Following the daytime program, two evening events were planned: a dinner at Hōsō Kaikan (then headquarters of NHK, Japanese national broadcasting, in Uchisaiwai-chō) and a play at the Imperial Theater:

e) At Dinner, about a hundred of our government officials and men of cultivated circles would also be invited, more than one thousand be expected to attend. For reference, cost of dinner to be served is five yen head and it is a limit that our populace could obtain as a daily food today.

Fuse probably intended the cost of the dinner to be covered by the participants, but it is unclear how he expected to cover the other considerable expenses for the events. The prospectus pledges that labor and expenses for the rally will be arranged by the organizers, but did Fuse really have this assurance? In any case, where there is an event, there must also be souvenirs:

f) Souvenir to be presented is a "Kasaban" type autograph of our promoters in a single sheet of "Shikishi" paper, which signifies one of statics [tactics] ever used by populace to defend against several oppressions frequently imposed on them during an era of feudalism; cost being 10 yen each.

Kasaban refers to a petition with signatures arrayed like the ribs of an umbrella. During peasant uprisings against Japanese feudal lords, it was common practice for the participants to show their determination and solidarity by signing a petition and sealing it with a fingerprint, often in blood. The person who signed first was considered the leader and was punished severely. To avoid this outcome, the practice was developed of signing in a succession of lines radiating from a center, much like the ribs of an umbrella radiate from the handle. This made it impossible to tell who had signed first and increased the possibility that the leaders might survive to continue the struggle.

The *kasaban* was a clever invention of people struggling to survive, but what did Fuse have in mind in presenting MacArthur with a *shikishi* (a large, square calligraphy card) with the organizers' signatures in this format? He may have wanted to let the occupation leaders know about the inventiveness of the peasants who struggled against feudalism, and it may have seemed advantageous for the rally organizers to present themselves on an equal footing. There is no indication that Fuse implied a warning that the people would rise in opposition if democracy were suppressed or that the organizers feared retribution. Everything in the letter suggests that his intentions were straightforward, even naive.

The evening was to end at the theater:

g) Invitation to the theatre means that we hope and expect Your Excellency and men could enjoy and appreciate, the performances played by the most progressive "Zenshinza" party of actors.

The Zenshin-za was formed in 1931. The troupe was dedicated to theater reform and democratic control through collective living. Fuse was legal counsel for the troupe and a lifelong friend of the leader Kawarazaki Chōjūrō. The group's first postwar performance was in

November 1945 at the Imperial Theater, with *Port of Toulon* and *Narukami* on the bill. It was an interesting combination of a French drama of resistance and a charming Kabuki play; at one point, the actor Kunitarō sang "La Marseilles" backstage while wearing the makeup for Taemanohime, the princess in *Narukami*. This was the performance that Fuse wanted MacArthur to attend.

Near the end of his letter, Fuse provides some information about himself. It is not a typical self-introduction, for he assumes that the occupation authorities already know something about him. He tries to correct any preconceptions:

> As to the standpoint of myself, I should like to add that I am nothing of communist as communicated in newspapers, but am convinced that "Tennoism" should not so much be knocked down as be aufgehoben [a term used in Hegelian dialectics to mean "sublated"].

It was true that Fuse had sacrificed his social currency by defending indicted members of the Communist Party, and he was a party sympathizer, but he had never been a member of the party. Fuse's complex relationship with the party is well explored by his eldest son Kanji, whose biography of Fuse is quite objective (he refers to his father throughout the book as "Mr. F").[3]

Fuse's prison sentence was commuted in July 1940 by an imperial amnesty in commemoration of the year 2600 (the number of years since Japan's creation, in the convention of the prewar and wartime era). He lived quietly during the war in his seaside home in Zushi. A year before the end of the war, he received the sad news that his third son, Morio, had died of illness in prison in Kyoto. Morio had also been indicted under the Maintenance of Public Order Act. Kanji quotes his father's notes from this period: "St. John was impatient and emotional, and to help the poor he engaged the rich in battle. The brave were drawn in by the fight, and as a result, St. John and the brave and the poor were all persecuted by the rich and made to suffer." Kanji added this remark: "Mr. F seems to have likened St. John to the Communist Party, and 'the brave' to himself."[4]

When he writes, "[Mr. F] was only using his Tolstoyan conscience as his guide,"[5] there is some bitterness in his tone, but Fuse's attitude toward the emperor system ("Tennoism") may reflect this very Tolstoyan conscience. Fuse recognized the Japanese people's strong support for the emperor system as a reality, and he believed that as the people's consciousness matured, that support would be supplanted (the Hegelian term he used, *aufgehoben*, means superseded but simultaneously preserved). At the same time, deep in his heart he had a feeling of honest gratitude toward the emperor. Fuse believed, according to Kanji, that "at a time when it was not clear how long the Pacific War would continue, it was the emperor's decisive resolution that prompted the acceptance of the terms of unconditional surrender."[6] It was the kind of perspective, colored by affection for the emperor, that one might expect of someone raised in the Meiji era. "Mr. F's heart was filled with gratitude for the occupation forces and the emperor who brought about the end of the war," Kanji noted.[7] Kanji makes no mention of Fuse's letter to MacArthur, but this was certainly an expression of his gratitude toward the occupation forces. That upwelling of gratitude ended in an almost comical affair, but first let me quote the end of Fuse's letter.

I believe that it is natural to promote the Welcome Mass-meeting for the Allied Troops; and that Your Excellency would kindly understand that if Your Excellency refer Mr. Juzo Nagata of Kyobunkan and Mr. Wataru Narahashi, president of the Legislative Bureau [director-general, Cabinet Legislation Bureau].

I am, Your cordially,
T. Fuse

Unfortunately, it seems that few of Fuse's comrades shared his feeling that it was natural to hold a welcome rally for the occupation forces. Kanji offers the following rather candid assessment of what ended up being a fruitless personal campaign:

Mr. F had obtained an unexpected liberation, and he felt the need to undertake something grand. In a word, he had been yearning for something to do for ten years. He was like a desperately hungry person presented with a feast, who wants to eat everything and feels that he can. After the "people's rally" at the Aviation Hall, Mr. F began plans to organize the "mass rally to welcome the occupation forces." At the end of October, he sent letters all over the country soliciting supporters, but the results were disappointing. It seems that many people regarded his efforts as Mr. F's way of selling his name to the occupation forces.[8]

Thus Fuse's plan for a mass rally came to naught. It may have been a time when many people, including the Japan Communist Party, were filled with gratitude for the "army of liberation," but perhaps even

Photo 2.2   July 19, 1946: Citizens of a Tokyo suburb used the occasion of the annual Bon festival, when food is traditionally offered to departed ancestors, to display thanks to General MacArthur for obtaining food imports to Japan, where shortages remained severe nearly a year after the end of the war. Source: U.S. Army

intellectuals didn't have any energy to spare for such an effort. Or perhaps it was just natural for people to shy away from publicly embracing
and lavishing praise on the victor that just yesterday was considered
the enemy and moreover had firebombed nearly every Japanese city
and dropped atomic bombs on Hiroshima and Nagasaki. MacArthur's
aide-de-camp Brigadier General Bonner Fellers prepared a short memo
summarizing Fuse's letter for the general, but there is no record of how
MacArthur responded. If the letter was ignored, as probably was the
case, then Fuse's efforts didn't even succeed in selling his name.

There is a sequel to this story. According to Fuse Kanji's account, his
father was unable to abandon his plan entirely, and he began to talk
with friends about organizing a "rally of gratitude to the emperor and
the occupation forces." The result was a gathering called the "people's
rally in gratitude for the end of the war," which took place on March 1,
1946, on the grounds outside of the imperial palace. It was organized by
the National Committee for the Festival Commemorating the Establishment of a Peaceful Japan. Kida Minoru, then a reporter for a French
news service (and later renowned as a perceptive analyst of Japanese society), recalls this event in his memoirs:

> One day, a foreign colleague was reading the newspaper. Suddenly his eyes popped
> wide with surprise, he laughed and asked, "What's this about?" I took a look, and
> it was an article about Fuse and others holding a "celebration of defeat." To an or-
> dinary Frenchman, celebrating defeat would usually be considered an act of trea-
> son, or at best, an attempt to win the favor of the Americans at a time when the
> government and ideology was in disarray because of defeat. I was at a loss as to what
> to say. I dodged the question by saying, "They must be Dadaists."
>   The truth is that, just like that reporter, I could not understand in the least why
> anyone would "celebrate defeat."[9]

Of course, Fuse was a Tolstoyan humanist and not a Dadaist, and his
desire to celebrate the end of the war was, in his view, entirely patriotic.
Also, when France was defeated, it was Hitler who marched into Paris,
but it was MacArthur, who considered himself an apostle of democracy,
who entered Tokyo. As we have seen, Fuse was extravagantly grateful
toward the foreign liberators. I have not found any reports in the Japanese press that described a "celebration of defeat," although it is possible that a foreign correspondent could have described the rally in this
way. In any case, the "people's rally in gratitude for the end of the war"

took place under a freezing rain. Facing a small crowd of participants, "Mr. F, drenched with the cold sleet, raised three banzais."[10] One wonders if the cheers were for the emperor or for MacArthur.

HEARTFELT INVITATIONS

MacArthur did not accept a single invitation from the Japanese. Despite his eloquence, he never directly addressed the Japanese people during the occupation. Fuse's schemes were thus destined for frustration from the start. In *The Riddle of MacArthur*, John Gunther commented ironically on the general's transcendental manner of governing: "God does not choose often to expose himself."[11] This very aloofness has been credited with the success of the occupation. Nonetheless, the Japanese continued to send invitations to the blue-eyed ruler throughout the occupation. The next letter came from the chief priest at Hachiman shrine in Kamakura and was written about the same time that Fuse initiated his call for a mass rally. It was typewritten in English in two parts, the invitation and the attached notes.[12]

24 October 1945

General Douglas MacArthur
Supreme Commander of the Allied Powers
American Embassy
1, Enokizaka-ohō
Akasaka-ku, Tokyo

Your Excellency,
   The visit of Your Excellency and the staff to the Kamakura Hachimangu Shrine last month was a source of great honor and pleasure to me and all the members of this shrine. It has since been my fervent desire to have an opportunity of furnishing Your Excellency with some form of entertainment as diversion in your daily life of arduous responsibilities.
   On the 28th of October, from one to three o'clock in afternoon, we are going to hold the annual Bunbokusai Festival of this shrine (Note 1). We would like to request the honor of the presence of Your Excellency, Mrs. MacArthur and your son on this occasion. We have prepared a special program of Japanese traditional

arts (Note 2), such as formal tea ceremonies, flower arrangements and classical dancing, hoping that the program would be of some interest to you.

I was afraid that it would be presumptuous of myself to send a formal invitation to Your Excellency under the present circumstances and have, therefore, taken the liberty of abbreviating formality and substituting this letter for an invitation card.

I have, for similar purposes as stated above, asked the presence on this occasion of the members of the staff of Your Excellency's Headquarter, Commanding General and the staff of the Eighth Army Corps.

With best regards, I am,
Very respectfully yours,

[signature]
Moriuji Saida,
Chief Priest
Kamakura Hachimangu Shrine

Note 1.

BUNBOKUSAI is a festival to commemorate Minamoto Sanetomo, Shogun of the Kamakura period. Sanetomo, although a soldier by profession, was a man of cultures at heart, endeavored to import the cream of civilization from Kyoto, then the cultural center of Japan, and this became the pioneer of the Kamakura period culture. He excelled especially in waka poetry and game of kemari (a kind of football played by the nobles of these times.)

Note 2.
PROGRAM

1. Tea ceremony and flower arrangements
2. Dance of Urayasu
3. Dance of the Lion
4. Dance of Shizuka (a famous court lady)
5. Tenor solo by Yoshie Fujiwara
6. Dance of the cherry blossom festival of Genroku period.

Twelve American soldiers claiming to be "MacArthur and his staff" visited the Hachiman shrine in Kamakura on September 2, the day on which the instrument of surrender was signed, but it seems doubtful that the supreme commander was among them.[13] Of course, this invitation requesting a repeat visit was not accepted. In addition to his general policy of declining all such invitations, MacArthur was constitutionally unable to indulge in diversions, except for the cowboy movies he watched late at night at his residence. It is amusing to imagine MacArthur among the Japanese enjoying the Dance of the Cherry Blossom Festival, but such an event did not fit his style of governing Japan.

One more charming invitation will close this chapter. The letter was written in Japanese with pen in rather large characters on two sheets of paper.[14]

INVITATION
July 28, 1948

The Honorable General Douglas MacArthur:

At a time of midsummer heat, I humbly offer my best wishes for your continued health and for the vigor and intelligence with which you are building the basis for world peace.

Please pardon my rudeness for suddenly submitting this letter. I am a simple fisherman living along the Iruma River. I make my living by going to the river every day to catch ayu [sweetfish] and eels. I believe that a defeated nation like ours is only able to live in peace because of the understanding of the Allied nations and your generosity and discreet guidance. From the bottom of my heart I express my gratitude for the outstanding ideals and skill with which you are carrying out the restoration and democratization of Japan, and for accomplishing for Japan and the Japanese what we could not bring about even through long years of intense struggle. We are simply too poor and meek to repay you for your supreme efforts and accomplishments, but within my capabilities, I have thought deeply about a way to express my gratitude for your unceasing efforts.

Since ancient times, the ayu in this river have been caught in a special way, prepared alive, and served to our guests on the spot amid the beautiful scenery. Traditionally, the ayu are also brought home as presents. Fortunately, this is the time of the year that ayu are fat and delicious. I beg of you to oblige me with your presence for a day of pure entertainment some day in early August, and I will have the opportunity to express my humble gratitude. If the good weather persists, ayu are bound to be caught. Right now, those ayu that swam upstream naturally and those that were hatched and stocked by the local fishing cooperative are lively and dancing in the river.

I will be waiting your notification of a convenient date and time when you may be able to take some time off from your busy schedule and come along with your gracious wife and son. The place will be Jisaki, Hannō-cho, Iruma-gun, Saitama Prefecture.

As soon as I hear from you, I would like to make more definite plans in consultation with your office.

This invitation and plan are my own doing; no one else is involved. Therefore, there is no need for you to worry about the participation of local officials. I also will refuse any type of payment.

I hasten to send this unofficial letter of invitation and I await your response. I will be most obliged if you will appreciate my sincerity and make plans accordingly.

Katō Ikkan
Kashiwabara-mura
Iruma-gun, Saitama Prefecture

This letter needs no explanation. The pseudonym Ikkan ("one fishing pole") probably was intended to mean "a simple fisherman," but his style and calligraphy suggest a man of considerable learning. In the letter he refers to "what we could not bring about even through long years of intense struggle"; whether he meant the abolishing of the tenant-farm system, the liberation of the Burakumin, or something else is not clear. However, he deeply appreciated the three years of MacArthur's occupation and found a way to show his gratitude within his means and without pretension. This is not sycophancy; it is an accomplished Japanese method of survival that opens one's heart even to a foreign ruler. By the summer of 1948, for Katō Ikkan, the occupation had become a familiar state of affairs.

3

"I DARE SAY . . ."

 The large majority of the letters sent to MacArthur were supportive, if not adulatory. Some Japanese, however, dared take up their pens to express criticisms of the Allied forces. The first of these letters was sent within days of MacArthur's arrival in Japan:[1]

Marunouchi, Tokyo
September 1, 1945

Gen. Douglas MacArthur
Commander-in-Chief of the Occupation Army in Japan

Dear Sir:
*   This is to inform you that our International Peace Society was organized and came into being on the third day after the termination of the war when the Imperial Rescript was proclaimed. Regarding the Society's aim and plan we expect to have them put in shape and made public in the not far distant future; but in essence, as its name indicates, we stand to contribute toward the promotion of international peace. In this premise, we have recently asked different sections of our citizenry to express their frank views, and do it impartially and without fear and concealment, on what they desire of your honor and the American Army of Occupation. And as a result we are in receipt of numerous letters including callers in person. Of the views so expressed we believe the following one is most timely and typical of the many, which we take the liberty of submitting to you as a reference for your kind considera-*

tion. We are most happy if you consider it a just protest of our Tokyo citizenry: (we quote a letter sent us by a Japanese lady.)

This letter, which was typed in English, is noteworthy not only for the formality and precision of its language but also for its date— September 1, 1945. The signing of the instrument of surrender on the USS *Missouri* took place the following day, so the Pacific War had not yet officially ended. At this early date, what appeal was this International Peace Society making to MacArthur? The rest of the letter is devoted to a translation of a complaint that had been sent to the society:

We learned some time ago from newspaper reports that when London was raided by German planes more than 80 per cent of London women became neurasthenic, of whom over 70 per cent verged on hysterics. Now recalling what took place in Japan, whenever a B-29 flew over our Kanto area there was no question but that it caused our people worry, unrest and loss of valuable time. Our house was subjected to attacks twice with incendiary bombs and finally burnt out. My sister in Hiroshima is missing as a victim of atomic bombs. Our family is keeping up an unhealthy living in an old air-raid dug-out. Our baby is barely maintaining its life with the scanty supply of milk from my breasts. And to aggravate the situation our store of foods is very low.

Yet if this was wartime we would have nothing to complain, but in spite of the fact that now it is peace time we are to hear the noisy American planes which are flying low our overheads almost everyday, be the acts intended for reconnaissance, intimidation, demonstration, or what not. We are seized of a very unpleasant feeling, sometimes causing us to think we might go hysteric, if not insane.

In exasperation when I spoke this to my husband he agreed with me. He said he himself was much bothered with the noise in his work, really making him to think that the American acts looked more than necessary for the carrying out of reconnaissance. He said further that once committed to a promise the Japanese are a people who will stick to it like going under a God's oath, as in fact they are a people most proud in this respect, being superior to all others in the world. Instead of living by betrayal and trickery, they would rather choose death as being more respectful. He thought it seems incumbent upon the Americans to first know this. This is what he so emphatically reminded me.

The letter continues, but even reading this far one is struck by the strong tone, uncommon for a Japanese woman. It could be that softer nuances were lost in translation, but what she is saying is quite clear— the noise of the airplanes is driving her crazy; the war is over, so it is not necessary to intimidate the Japanese anymore; and since the Japanese have opted for surrender, they will stand by their word.

This could be considered a legitimate complaint. With Japan's surrender the war had ended, and peace should have been restored as soon as possible. Anyone living through that time would have dreaded the sound of airplanes, which reminded them of the firebombing of their city. On the other hand, the American forces had just begun their occupation, and this request must have seemed quite self-centered. It is not so easy to bring the enormous apparatus of war to a halt. The remnants of Japan's kamikaze units had still been massed at Atsugi air base outside of Tokyo until a few days earlier, with some talk of attacking American planes. MacArthur had arrived at this same airfield only two days before this letter was written. He made a show of getting off his plane carrying no weapons, but the area was surrounded by heavily armed American troops. As far as the American military was concerned, the war with Japan continued.

Whether the woman who wrote the letter understood the situation is not clear, but she does go on to say that, if the American planes had to fly, she wished they would fly somewhat higher:

Now should the American acts have been carried out for the purpose of reconnaissance or for the maintenance of their dignity, I would have been the first to recognize the superiority of the American air force. But even if I recognize their superiority, there seems to be no necessity to disturb the sick people in beds or irritate the sensibility of women and children. Of this feature, I wish the American authorities would give a special attention. If in any event their conducting of reconnaissance be in need, and that repeated almost daily, I wish they would fly around in a little upper air. This is our earnest wish arising from living our present life.

And if my wishes were granted, I would hope that those American planes will refrain from flying around over our most respectful Imperial Palace.

Finally, it is my firm belief that by attending to the care of these matters the amity and friendship between the Americans and Japanese will gradually be promoted.

Yours very sincerely,
[signed] Iwao Tomimoto
International Peace Society

The woman's hope that American planes not fly over the imperial palace illustrates that immediately after the war, even in defeat, many people still did not want the honor of the emperor to be infringed upon. In later chapters, we will explore popular perceptions of the emperor and the imperial system. As to the activities of the International Peace Society, I have found no record aside from this letter to MacArthur. Ordinarily, an organization like this engages in public programs in support of its agenda, but I have encountered no evidence of such activities. It could be that this group never accomplished anything beyond sending this letter to MacArthur.

The letter is marked "MacA" in MacArthur's handwriting, evidence that the general read it. He added a note, "To the chief of staff for file. No reply." At least two more sets of initials appear, indicating that GHQ officials took letters of this nature quite seriously.

ON THE BEHAVIOR OF AMERICAN GIs

In the history of war, occupation typically follows in the aftermath of a land battle. During the Pacific War, however, no fighting took place on Japanese soil or involved the civilian population, with the notable exception of the battle of Okinawa (although there were intensive and prolonged aerial attacks on Japan). When the Allied troops arrived on the mainland, they did not appear as an invading or a conquering army, but as troops being stationed in Japan, which was easier for the public to accept (in fact, the occupation forces were generally referred to as *shinchūgun*, which is a rather neutral term that translates as "stationed army," rather than the more direct *senryōgun,* or "occupation army"). Moreover, compared with the Japanese Imperial Army that perpetrated atrocities on the civilian populations of China and Southeast Asia during the war, American soldiers were generally orderly and perceived as "happy soldiers."[2]

There were, of course, incidents that reflected the victor's arrogance of the American army, and it was hardly surprising that young GIs, liberated from the stress of the war and finding themselves in the land of the enemy, would engage in rowdy behavior or worse. Still, MacArthur issued a statement in mid-October saying, "I wish to pay tribute to the magnificent conduct of our troops. With few exceptions, they could well be taken as a model for all times as a conquering army."[3] That may have been why ordinary Japanese citizens believed that it was their duty to report improper conduct of GIs and why MacArthur would pay attention to these reports, which were numerous.[4]

Photo 3.1   General MacArthur reviews the troops outside of the U.S. embassy, April 19, 1946. From the general's perspective, the conduct of the troops was exemplary and should be seen "as a model for all times as a conquering army." Source: U.S. Army

The first such letter we will examine here was written by brush with a free style on two sheets of writing paper, clearly by a woman's hand. The first line reads, "I state to Mr. MacArthur," and her boldness is surprising:

I state to Mr. MacArthur:
Congratulations on Your Excellency's bountiful happiness.
Ordinarily I am one who breaks down the barriers of nationality, and I even smiled at reports of Your Excellency's high praise for American soldiers. But on the night of October 17 at 7 P.M., I was in the women's side of a public bath on Asakusa Dōri [avenue] in Mukō Yanagihara 2-chōme—a person bombed out by the war, washing away the day's toil from my tired body— when a commotion began: "An American soldier is peeping." I could not believe that an American soldier with any intellectual pride would do this, but I happened to see your country's soldiers taking turns laughing and peeping

Photo 3.2   Japanese women dance with GIs at a "recreation and amusement" center set up with the support of the Japanese government. Many of these centers were officially sanctioned prostitution facilities, established to service and contain the sexual drives of the U.S. troops. The occupation put an end to public prostitution in January 1946. Source: *Kyōdō News Service*

from a small window by the side of the bath. If Your Excellency were to hear about this incident, I knew you would be deeply aggrieved, and I secretly felt sorry for you. You have said that Japanese soldiers may have done so and so, and I do not wish to negate your words, but not all of the young Japanese men sent to the front were uncivilized. There were many who were capable of human reflection and cherished refined aesthetics. Your Excellency, please bear in mind that there are some among your soldiers who have the lowest tastes. Women of your country and my country too are all God's children. I pray the best of health to you.

Butsuko

The address on the envelope reads, "Mr. MacArthur, MacArthur Headquarters, Kojimachi-ku, Tokyo." The reverse of the envelope says, "Butsuko, Asakusa Dōri, Tokyo, October 20, 1945." The name Butsuko, meaning "child of Buddha," is undoubtedly a pseudonym that was used to emphasize the point that Japanese and American women are all children of God. The writer is from Asakusa, where there is a famous Buddhist temple, another reason she may have considered herself Buddha's child. She makes her points with certain degree of irony and style, indicating that for a woman of the period she must have been quite well educated.

As mentioned above, MacArthur issued a statement on October 16, when the demobilization of the Japanese armed forces was completed, pointing to the low standard of behavior of the Japanese army during the war and praising the American troops. The writer shows her mettle by referring to that statement and suggesting that MacArthur bear in mind that not all of his soldiers were saints, nor were all Japanese soldiers uncivilized.

The next letter was written on a postcard and also gives an account of GI misconduct, but this one has neither name nor address.

October 19 [1945]

To the Honorable Supreme Commander, Dear General MacArthur:

May I say that American soldiers, with their strict discipline, have taught us Japanese a lesson that strikes the bottom of our hearts, but there are those among them whose conduct is not acceptable. On the 19th of October shortly after noon, two members of the American occupation army appeared at the provisions depot [of the former Japanese army] at the Ibaraki Golf Club, Kasuga-mura, Mishima-gun, Osaka Prefecture. They loaded a truck with sake and beer and sold them at black market prices along a road in [the village of] Shimohozumi.

There may be ways to explain this activity, but there must be a more fair and rational way. I believe this was not done legally, so I am notifying you. It was also wrong for the Japanese to buy the goods, but we are like hungry wolves, so I feel those who instigated the wrongdoing are to blame.

Incidents like those mentioned here happened throughout Japan, and some reached scandalous proportions. For example, in 1948 it came to light that high-ranking GHQ officers had taken bribes in a scandal involving loans to the Shōwa Denkō company. The point here, however, is to appreciate the sincerity of the Japanese people who took MacArthur at his word when he promised that discipline would be maintained.

WHAT ABOUT AMERICA'S WAR CRIMES?

There are a number of letters that give the impression that the writer did not shy away from challenging the victor, even in the immediate aftermath of the war. These assertive statements stand in sharp contrast to the letters quoted in the first chapter, which reflect a loss of self-esteem among the people.

The following postcard, dated November 28 (probably 1945), was written in pen in a mix of *hiragana* and *katakana* scripts, with quite good calligraphy. The note is signed Murayama Sakuji, with an address in the Ōtemachi section of Tokyo. If this was his actual name and address, one has to marvel at his boldness.

The problem of democracy should be addressed after ample food has been obtained. Let the people have a "bare livelihood" [demo kurashi, a pun on "democracy"].

Photo 3.3   People line up to receive a free distribution of potatoes at the black market in front of the Hankyū department store in Osaka, November 20, 1945. Source: Mainichi Shimbunsha

This is not a time for ideological debate. Where is justice when only American soldiers have full stomachs and the Japanese people are on the verge of starvation? Have you forgotten the American spirit? Import a large quantity of staple foods immediately. Otherwise the people will not respect America; they will alienate themselves. I dare ask, "Are you planning another mass killing of the people with a passive atomic bomb?"

This letter can be seen as a bluff by the loser who demands of the victor, "Give me rice and I will be quiet." By equating the problem of hunger with the atomic bomb, he figured he would be getting under the skin of the Americans.

The next letter is a more systematic critique of the self-righteousness of the American victors, and it is striking in the directness of its challenge to MacArthur. The focus is a criticism of the Tokyo war crimes tribunal and the issue of responsibility for the war. The date, March 15, 1947, perhaps indicates that the Japanese people had reached a point where they could view the American occupation with a certain objectivity and express themselves with some confidence. The writer identifies himself as a primary school teacher from the city of Kōfu.

To Commander MacArthur:

As a Japanese, I feel that it is extremely unfair that the term war crimes is being used at the Tokyo tribunal that is now taking place.

Since it was a world war, it would be most fair to judge right as right and wrong as wrong through a world war trial.

During the trial, whenever testimony refers to illegal acts of American forces, the judges always avoid the subject and seal the testimony. Can this be called a fair trial? War is the act of fighting over lives, and many kinds of extreme, bloodthirsty actions occur. But today, after surrender, I don't think one should be judging the killing that took place in wartime.

We Japanese, for our part, when undefended cities like Kōfu were incinerated, five hundred innocent lives were lost. Also, clearly marked hospital ships were sunk during battle, and on Guadalcanal Island wounded Japanese soldiers were flattened like paper under a steam roller; these are memories that cannot be erased from the mind of a parent like myself who sent his child to war. I am impressed that a race of meat eaters is sweet toward women but then takes pleasure in committing such cruel deeds.

Photo 3.4   An American ex-prisoner of war testifies at the Yokohama war crimes trial on May 27, 1946, identifying a guard from a prison camp in Manila as the "man who beat me." Aside from the Tokyo tribunal, where the top leaders of the Japanese war effort ("Class A" war criminals) were tried, the Yokohama trial of "Class B" and "Class C" war criminals was the only one to take place in Japan; others were held throughout the Asian war theater. Source: Mainichi Shimbunsha

There is a lot of fuss being made at the Tokyo tribunal right now over whether the twenty-four defendants are guilty or innocent. However, as the American lawyer has stated, when the Japanese tried to ease their population growth by emigrating to America with its vast territory, the American government banned immigration. When we began, out of necessity, to colonize Manchuria, the United States and the Soviet Union interfered and threatened us with economic boycott. When the tightening of the ABCD encirclement[5] coerced Japan, the Japanese, like a cornered mouse biting a cat, began the war as a legitimate act of defense or self-defense. This is what most of the Japanese people believe. The twenty-four defendants only acted in order to help the people; they only took unavoidable measures for the country's sake. From the American standpoint, it may have been a burdensome war, but its cause originated in the American exclusion of Japanese immigrants, it is your own fault, so I think they should be found not guilty. You should lecture them that resorting to arms was an overreaction and set them free, thus displaying the magnanimity of a civilized country. Punishing the twenty-four defendants is the same as punishing all of the Japanese people.

Given the current state of the Tokyo trials, one would have to delete the term "measures for self defense" from the language, because it has lost its meaning. After these trials, where will the people of the world turn to hold trials for the crimes of burning a defenseless city, or incinerating civilians, or murder with an atomic bomb? Unless America provides appropriate acknowledgment that what is wrong is wrong, even a defeated people cannot accept American methods as fair.

American dignity would also be damaged if the Soviet Union's violation of its treaties with Japan is left unaddressed. To only focus on Japanese treaty violations cannot be considered judging the truth, can it?

These are the thoughts of a victim of the bombing whose house was burned. Please place your hand on your heart and think about it. I know these thoughts are not illogical. I have dared to submit this letter in the hope that Your Excellency will give it fair consideration.

At home, sitting on straw mats,
An elementary school teacher, citizen
March 15, 1947

This man was likely moved to write to MacArthur out of anger at his home being destroyed in the bombing; his sharp words cut to the heart of American self-righteousness. His reference to the atomic bombs and the firebombing of Japanese cities is worth noting. In spite of the fact that most major Japanese cities had been devastated in the last years of the war by Allied aerial attacks, resulting in hundreds of thousands of predominantly civilian casualties, remarkably few of the letters express anger toward the Allies for these acts, as this letter does. Anger of this sort appears to have been directed at the Japanese wartime government and military leaders, rather than at the Allies. This letter is a notable exception to that rule. On the other hand, it would be hard to deny that the writer's complete failure to address Japanese aggression in the Pacific War makes his logic self-serving. The writer had the courage to include his name and address, Ōno Hideo from the city of Kōfu, on the envelope.

The next letter was written a half year later, and it is a severe criticism of the policies of the entire occupation.

2-457 Ikebukuro, Toshima-ku [Tokyo]
September 18, 1947

The Respected and Beloved Honorable General MacArthur
Dear Sir:
The cool autumn has arrived, and I offer my best wishes for Your Excellency's health and diligence in the handling of your duties. Without respect to proper protocol, I am submitting this letter because I harbor some questions about your "occupation policies." Many Japanese people are also dissatisfied.

Since the end of the war, we have breathed the air of freedom, and through your good policies, the slaves of the emperor have become free citizens and have come to value democracy, and the labor movement and farmers' movement have grown by the day. I am truly grateful and moved from the bottom of my heart in so many ways.

Recently, however, the excesses of the soldiers of the occupation have become intolerable: incidents of rape, armed robbery, and violence are too numerous to count. The present situation is that after dark women and children and even others do not want to pass near the barracks of the occupation forces, so they choose a roundabout way. How about the wages of those who work for the occupation forces? Are you aware of their complaints? It seems that interpreters and others are living in luxury by selling military goods on the black market.

These problems easily reach the eyes and ears of the Japanese people; they spread to the whole population in no time and foster mistrust of America. Absurd ideas are spreading: "We lost, so we cannot help it. We are under occupation, so even if communism is right, let's do as America says for now. Then, we'll distinguish ourselves in an American-Soviet war. We should attack America later."

Mr. Truman, General Eisenhower, and your country's top government officials praise America as the only democracy and insist that the Soviet Union is a dictatorial and totalitarian state.

Even people who once believed this view, as propagandized in progovernment newspapers, are now experiencing an antidemocratic America through your occupation policies. More and more people are beginning to feel that the word dictatorship does not apply to the Soviet Union alone.

Basically, the writer approves of MacArthur's policies, but the letter shows that after two years, the people had become tired of the occupation. MacArthur himself had pointed to the danger of a prolonged occupation: "After about the third year, any military occupation begins to collapse of its own weight," he was quoted as saying.[6] Morale among the occupation troops was falling as they grew tired of routine military duties, as the writer of this letter pointed out. It was typical of this type of outspoken letter to move directly from criticizing occupation policy to pointing to the complacency of American democracy, and then to proceed to sympathy for the Soviet Union. It does not appear that the writer had any real knowledge of the reality of Soviet socialism, and this type of letter must have irritated MacArthur. The writer moves on to discuss food imported from America. The Japanese had survived food shortages, and now they were beginning to lose patience with the poor quality of imported food.

Regarding the distribution of corn meal:

In the southern part of the USA, a bumper crop of potatoes was sprayed with kerosene and burned. A member of Congress protested, and as a result, an order was issued, "Do not spray potatoes with kerosene." There is also the issue of what is being done with food other than potatoes, and then chickens are not being fed corn anymore, they are fed wheat flour, while the people of Japan have to eat chicken feed [corn] that is more expensive than rice.

Is this a false rumor?

At any rate, freedom of speech, assembly, publishing, and association are like rice cakes in a picture, and many young Japanese are pledging to overthrow the United States. Some serious young men are watching with great interest the actions of the Japan Communist Party and its policy of sharing life with the masses.

The fascist Truman, they say, manipulated by the American fascist [J. Edgar] Hoover, has mobilized Japanese propaganda organs. A middle-aged newspaperman of about forty said, "I have been called a rotten labor union leader, but I am surprised at Mac. I do not want American democracy anymore, it's worse than Tōjō."

I have dared to quote his words, but as I said earlier, this kind of thinking is reflected in the people.

"The Soviet Union said so and so at the Allied Council of Japan meeting."
"The plenary session of the United Nations is thus and so." These words do
not serve as propaganda without good policies.

I wonder if the time has not arrived for a change in your occupation
policies?

Yours most respectfully,
Matsubara Tōru

Although the writer quotes other people's opinions in the third person, it still took a great deal of courage to criticize "Mac" in a signed letter. However, despite the boldness, the letter is less than convincing. At the time of this letter, the Japanese Communist Party's honeymoon with the occupation forces was still in the recent past, and it was not until considerably later, when the anticommunist "reverse course" reached full swing in 1949, that the various freedoms began to look like "rice cakes in a picture" to the Japanese people. In short, this letter airs the frustrations of a dauntless man who had grown weary of the occupation earlier than most Japanese.

While these letters showed great spirit, few of them went beyond criticism of the occupation to engage in critical self-reflection. As such, they provide a revealing measure of a people's self-respect and dignity—and their limitations—in speaking their mind to a foreign ruler who exercised such awesome power and carried so potent a personal image as MacArthur did during the occupation.

4

"PLEASE PROTECT THE EMPEROR"

December 16, 1945

The Honorable General MacArthur,
Supreme Commander for the Allied Powers:

The emperor is our life. We cannot live without the emperor. Please do not make His Majesty suffer. This is the ultimate and most earnest request of the Japanese people. Please accept our request.

Takemoto Rihei
Tawaramoto-chō, Shiki-gun
Nara Prefecture

This letter is written in large, bold characters, as if the writer tried to carve the words into the paper. His earnest support for the imperial system and his heartfelt defense of the emperor are noteworthy, but the date of the letter is also important.

In the eyes of the Japanese public, the emperor's position under the occupation was largely established by a historic photograph of Hirohito together with MacArthur at the American embassy on September 27, 1945. MacArthur, standing haughtily with his hands on his hips, was clearly the new ruler of Japan, and the emperor, stiff and diminutive, was just as clearly subject to his authority. The photograph almost mercilessly captured the power structure of the occupation.

In fact, MacArthur's agreeing to meet the emperor and be photographed with him was an early signal that the general would support

Photo 4.1   This famous photograph, taken when Emperor Hirohito made an official visit to General MacArthur at the American embassy, appeared on the front page of Asahi shimbun *and other newspapers on September 29, 1945. The Japanese Home Ministry attempted to ban distribution of the newspapers on the grounds that the photograph compromised the dignity of the emperor, but GHQ overruled the ban.* Source: Asahi Shimbunsha

the continuation of the emperor system, but the photograph also left the strong impression that the emperor's fate was in MacArthur's hands. From around October 1945, after the initial shock of defeat began to dissipate, and continuing until the beginning of the next year, the concern and anxiety of many Japanese was focused on the future of the imperial system and whether the emperor would be indicted for war crimes. Most of the letters to MacArthur appealing for clemency for the emperor and the maintenance of the imperial system date from this period.

This is reflected in a file of letters concerning Emperor Hirohito, upon which this chapter is based. While most of the GHQ/SCAP documents were kept at the National Records Center in Maryland (now stored at the National Archives II), some important documents have been kept at the National Archives in Washington, D.C. Among these are documents from the International Prosecution Section (IPS) of General Headquarters, which was responsible for the International Military Tribunal for the Far East, better known as the Tokyo war crimes trial. The documents include transcripts of interrogations, research reports, and reference materials on "Class A" war crime suspects and various witnesses. File number 254, Emperor Hirohito, consists primarily of letters from the Japanese people to MacArthur and GHQ.

The IPS documents were given special treatment as confidential material until 1975, and their very existence was unknown for many years. When I began searching the archives for letters to MacArthur from the Japanese, it seemed that there were too few letters concerning the emperor and the imperial system, until it became clear that those letters had been placed in a separate file. As I noted earlier, letters from the Japanese were translated and passed on to the appropriate sections within GHQ, where they were utilized in planning and carrying out occupation policies. Letters concerning the emperor were sent to the International Prosecution Section, where they played a role in determining whether Hirohito should be held responsible for the war.

There are 164 letters in the file, the majority written between November 1945 and January 1946 (including twenty without dates that are presumed to have been sent during the same period). By that time, American authorities had already decided to retain the imperial system as a means of exercising political control of Japan, but it appears they were trying to assess the sentiment of the Japanese people regarding the form the system would take. When representatives of the Japanese imperial government accepted the Potsdam Declaration, they demanded as a condition for surrender the "preservation of Japan's national polity." The Allied powers responded that the authority of the emperor and the Japanese government would be subject to the supreme commander for the Allied powers, and the ultimate form of the Japanese government, including the imperial system, was to be "established by the freely expressed will of the Japanese people." The letters from the Japanese people to GHQ were considered an expression of that will.

However, more than the future shape of the imperial system, the people's immediate concern was whether the emperor was to be held responsible for the war and indicted as a war criminal. The Japanese news media had reported that, among the Allied powers, China and Australia were the strongest proponents of indicting the emperor. In the United States, there were two opposing groups. One, centered in the armed forces and including Dean Acheson, assistant secretary of state, insisted that the emperor be held responsible for the war; a second, including Japan specialists such as former ambassador to Japan Joseph Grew, argued that the emperor should be exempt from prosecution. Consequently, the State-War-Navy Coordinating Committee sent an inquiry to MacArthur (SWNCC 55-6), requesting his opinion. The question put to MacArthur was whether it would be possible to carry out the policies of the occupation if the emperor was put on trial. In essence, MacArthur was asked to make a political judgment, not a legal determination, that would decide the fate of the emperor.

MacArthur's reply was dated January 25, 1946, and addressed to army chief of staff General Dwight Eisenhower. In this famous long telegram he characterized the emperor as the equivalent of twenty military divisions. He concluded that the emperor did not bear responsibility for the war, and that an indictment would force major changes in occupation plans because the whole nation would turn to resistance, all government institutions would collapse, and guerrilla warfare would take place in the mountains. This would make it necessary to station an occupation army of at least a million in Japan for many years.[1]

It is now known that, from the early days of the occupation, MacArthur believed that retaining the emperor would assist his governing of Japan, and he had no intention of indicting him as a war criminal. His reply, backed by his authority as the top commander in the field, put an end to the division in American policy on the treatment of the emperor.

How did MacArthur reach his conclusions? Why did he believe that the Japanese people would rise up in resistance if the emperor were to be indicted? There is no evidence that GHQ engaged in a thorough examination of the emperor's responsibility for the war. MacArthur stated that 90–95 percent of the Japanese people supported the emperor in a secret poll, but again there is no record of any survey being conducted to obtain these results.[2]

However, around that time private sector public opinion research firms in Japan did conduct several polls concerning the emperor and the imperial system. The results appeared in the press, under such headlines as "Support for the Imperial System—95%" (*Yomiuri hōchi shimbun*, December 9, 1945), and "92% to 8% Overwhelming Majority Supports Imperial System," (*Asahi shimbun*, January 23, 1946). These figures match the percentages that MacArthur reported as results of his "secret poll." But these figures were perhaps misleading. As Takeda Kiyoko has pointed out, the polls did not differentiate between the emperor and the imperial institution; after the occupation issued a directive disestablishing Shinto as the state religion, and the emperor himself made a New Year's declaration renouncing imperial divinity, the emperor was reduced to symbolic status.[3] In other words, the majority of the people who favored maintenance of the imperial system were supporting an elephant with its tusks removed.

Yamauchi Tōru has also examined the IPS documents thoroughly, and he concluded that as far as the Emperor Hirohito file was concerned, there were only 138 letters from the people to GHQ, and no record of any investigation on the emperor.[4] I agree with the gist of Yamauchi's conclusions. However, as noted above, the total number of letters is 164 (34 letters and 130 cards). Also included in the file are sixteen documents, all in English. These include a translation of an abstract of Konoe Fumimaro's June 1941 letter to the emperor asking to be relieved of his post as prime minister; three copies of the complete translation of an essay on the responsibility of Kido Kōichi, lord keeper of the privy seal, by Konoe's close associate, Iwabuchi Tatsuo, which appeared in the first issue of *Shinsei* in November 1945 (Iwabuchi argued that the emperor had no responsibility for the declaration of war, while Kido bore some responsibility because he recommended Tōjō Hideki for prime minister); and an internal IPS memorandum regarding the necessity of establishing the extent of the imperial family in order to select defendants. As Japanese mail was regularly censored by the occupation, the file also contains parts of ten Japanese letters translated into English for their opinions concerning the imperial system. The number of these additional documents is small, however, and none of the material contained any definite proof as to whether the emperor was responsible for the war. The real significance of the Emperor Hirohito file lay in the contents of the letters from the Japanese people, and, more to the point, in the effect the letters had on MacArthur. Did their contents significantly affect MacArthur's opinion concerning the emperor?

"THE EMPEROR IS MORE THAN A GOD"

Let me return then to the letters themselves. Here are several more in the same vein as the one at the beginning of this chapter. First a postcard:

You must not put the emperor on trial.
The emperor is not responsible.

The front of the postcard, postmarked December 2, was addressed to "General MacArthur, Headquarters of the Allied Forces, Tokyo." It was sent by Fujino Sawako, of the town of Futase in Fukuoka Prefecture. The faltering handwriting in pencil makes one think that it was written by an elementary-school girl.

Another card, postmarked December 12 and sent by Koretsune Hitoshi from the same town, has identical wording, but the writer is an adult because he used Chinese characters for *saiban* (trial) and *sekinin* (responsibility). The next is a postcard addressed in beautiful handwriting to "c/o MacArthur Headquarters, Tokyo"; the postmark is illegible. It says:

You must not put the emperor on trial.
Please, absolutely, do not put the emperor on trial.

Satō Susumu
Soda, Higashi Ueta-mura, Ōita-gun, Ōita Prefecture

Eighty of the letters in the file, or over half of the total, are from Ōita Prefecture. Since the contents and even the wording are similar, it seems as if there was an organized effort to petition for the emperor's life, although it is strange that it should have happened only in Ōita, and the number of letters is small for a campaign. In any case, I will include one more in the same vein. It is also a postcard, addressed "c/o MacArthur Headquarters, Tokyo"; the return address is "Okusako Tetsuji, Mihara Tofu Business Association, Hon-machi, Mihara-shi." The card was written on the printed stationery of the tofu association. It is dated December 20.

The emperor is not a war criminal.
The emperor is a parent to us, the people.
The emperor and the people exist absolutely in peace.
The emperor is a person who prays for the happiness and peace of the people of the world.

The basic pattern of these short letters was to assert that the emperor had no responsibility for the war and to portray him as a symbol of peace. The messages are short and simple.

Let me introduce some longer letters. The following is interesting because the writer uses the first half to confess the spirit of selfless devotion to his country that he embraced during the war.

December 13 [1945]
The Honorable General MacArthur:

Dear Sir:
The cold weather has come. Ever since Your Excellency arrived in Japan, you have been blessed with good health. As one Japanese citizen, I offer my heartfelt gratitude and awe at your ceaseless efforts for Japan's postwar reconstruction, the building of a democratic nation, and the establishment of world peace. I am an uncultured person, and as the saying goes, "The uncultured do not follow decorum." Some of what follows may be improper, but I hope you will forgive me. What I say here is neither false nor exaggerated. I will only honestly say what went through my mind. On December 8, 1941, when the imperial edict for the Greater East Asia War was issued, I jumped with joy and spontaneously shouted three banzais. I felt a great sense of relief. I wrote this poem to express my feelings:

> *Why shouldn't we attack America and England*
> *For the sake of the one billion people of East Asia?*

> *When I think of the boundless mercy of the emperor,*
> *I feel I should give all of myself.*
> *His mercy is deeper than the sea and higher than the mountains.*
> *How sad, I cannot repay my debt to him.*

As a poorly educated and untalented person, I knew nothing about Japanese–American relations at the beginning of the war or about international relations before that. I only knew what appeared in the newspapers and what I heard on the radio. I believed that America and England were despicable, and that we could not share the same sky because they excluded and isolated Japan and used the world as they pleased. They were worse than contemptible. When sparks fall on you, you must brush them away. I felt that we absolutely must win this war, and to win, we must endure whatever shortages and hardships come our way, so I obeyed government orders religiously. But the war continued to go against us. I thought we would definitely hold Okinawa, but Okinawa fell too. The former prime minister, Suzuki Kantarō, said Kyūshū would be the decisive battle. He said we were bound to win in Kyūshū, so I was confident about Kyūshū. Combat troops and civilians would join together in defending Kyūshū, and I decided that I would give my life to the nation. To sever my worldly attachments, I was ready to kill my two darling grandchildren first and then fight to the end for my country. But on August 15 [1945] the emperor's decision to end the Greater East Asia War was announced, and I felt torn up inside with indignation. Afterwards, however, newspaper and radio reports gradually clarified the situation, and I began to understand that it was inevitable that Japan suffer defeat. Ever since Your Excellency and your armed forces arrived to occupy Japan in accord with the Potsdam Declaration, I have observed your activities, and my previous way of thinking has completely disappeared. I regret my early convictions; I am filled with gratitude now. Especially, when I think of the generous measures Your Excellency has taken instead of exacting vengeance, I am struck with reverent awe as if I were in the presence of God.

So far, this is a letter of confession. A man who was so full of animosity toward the United States and Great Britain came to feel that Japan's defeat was a deserved consequence and was offering his gratitude to the occupation forces. His real intention, however, was to say, "Therefore listen to what I now have to say." The letter continues:

I have a favor to ask Your Excellency. According to recent newspaper reports, accusations of responsibility for the war may reach His Majesty. This news was so unexpected, I was stupefied. This has to be prevented at all costs. I considered this and came to the conclusion that I have no other means but to plead to Your Excellency for mercy.

In our country, the emperor is absolutely unique and exists above God. He is the object of the people's faith. I hesitate to make a comparison, but he is like the rudder to a ship. If something should happen to His Majesty, we the people would lose our direction. For the past three thousand years the people have received deep affection from the imperial family. If something should happen to His Majesty, we the people would lose our purpose in living. A country without purpose would be like a Buddhist statue without a soul, and I would not want to see this. Please exercise Your Excellency's power and see

Photo 4.2   After delivering his "declaration of humanity" in January 1946, Emperor Hirohito embarked on a series of visits to towns and cities throughout Japan. Here he stopped his car to greet war refugees lined up outside a temporary barracks on the road between Tokyo and Yokohama on February 19, 1946. Source: Mainichi Shimbunsha

to it that nothing happens to the emperor. I would gladly give my life if this were required. Please heed my plea. Lastly, I pray to God for your country and for Your Excellency's prosperity and happiness.

Tashiro Kakutarō

This man changed his perspective on the Allies and acquiesced in the occupation itself, but his belief in the emperor remained unshaken. His willingness to give his life for the emperor was unchanged from before the war. The very simplicity of this letter adds to its weight.

Next is a fiery missive arguing that the emperor is a pacifist.

December 18, 1945

Mr. MacArthur
Allied Headquarters

Despite my humble status, I offer these words to my dear General MacArthur. I hope you will accept them.

The emperor of Japan is absolutely not a war criminal. I see articles in recent newspapers treating the emperor as though he is a criminal, but the articles are written by people with some misunderstanding. The emperor is an advocate of world peace, and we, the Japanese people, all revere him. As you know, the bullies—his counselors, the militarists, and the government—because of their own wrongheadedness, were not able to understand the emperor's mind, nor his great intentions, and they started a hopeless war. They used the emperor because they were wrongheaded.

The emperor is not a militarist or a warlord or an imperialist. The Japanese emperor is a pacifist and a person who advocates peace. For your reference, I will give one or two examples. During the previous European conflict, he wrote the following poem:

> *I thought the world's oceans were brothers;*
> *Why the tumult of roaring wind and waves?*

Explanation: The emperor felt all the people in the world were brothers. He is asking, Why do they wage wars and kill each other's soldiers and cause each other pain? He has always been a pacifist with great passion and love.

Over three thousand years ago, the emperor's ancestors established the great ideal that all peoples of the world are equal and, as human masters of all creation, they should get along like members of one family. To carry on their great work, successive emperors have inherited the same ideal, and it has continued to the present 124th generation.

These are only a couple of examples. If you study the edicts issued by the emperors over the generations, you will clearly understand my point. To the Japanese people, the emperor is a teacher who has shown us the way; he is a parent to the nation.

Please, General MacArthur, I ask you again and again, do not put the emperor on trial. I petition you despite my humble position. Please forgive my poor penmanship.

Enju
2805 Fujisan-mura, Koagata-gun,
Nagano Prefecture

It seems it did not occur to this writer that the emperor, as head of state, had the political responsibility for declaring war. All that mattered was that the emperor loved peace in his heart, and it was his counselors who were to blame. But if the counselors were to be held responsible for leading the emperor astray, what about the responsibility of the person at the helm—the emperor himself—who steered the ship of state accordingly? Those who asked for the emperor to be spared refused to address this issue.

FILLED WITH EMOTION

At this point, let me introduce a letter from a person who seems to have had leadership and influence at a local level. A portrait of the rural intelligentsia of prewar Japan emerges from this long letter—three meters in length, written on a roll of paper in beautiful calligraphy. The writer's distorted view of the United States, his twisted view of history, and his blind reverence for the emperor make for a complex letter that at times feels suffocating in its logic.

December 16 [1945]

The Honorable, and Respected, General MacArthur:

Japan's extremely cold winter has arrived. I offer my profound sympathy for the hardship facing Your Excellency in your old age, fulfilling your duties as commander of the Allied forces during the winter in a strange land.

As one Japanese citizen, I would here like to honestly express my feelings and opinions and receive Your Excellency's criticism. Truth is always the most valued treasure.

Although a citizen of a defeated Japan, I believe that I too have the freedom to speak the truth. What feelings do the Japanese have toward the United States? I cannot say that my feelings are those of all Japanese, but most people think as I do.

The general atmosphere before the beginning of the war was pro-American, as Your Excellency knows. But this pro-American feeling was not without reservation. I believe that this was because of oppression toward Japan. During the forty years of the Meiji era, the United States was Japan's friend. After the Russo-Japanese War, American involvement in East Asia grew steadily, and unfortunately our countries became competitors. Then two developments occurred that the Japanese were unable to forget—the Washington Conference and anti-Japanese immigration laws. These were the fundamental reasons that they supported Japan's war against the United States years later.

From the beginning of this letter, it is clear that the writer has quite a bit of nerve. These letters typically begin with praise for MacArthur's governance of Japan, but here the writer offers his sympathy for the burdens on the supreme commander's old age. It seems likely that if MacArthur understood the nuance of the phrase, he grimaced.

It is true that pro-American tendencies were pronounced in prewar Japan. They were so deeply rooted, in fact, that the military, along with promilitary writers and artists, had to aggressively cultivate the anti-American sentiment that arose in the 1920s in the wake of the Washington Disarmament Conference and the movement against Japanese immigrants in California. The writer makes no mention of that effort but instead attempts to lay the blame on the United States so as to justify the war.

He goes on to argue that anti-American sentiment did not put down roots and that in fact Japan did not develop deep hatred for its other enemies:

During the war, the Japanese did not feel an upsurge of animosity toward their enemy, the United States. It was the same toward China and Great Britain. It is strange that in such a major war there was no flood of ill will toward Japan's enemies.

The old-timers who had experienced previous wars would say, "The people's spirit is entirely different from what it was during the Russo-Japanese War. We cannot fight a war this way. The Japanese are not in the spirit of fighting a war." I heard this said very often.

In June of this year, I stood in the middle of a city that had been bombed by B-29s. As far as my eyes could see, nothing survived the merciless destruction to remind one of what the city had been. But even at that moment, I only felt a sense of resignation as if it had been a natural disaster. But if you were to ask me, "Were you a bystander during the war?" I would answer clearly, "No, no, I did everything I could for the defense of Japan." I was not drafted by the military, but if I had been, I would have volunteered for the front line, and if allowed I would have been a member of the special attack [kamikaze] corps. This is the honorable duty of any Japanese.

I cannot begin to resolve the contradictions in this writer's thinking. He did not feel animosity toward the enemy, and destruction from the war seemed like a natural disaster, but he is proud to have done what he could for the war effort. Were these words a show of courage, to say that the Japanese should not be demeaned? But now the writer bows low once again:

The end of the war came suddenly. It was a reality too cold to accept. Your Excellency is familiar with the postwar attitude toward the United States. I have honestly described here Japanese sentiment before and during the war. I now truly feel that "a friend comes from afar."

The writer again sings his chorus that the Japanese were originally pro-American. It seems far-fetched to say that the near kowtowing of the Japanese welcome of MacArthur and the hospitality extended to

the occupation forces immediately after the war was simply an extension of prewar pro-American sentiment. I prefer to see it as a national
characteristic of subservience to authority, in this case a foreign ruler,
but this does not seem to occur to the writer of this letter. Even so, it is
astonishing to read the occupation described as "a friend comes from
afar" (a quote from the Confucian *Analects*). The tone of the letter
shifts now to an indirect warning to the occupation forces.

However, I must express my most important honest feelings here. This con-
cerns the present and the future.
　　A defeated Japan! It is an extremely deep wound in my heart. To think that
Japan, which had not been invaded by another country for three thousand
years, is now under occupation gives me endless grief. Japan is steadily being
reformed through Your Excellency's just measures, and I am truly delighted to
see the dawn of hope for a new Japan. The causes of the recent war must be
eliminated. I feel that major reform may be possible because the occupation
forces are here. But does this mean that the Japanese are not capable of re-
form themselves? Absolutely not. I believe the Japanese by their own strength
are able to return to their innate character. It is true that it will be easier for
the occupation army to carry out reform, because the occupation army has
power. The dangers of excess and misdirection come with this power.
　　I described Japanese sentiment toward the United States earlier. As it was
in the past, I pray it will be for the present and the future, but I have to say
that sentiment is changing.
　　Number one is the fact that we are being occupied.

"A friend comes from afar," the writer had remarked, but his anger
over defeat and occupation continues to rise to the surface, apparently
beyond his control. The factors that led Japan to war must be eliminated, but the Japanese have the ability to reform themselves. The occupation forces can readily carry out reform because they can rely on
their power, but if power is misused, pro-American sentiment will dissipate. Being occupied is already aggravating the situation. This writer's
true motive is gradually emerging.

Number two, the occupation forces have made a grave mistake, and that
is the detention of Prince Nashimoto Morimasa. No matter how high one's

position might be, as long as one is a subject, it is natural to give one's life for his country. This applies even to those who serve close to His Majesty. However, the imperial family is another matter entirely. This is because the imperial family is the nation itself. The Japanese people's absolute reverence for the imperial family may be difficult for Your Excellency, as a foreigner, to understand. For the Japanese, the imperial family is beyond criticism. This is not the result of education, and it is not a belief we have from coercion or distortion. It is a spontaneous feeling the Japanese people have had for three thousand years. To anyone who says that this reflects the feudal thinking of the Japanese, I think it is enough to reply, "Take off your colored glasses and study Japanese history."

Many people had expected the arrest of wartime leaders like the former prime minister Tōjō, and some even expressed support for such measures. But people were shocked when on December 2 an arrest warrant was issued for the emperor's relative, Prince Nashimoto, and the seventy-two-year-old army general was confined to Sugamo Prison as a suspect in war crimes. The arrest raised the concern that if a member of the imperial family could be arrested, the emperor himself might not be able to escape indictment as a war criminal. But few made their concern known publicly. For the writer of this letter to inform MacArthur that it was "a grave mistake" required considerable courage; his reverence for the imperial family undoubtedly emboldened him. His perspective on the unique status of the imperial family can be seen as a carryover of popular sentiment from prewar days, though describing the imperial family as beyond criticism reveals how totally caught up by the imperial system the writer is. Even so, it was daring for a Japanese of that era to suggest to MacArthur that something may be hard for a foreigner to understand or that he should study Japanese history without prejudice.

The writer abruptly turns his attention to global affairs and U.S.–Soviet friction. As we read on, it becomes clear that this is his grand design for preserving the imperial system.

Recently, there has been talk of a war between the United States and the Soviet Union. I have always said that this was impossible. This is because America does not want a war, and because it is so obvious the United States would win any such conflict that the Soviet Union would avoid it for the time being.

However, what effect would a U.S.–Soviet agreement have on Japan? It makes me tremble to think that the Soviet Union would be allowed to make inroads simply because the United States does not want a war.

I suspect the detention of Prince Nashimoto is the first manifestation of such a compromise because the action will enable the Soviet Union to prevent reconciliation between the United States and Japan forever. Japan and the United States are being forced down a path toward perpetual confrontation across the otherwise peaceful Pacific Ocean.

Japan, which could not fire up animosity even during the war, is now after the war coolly observing the changes occurring within its heart.

By this time, U.S.–Soviet confrontation over the disposition of Eastern Europe had already become apparent. The writer does not advocate compromise between the two powers but argues that the United States must never give in to the Soviet Union. The Soviets had been pressing for a voice on matters concerning the occupation of Japan, and they had made clear their support for abolishing the imperial system. The letter continues:

The next matter that might arise could be the harming of the imperial system or the emperor himself. This would obviously bring about the world's greatest tragedy. It would succeed only after the complete annihilation of the eighty million Yamato [Japanese] people. I think that the United States has no desire to see this happen. So why is this a possibility? It depends on how much the Americans give in to the Soviets.

"Over my dead body," the writer might have said, implying that eighty million Japanese would fight until death if any harm were inflicted on the emperor. Of course, he goes on to stress that he is among those seeking peace, but his strategy for peace comes as a total surprise. He continues:

I do not hope for confrontation between the United States and the Soviet Union. All of humankind forever desires peace.

The emperor said we should establish peace to last ten thousand genera-
tions. How can we bring about a lasting peace? Through reconciliation be-
tween the United States and Japan, and in the long run, unification of the
United States and Japan. It should be a complete and coordinated unification
encompassing culture, the economy, and industry, based on mutual respect
for each country's history and traditions. The United States and Japan should
thoroughly understand each other, standing on an equal footing. This might
be called a U.S.–Japanese alliance, but its character would be totally differ-
ent from previous alliances. You may say that Japan should faithfully observe
the Potsdam Declaration and leave other discussions for the future, but I fear
that a U.S.–Japanese reconciliation will be lost forever while the terms of the
declaration are being carried out.

The writer argues that U.S.–Japanese unification is the path to a lasting peace, but how could such fundamentally different countries be uni-
fied? How would the issue of the emperor system be resolved? Is it possible for two countries with such different cultures and histories to truly
understand each other? The writer then argues that an alliance between Japan and the United States should take precedence over observance of the Potsdam Declaration, but the Potsdam Declaration was
meant to deal with Japan's war responsibilities. There is not the slightest sign of repentance for the war in this man's letter. His plan of alliance with the United States had only one purpose—to safeguard the
imperial system.

As we have seen, quite a number of the letters to MacArthur suggested that Japan become a dependency or a state of the United States.
Defeat in war had resulted in a loss of national confidence, and the idea
of joining the United States was raised by some as a joke and by others
as a serious proposition. The writer Kume Masao published a "Thesis on
Japan as an American State," arguing that Japan would be better off as
the forty-ninth state of the union.[5] He reasoned that the emperor would
be safe if the country was annexed by the United States, a theory shared
by the writer of this letter.

The writer was proposing a unification that would extend to a spiritual merger between the two countries, but considering the balance of
power between victor and vanquished, would this not mean the loss of

cultural independence for the defeated Japanese? Would it not result in the Japanese becoming compradors for the Americans in order to save the imperial system? Did this amount to defending the imperial system, regardless of the cost? The letter ends in the following manner, with a plea for the imperial family and friendly relations with the United States.

Nothing would grieve me more than to have Japan suffer further because I expressed my true feelings. I only pray that Japan and the imperial family may emerge from their present sorrow as soon as possible and move forward hand in hand with the countries of a bright world.

Your Excellency, General MacArthur: I have written a very long letter. The true heart of the Japanese lies in absolute respect for the imperial family and everlasting peace with the United States. I would be most happy if you were to understand and give us your assistance.

Totsuka Hideji

The address on the envelope reads "Nishi-Yamaguchi Village Primary School, Ogasa-gun, Shizuoka Prefecture," and judging from the contents and the penmanship, the writer must have been an accomplished teacher or perhaps a principal. The letter has a persuasive power of a sort, based more on its emotional force than its logic. Such local intelligentsia were often the very ones who herded the people into the war effort but then after the war turned around and propounded their own theories of peace.

THOUGHTS EXPRESSED IN BLOOD

For the Japanese, it is not an easy task to make a rational argument about the emperor or the imperial system. The letter we have just examined is, if anything, one of the more well-reasoned examples. In the shock of defeat, people who sensed a threat to the emperor expressed intense feelings to MacArthur in many forms. The extreme cases were letters, like the following, written in blood.

December 13, 1945

To the Honorable General MacArthur,
I respectfully petition:
Please exclude His Majesty the emperor from responsibility for the war. For us Japanese, His Majesty is absolute, and he is the life of the Japanese people. If Your Excellency contemplates the future of Japan and desires true peace in the world, you will realize that a policy of leaving His Majesty in place in Japan is advantageous not for Japan alone.

If it ever happens that His Majesty is brought to trial, not only I but many Japanese, whose loyalty is close to a religious belief that has deepened through history and tradition, would hold a tremendous hatred not only toward you, but toward all Americans forever. Unexpected incidents would be certain to occur, and as Japanese living today, even if we were to die of indignation, how could we face our descendants?

Your Excellency: With my life I beg you with a petition written in my blood. Please do not inquire into His Majesty's war responsibilities. I am one lone person, a scholar of Western paintings who graduated from the political science department of Waseda University, but if you so desire, I swear to God that I am willing to offer my life. Please understand my humble feelings.

A Subject of Japan
Yoshida Yukimoto
[handwritten seal]

The letter was written by brush with a sure hand on a sheet of writing paper. After forty years, the color of the blood had turned brown and it showed signs of fading, but the writer's determination was still visible throughout the letter. The writer was probably sincere in pledging his life for the emperor. The Allies had fought a war with Japan to eliminate this kind of fanatical patriotism. Unfortunately, there is no record of how MacArthur felt if he read this petition in blood. But such letters were certainly consistent with and may have contributed to his belief that preservation of Hirohito on the throne was essential to stability in occupied Japan.

A woman living in Nishi Ogikubo, a suburb of Tokyo, wrote to MacArthur almost every day during the month of December 1945. Some letters were short, others were long. The following is an example:

December 7 [1945]

Your Excellency:

How have you been? We feel closest to Your Excellency, the supreme commander, and rely upon your kind heart. Knowing that we depend on your heart alone, I am once again sending you a letter.

You may consider it troublesome and redundant, but please bear with me and listen to the pleas of the Japanese people.

Today's newspaper has made us feel disheartened again. Of course, it hurts us to read about fellow Japanese being arrested for war crimes, but when the article gives us the sense that the emperor may be questioned about his responsibility, it pains us without limit. As citizens of a defeated nation, we are willing to accept any amount of hardship; our only pride as Japanese is that we not show ourselves to be cowards. We are determined not to utter one word of complaint despite any hardship, but the one thing we cannot endure is any misfortune visited upon the emperor. No matter how small the misfortune, we cannot stand it.

The present emperor is burdened with troubles and is the most unfortunate of all the emperors. Whenever I think of this, tears come to my eyes. The pain we feel about visiting more hardship on the emperor may not be conceivable to Your Excellency because you do not have an emperor, but this feeling is not the blind or crazy belief of the uneducated. To us, the emperor is not a god to be treated as an idol. Our reverence and affection for the emperor are much, much more intense, much, much larger and abundant. As I said yesterday, this is something that flows in the blood of the Japanese.

I want to say that the present emperor did not have a single good retainer. How we detest those who severed the bond between the emperor and the people. If there is even one coward among the suspects who tries to escape his responsibility by laying it on the emperor, we would consider it the greatest disgrace for Japan, and if Your Excellency were to make this public, I know the shame would pierce our hearts.

The essence of the Japanese emperor is a love of peace. I am truly embarrassed toward the world that there are some Japanese who have forgotten the kindness of the emperor, who tried sacrificing himself in order to save them.

The present emperor is not responsible. Attendants close to the emperor forced him into a quandary. Please, Your Excellency, do not judge all of the Japanese people from the ugly Japanese you happen to come across. I was one of those who once believed ourselves to be a superior people, but now, what I see and what I hear brings me nothing but shame and sadness.

Young girls who display their coquetry like prostitutes, those who disregard hungry fellow citizens and get fat on the black market, those who are trying to expel the emperor even though they were born in Japan, those retainers who are trying to evade their responsibility, etc., etc. Why can they not bravely accept defeat with the pride they inherited from their ancestors? It only makes me feel ashamed and humiliated.

To protect the emperor, we will gladly offer our lives to Your Excellency's country if you will guarantee the emperor's safety.

Your Excellency, I beseech you, please understand the emperor of Japan.

Please forgive me for this long and poorly written letter.

The weather has been fine both yesterday and today. We call this type of weather frosty sunshine.

As long as our lives last, we will love and revere the emperor, Japan, and beautiful Musashino [a plain to the west of Tokyo] with all our strength.

I pray for Your Excellency's health.

Itō Taka
[thumb seal]

There is no doubting this woman's determination to give her life to ensure the emperor's safety. The daily letters she sent all closed with her signature and her thumb seal in blood. This is the kind of sentiment that lay behind the writer Takeuchi Yoshimi's famous characterization that "the emperor system permeates every living creature" in Japan.[6] For MacArthur, whose main goal was a successful occupation, it may have been a wise strategic move to avoid tackling the imperial system head-on. But, as we shall see in the next chapter, others in Japan were not so willing to leave the emperor in place, and the persistence of the emperor system remains controversial to this day.

5

"DEPOSE THE EMPEROR"

 The large majority of the letters in the International Prosecution Section file on Emperor Hirohito supported the emperor and the emperor system. However, there were nine letters in the file that accused the emperor of responsibility for the war and appealed to MacArthur to abolish the imperial system. We will look at these letters in this chapter.

THE EMPEROR SHOULD ACCEPT
TOTAL RESPONSIBILITY FOR THE WAR

(From a country farmer in the northeast) [sic]

Dear Sir:

Today's newspapers quote American newspaper reports that the emperor may be held accountable for the war, and we farmers agree. All Japanese begin and end a war through the emperor's edicts. The people have no responsibility whatsoever. What contradiction is there in the emperor taking full responsibility at this point and becoming a war criminal? However, the high officials, the military cliques, the bureaucrats, and the zaibatsu who participated in the imperial plots and put the emperor in his present situation also bear a heavy responsibility. Especially the rich with more than a half million yen, members of the Diet, field-grade military officers, bureaucrats above the Higher Third rank, etc., should be arrested collectively as war criminals, and some will face the death penalty. If not, within the next twenty years these people will rise again, and in the name of the emperor will arouse the people and start a war. Farmers are sick and tired of war. All we want is to be able to live happily. Even if there were no emperor, we would be satisfied as long as we can eat our fill of rice and lead a happy life. My dear General MacArthur! It is right to arrest the leaders as war criminals, but unless you seize the young military officers, the Diet members, and the aristocrats, I am afraid the spirit of militarism will not disappear from Japan. Thus, I have dared to write this letter.

Written on one page of rough newsprint, the quick movement of the brush makes it appear as if it was carelessly composed, but the man is a capable calligrapher and quite articulate. This is one of the most frank and direct of all the letters arguing the emperor's war responsibility. Although he identifies himself as "a country farmer," the writer was probably quite well educated.

The writer lays all of the blame for the war on the emperor and the leaders who surrounded him, while absolving the people of all responsibility. Very few writers of the time, regardless of political persuasion, raised the issue of popular responsibility for cooperating with the war effort. They were likewise content to leave it to the occupation authorities to cleanse Japan of the elements that led the country into war. The writer's passivity is evident when he suggests, "Even if there were no emperor, we would be satisfied as long as we can eat our fill of rice and lead a happy life."

Could it be that this "country farmer" was counting on the new "emperor" of Japan, MacArthur, to deliver benevolent rule? But if he was thinking along these lines, why did he not identify himself? Throughout the history of Japan, especially in the modern era, it was unheard of for people to express opinions on such matters as the emperor's responsibility or measures that might be taken against him. To do so would have put the writer's life in jeopardy, and even then, there would have been no chance for his voice to be heard. Defeat made such expression possible for the first time. The structure of authority had crumbled in defeat, and people wrote MacArthur believing that the foreign ruler would listen to their opinions on the emperor. Still, the traditional taboo persisted, and in a daring letter like this one, the writer hesitated to use his real name.

The next letter is also anonymous, written on twelve pages of lined paper with a thick pen in large characters (the date is illegible):

Why has the present emperor not been arrested as a war criminal? The emperor of Japan has great power unparalleled in the world. He started the war, and he ended it. To his own advantage, he is only taking responsibility for ending the war.

The Japanese people are also unparalleled in their egoism and cowardice. During the war they never attacked the militarists, but now that there are no militarists, they attack the militarists. After the occupation forces leave, they will just support the emperor system and the maintenance of the national polity to protect themselves under the emperor system. No one thinks of the emperor from the heart. They're only trying to protect themselves. Even during the time of Kusunoki Masashige [a fourteenth-century loyalist], all of the people were on the side of Ashikaga Takauji, who opposed the emperor. If the present emperor is not tried as a war criminal, trying petty Japanese officers for mistreating prisoners of war seems to us more like simple vengeance than justice. To achieve true legal justice and human righteousness without shame before the world and before God, we ask you to strictly punish the present emperor as a war criminal. If you leave the emperor untouched simply to manipulate the people, then I believe that all the well-meaning policies of the Allied forces will come to naught after you leave.

It has been common practice, up until the present day, for those who uphold the status quo to ignore the emperor's responsibility for starting the war while praising his decisiveness in ending it. The writer of the letter openly argues that the emperor must be held responsible for starting the war, and his insistence that war crimes trials cannot claim to mete out justice if the emperor is not indicted is a biting criticism of the approach later adopted at the Tokyo tribunal. In addition, he had grasped the American policy of retaining the emperor to ensure a smooth occupation of Japan and shrewdly indicated the danger that this would provide a base for later reactionary movements. His opinion of his fellow Japanese as egoistic toadies begins to sound almost masochistic as his letter continues:

The Japanese people are extremely cowardly. Even if the present emperor is indicted now, Japan will not be thrown into chaos. Those who support maintenance of the national polity do so for self-preservation, so they will quickly drop their assertions and follow the trend. All the shouting about defeating the United States and England during the war, and now they dare to cheer for democracy: such is the incredible conversion of this faithless people. From birth they were taught to see the emperor as a living god, and they accepted this wholly unscientific history without questioning. A scientific analysis would show that the most egoistic person in Japan is the emperor. When it is in his interest, he can deceive the people by calling them His Majesty's babes, and when things go wrong, he can blame it on Tōjō and absolve himself. If the war had been won, the guy who would have gained the most is the emperor. In defeat, he scurries to cast his babes as war criminals and escape himself. The British monarch and the Japanese monarch are totally different. The Japanese emperor made the country go to war with more power and authority than Hitler. If this guy is allowed to escape punishment for war crimes simply as means of governing Japan, there will be no justice and all war crimes trials will lose their meaning. Please do not get carried away cutting only the leaves and branches, cut down the trunk. For the sake of humanity and for the sanctity of law, I implore you.

The writer's critique of the Japanese is as insightful as it is self-deprecating. The Japanese are cowardly and quickly change their colors, he argues, so people would adjust if the emperor were dethroned. Maybe he was right. However, neither the United States nor MacArthur dared to undertake this grand historical experiment. In any case, Japanese support for the emperor's indictment, his abdication, and the abolition of the emperor system was insignificant. The Japan Communist Party slogan, "Down with the imperial system," did not receive much support and quietly disappeared. I have found a few letters to the editor in the newspapers of that time that supported, in an indirect manner, the pursuit of the emperor's responsibility for the war. It is possible that newspapers chose not to publish letters that more directly addressed the issue of the emperor's responsibility, but the most candid and articulate, and the least ideological, expression of this perspective is found in these letters to MacArthur. This is an indication of how difficult it remained for the Japanese to openly criticize the imperial system even after the war.

The letter continues, repeating the earlier arguments, suffused with an anger rooted in the hardship of the writer's life:

We have been made to suffer for him for two thousand years. He sits at the top of the privileged classes, and as long as those who use his status manipulate politics by making the imperial family the foundation for the sacredness of Japan's history, rationing [of basic commodities] will never be fair. This is because the emperor stands above the rationing system with more than enough to wear and eat. The imperial family follows, officials of the imperial household receive their shares, and the prime minister and other high-ranking officials are all exempt from the rationing system. As such, they are unable to condemn dishonesty among their subordinates. This is why Japan's rationing is blurred like a painting and can never be fair, and the people are on the verge of starvation.

He robbed the people of their riches, and his own family lived in luxury beyond words. The war was not begun under Tōjō's authority. It was started under the authority of the emperor. Even Tōjō's power was less than a billionth of the emperor's. The Japanese people are cowardly but clever. They support the maintenance of the national polity and the emperor system only to protect themselves for the future. Please wipe out immorality and dishonesty. Please punish the emperor's war crimes harshly.

We believe in the honesty and courage of the Allied forces. We do not want to be enslaved Japanese or cowardly Japanese; we want to be strongly righteous Japanese, living in an open rather than a divine Japan, peace-loving rather than militarist. Please help us.

Please convey this message to General MacArthur.

Although the letter was addressed to MacArthur, perhaps the writer was afraid that it would get no further than the Liaison Office, so he added the final request. His condemnation of the emperor is almost a curse, but it is based in a very real grievance about rationing. There is a grief-stricken tone to his final words of longing for Japan to become an open and peaceful nation, and for the Japanese to become a righteous people. Perhaps we can call this postwar naïveté, but when he describes his belief that the honesty and courage of the occupation will help Japan achieve rebirth, one senses the immensity of his faith in and expectations of the occupation forces. At the same time, it is evidence of the loss of self-confidence suffered not just by this writer but by the nation as a whole. The next letter reflects this even more vividly:

Item: The emperor [system] should be abolished. For the Japanese, as a people, the emperor is a hindrance to democratization. I believe that as long as the imperial system exists, democracy cannot be achieved. Only if the people's fixation is removed can a conversion to a peaceful democracy be possible.

Item: The imperial family and aristocracy should also be abolished. For a long time, the privileged class has enslaved and exploited the people. They have not contributed to the nation; on the contrary, they have caused damage. Their extravagant expenses are paid for with the people's blood and sweat.

Item: There are at least one hundred thousand war criminals. There are many among the civilian population, including all of the leader class. They all deserve the death penalty. However, if crimes committed by lower ranks were done on orders from superiors, they should be pardoned.

Item: Japan should be occupied forever. If possible, please make Japan a colony. If your forces leave, the bad ones will make the people suffer again. Please severely punish the leaders of every circle of society.

Item: The Japanese are sincerely glad about the defeat.

Item: Prefectural governors, mayors of cities, towns, and villages, the heads of hamlets, policemen, etc., all forced the people to suffer during the war, and they should be indicted as war criminals.

To be "glad about the defeat" is comparable to the psychology of welcoming the occupying forces as liberators, but words of this sort do not come easily from those with self-respect as a people. Because he had lost self-respect, the writer could ask that Japan be colonized and make overheated claims that there were a hundred thousand war criminals, down to the heads of hamlets. Compared to this writer, the supporters of the emperor system we encountered in the previous chapter had stronger backbones.

The assertion that democracy cannot be achieved as long as the emperor system exists is understandable for those who lived under the prewar and wartime imperial system, sustained by the organized violence of the state. Removing "the people's fixation" implies the need to abolish the emperor system that the people revere, but how much could one expect such an action alone to transform the country into a peaceful democracy?

This letter was written neatly with pen on a postcard. It was addressed to "General MacArthur, MacArthur Headquarters, Tokyo," and the return address is "Itabashi-ku, Tokyo," with the complete street address and full name. This was a person who was brave enough to sign his own name when appealing directly to MacArthur to abolish the emperor system. We shall see that he was not the only one, which I would argue shows strong confidence in MacArthur that names would not be passed on to the Japanese government. I will identify the writer here only as "U.K."[1] There is a large "Confidential" stamp on the front of the letter, which was postmarked January 19, 1946. The emperor's "declaration of humanity" of January 1 seems to have had little effect on this person's opinion.

JAPAN SHOULD BE MADE A REPUBLIC

The next letter is a thorough and well-organized presentation of the same arguments as the previous three letters, that the emperor's war responsibility should be pursued and that the imperial system should be abolished in order to democratize Japan. This letter is also filled with the sense of liberation that followed the war, and one can almost feel the spirit of the time—that people were finally able to freely express themselves. Written in pencil filling four pages of letter paper, the writer gives his full address in Kawasaki, Kanagawa Prefecture and his full name, but I will identify him only as "A. M."

Photo 5.1   Emperor Hirohito (on platform at right) responds to the shouts of banzai from schoolchildren at an elementary school in Miyagi Prefecture, August 7, 1947. These visits were intended to emphasize the humanity of the emperor, but they also revealed the persistence of emperor worship among many Japanese, a point that was not lost on opponents of the emperor system. Source: *Kahoku Shimpōsha*

On Abolishing the Imperial System *[appears in margin]*
To: General Douglas MacArthur
December 23, 1945

I offer this letter to the person I respect and love, General Douglas MacArthur, who is striving to establish a democratic Japan.

I am only a humble citizen of Japan with neither education nor status. I am deeply impressed with the enthusiasm of the General Headquarters of the Allied forces in their effort to eradicate Japan's existing feudal, reactionary, and barbaric power structure that constrained, oppressed, and exploited the masses of the people, and to allow the great majority of the Japanese to truly enjoy political, economic, and social democracy. With gratitude and compelled by galloping emotion, I dare send this letter despite my poor penmanship and lack of education. Please hear this as the voice of one citizen who is deeply concerned about the future of democratic Japan.

At present, on the issue of Japan's national polity—the emperor system—there are those who advocate its continuation, and there are those who desire the abolition of the system. I am one who insists that this is the time to decisively abolish the system. I give the following reasons:

1. To continue the imperial system means that in the future when the Allied occupation army in Japan withdraws, the feudal powers and reactionary powers, e.g., the militarists, the bureaucrats, the capitalists, the landowners, the aristocrats, who recklessly and stupidly led Japan to war against the United States, will restore their control over the Japanese people, democracy will collapse, and the resurgence of militarist Japan will be inevitable.

2. Maintaining the imperial system is the greatest obstacle to the democratic education of the Japanese people. This is because the Japanese people, whose political standards are lower than Americans and Europeans, have been taught, since the Meiji Restoration, to believe that the emperor is a living god by the ruling class of militarists and bureaucrats, who have strengthened their control over the people by using unscientific mythology and legends to mystify and sanctify the emperor. As a result, the ignorant public still worships the emperor as if he were a god. Under these conditions, it is absolutely impossible to convert Japanese minds to think in a democratic way. To achieve this, the emperor's feudalistic, undemocratic, and militaristic ways must be completely exposed, he must be removed from his position, and it is absolutely necessary for Japan to become a republic.

"Compelled by galloping emotion," as the writer admits, the letter be-gins with intense fervor. One can well imagine the spirit of the times that made people write letters like this one, the level of trust in the occupation army that received the letters, and the magnetic power of MacArthur, the symbol of the Allies. The writer of this letter tackles the imperial system head on. To him, the imperial system is the source of traditional ruling au-thority, and if the occupation forces withdraw with that authority in place, militarist Japan is bound to revive. This is because, since the Meiji era peo-ple had been taught to believe that the emperor was a living god. Thus, exposing the nature of the emperor system and abolishing the emperor were prerequisites to the democratic reform of Japan. This is certainly a logical progression. But, what about the "republic" this man advocates? What form would it take, how would it be brought into existence? It seems that such questions never entered the writer's mind.

At this point, right after Japan's defeat, the former power holders, in-cluding the emperor, had lost the trust of the people. This power vac-uum was filled by MacArthur, a foreign conqueror, but how much was the writer of the letter aware of this? It is hard to believe that this man had a plan for the "republic" of Japan after MacArthur left. Let us re-turn to his letter:

3. Maintaining the imperial system will become the greatest barrier to the political, economic, and social democratic reform of Japan. The reason is that the ruling class of militarists, aristocrats, politicians, capitalists, and landown-ers have the imperial system as their fortress and would likely resist Supreme Commander MacArthur's orders for democratic reform, or the Japanese peo-ple's demands for democracy that rise up from below. Just as we are seeing right now, haven't they tried to obstruct the passage in the Diet of the agri-cultural land reform act and the labor union act, with the excuse that there has been insufficient deliberation?

The Lower House of the Imperial Diet at that time was composed of members chosen through wartime elections, and the House of Peers was of course made up of loyalists to the emperor. These Diet members themselves represented the "fortress" of the imperial system. Delibera-tion on democratic reforms had to be entrusted to this stronghold of es-tablished power because of GHQ's urgency to reform and democratize

Japan, even if in form alone, and because the occupation was bound by its own policy that democratization come as a spontaneous movement of the people. The first land reform bill, introduced in the fall of 1945, was modest to begin with, and it was further diluted by this Diet; there was likewise resistance to the reform of labor laws. This situation was largely corrected with the purging from public office of all leading politicians early in 1946 and the general election that took place the following April. But at the time this letter was written, the power structure that supported the emperor system was still in place. The letter continues, taking aim at the emperor's war responsibility.

4. *The Japanese emperor is a war criminal who triggered and carried out the Japanese–U.S. war. The Japanese–U.S. war was approved before the hostilities began by the so-called Imperial Council attended by and sanctioned by the emperor. Ignoring international law, the Pearl Harbor incident occurred because the emperor expressed agreement with the jingoistic Japanese militarists' plan to launch a dirty "sneak attack" on the U.S. Pacific Fleet. The Japanese defense that the emperor signed the declaration of war after the attack on Pearl Harbor has been undermined by indisputable evidence. The emperor is the greatest war criminal. He should be arrested immediately and put on trial.*

For these reasons, I support the abolition of the emperor system.

Wise General MacArthur: You must realize that maintaining the imperial system will make the construction of a democratic Japan impossible, and that it will provide an opportunity for the militarists to plan a war of revenge.

The abolition of the imperial system is also necessary for the everlasting peace between the United States and Japan. After the abolition of the imperial system, it is essential that the political and economic privileges of the emperor and imperial family be eliminated so that their revival will not be possible.

Respectfully,
[A. M.]

This part of the letter dwells on the emperor's responsibility for starting the war. The accusations are strong, on both legal grounds—ignoring international law—and moral grounds—authorizing a surprise attack. The writer seems to have been well-informed about current affairs, since he was aware of the failed effort to clear the emperor of responsibility for Pearl Harbor (perhaps he followed the occupation forces' announcements on the radio and in the newspapers). He not only demanded the emperor's arrest as the "greatest war criminal," but he also argued that the existence of such an emperor was itself an argument for the abolition of the imperial system.

An interesting point here is the view that maintenance of the imperial system would not only make the democratization of Japan impossible, it would also provide the militarists an opportunity for revenge and represent a barrier to lasting peace between the United States and Japan. As we saw in the previous chapter, supporters of the imperial system warned that eighty million Japanese would fight to their death if the emperor or the imperial system were harmed, a catastrophe for both nations. Viewing these contradictory opinions, one cannot help but marvel at the importance of the emperor in the consciousness of the Japanese.

IMPERIAL ORDERS AND DECREES SHOULD BE ABOLISHED

The next letter is interesting because it reveals a great deal more of the writer's personality than the other, more theoretical critiques of the emperor system we have examined. The writer appears to be quite an intellectual. The letter is dated December 16, 1945. Only a partial address is included in the letter, although the full address may have appeared on the envelope. The writer's full name is used, but I will identify him as "S. I." Written in pen on four pages of letter paper, S. I. begins by arguing that the concept of lese majesty is unjust.

To Our Great Emancipator,
The Honorable General MacArthur

Dear Sir:
Our great liberator, General MacArthur, please listen to a citizen's earnest letter.

Recently, freedom of speech has been recognized to quite an extent, but when it involves the emperor, a great deal of pressure is still applied.

First is the law of lese majesty. The emperor is a human being just as we are. He is neither a god nor a monkey. It is unbelievable that the slightest use of language concerning this human can be punished as lese majesty. After all, the emperor is nothing but a descendant of the foreign chieftain who conquered this island country, Japan. He may not even be a true descendant. There is also a great abundance of evidence that our ancestors were part of a conquered race (from the northeast).

Is it not irrational that we cannot speak freely about this emperor? My grandfather and others used to refer to the residence of the former daimyō (whose descendants are now aristocrats) as "the palace," which implies that the conqueror, good or evil, was on a par with the emperor.

There is no need for us to give this wealthy man called the emperor protection as someone above the law. We ourselves should select the leader who will be the center of the people.

Thorough indoctrination from early childhood about the imperial family had a great effect on many people, so it is a sad thing for Japan that there still are those who blindly and uncritically support the imperial system. It is certain the emperor will be used again by cunning people.

The true and clear history of Japan should be made public as soon as possible to awaken these people who are asleep.

Until the defeat in the war, the Japanese people were not allowed to utter words like, "The emperor is a human being just as we are. He is neither a god nor a monkey." Penalties for those who questioned the emperor's divinity were not limited to the legal provisions of lese majesty; mental and physical violence was administered in the military, in schools, and in every part of Japanese society. Defeat and the onset of the occupation should have eliminated the taboos surrounding the emperor. However, the Japanese government still intimated that lese majesty laws would be enforced, and in May 1946 Matsushima Matsutarō was charged with lese majesty for producing a placard that read, "I [the emperor] am eating a bellyful; you people, starve and die," which was displayed during a demonstration over food shortages (the Food May Day). The charges were later changed from lese majesty to libel, under pressure from GHQ, but it was not until November 1947 that lese majesty was removed from the penal code under the direction of the Government Section of GHQ.

By the time the law was changed, taboos regarding the emperor had already lost much of their strength, a trend that was accelerated by the emperor's "declaration of humanity" issued on New Year's Day of 1946. However, this letter was written before that watershed and thus provides a significant indication of public consciousness. Ancient historical texts clearly indicate that the imperial family was descended from invading conquerors and that the claim of "ten thousand generations of unbroken rule" was highly dubious. Word of this had quietly spread among the people.

S. I. says the people will select their own leader in place of "this wealthy man called the emperor," once again endorsing a republican form of government. The writer is quick to advocate abolition of the emperor, but his argument does not go into detail on how to bring this about. As in previous letters, one gets the strong impression that he believes that His Excellency, General MacArthur, will find a way to abolish the imperial system. In the face of such strong belief in MacArthur, it might be considered typically Japanese to open one's heart as well. The letter suddenly takes a personal turn:

Please listen to the desires of one citizen and help to build a nation in a world where we can all equally enjoy peace. I am an engineer, a graduate of a national technical college. I am thirty-one years old. I regret that I cannot speak English fluently.

One more thing: In Japan, we have words like "imperial orders" and "imperial decrees." These terms should be purged first. As it is, we might someday again be forced into useless acts through an imperial order.

During the two years I served as a conscript in the army, how I suffered under the emperor's orders! In the name of the emperor's absolute authority, I was beaten for no reason. I regret that I was forced to waste several years of my youth instead of contributing to my fellow citizens and mankind.

Am I wrong to think this way? If I am, I would have to change immediately, but I cannot do so without first hearing an argument that would overturn my convictions.

I sincerely request that you please issue clear directives on the above matters as soon as possible.

The wishy-washy attitude of the present cabinet members is not acceptable. There are many points I cannot support in the speeches of the Diet members. The name and membership of the House of Peers should be reformed immediately.

*I have written a very long letter, but I ask you again to please take action
as soon as possible.*

[S. I.]
Ōmori-ku, Tokyo

Graduates of prewar technical colleges achieved higher levels of
scholarship than postwar college graduates, which is why I described
the writer as something of an intellectual. Nonetheless, he would have
been drafted as a common soldier, and he may have suffered greatly in
the unjust class system of the army. He unburdens himself of these
memories to the "Great Emancipator," since airing his resentment to
any Japanese leader of that time would have been futile. He must have
found catharsis in writing to a foreign ruler who stood above them all.

His urge to speak out and his emotions get entangled, and his logic
becomes scattered, but this gives the letter its human touch. In hindsight, it is ironic that rule by imperial decree was one thing that
MacArthur dared not abolish, for it is well-known that the "Great
Emancipator," in the urgency of enacting occupation policies, did not
wait for the Japanese to enact laws and ordinances, but instead relied
heavily on what amounted to "imperial Potsdam decrees."

The institution of the emperor was very useful to the occupation.
These earnest appeals for an end to the emperor system and the pursuit
of the emperor's war crimes, in the name of Japan's democratization and
legal justice, were ignored for the sake of political expedience, and the
imperial system persisted. How much did the people who wrote to
MacArthur know about this cold political calculation? These letters all
reflect the naïveté of the Japanese people. The last letter I will introduce in this chapter is far less naive.

THE LAST NATIONAL ANTHEM

The Honorable General MacArthur:
    *You have said that you are going to make Japan into a democratic country.
We truly appreciate that, but Your Excellency has not been able to cut to the
root of the matter. That is the emperor.*

Their clan is one that drifted over to Japan in ancient times. They conquered the Japanese archipelago with their advanced weapons and intelligence. They imposed a system of feudal slavery on the foolish Japanese natives. They called themselves descendants of gods and deceived and intimidated the Japanese natives, while they continued to lead a life of extreme luxury and promiscuity.

In recent times liberalism, like a surging tide, has spread over the foolish Japanese natives. This of course is a major problem that threatens the basis of [the imperial family's] livelihood. Our history proves that the people cannot be governed by simply suppressing [liberal thought]. Following the lessons of history, they decided to divert the people's attention elsewhere. Of course, these were the Shanghai Incident, the Manchurian Incident, the China Affair, and the Greater East Asia War.

Your Excellency, you have arrested a soldier here and a politician there as parties responsible for the war. No doubt, they did work in the name of the emperor and stood to gain from it, so they are war criminals, but their crimes are trivial, because they acted under orders from the emperor.

Your Excellency is arresting only the petty criminals. I fear that Your Excellency might leave Japan without touching the emperor. The situation is that, with the exception of a few, the foolish Japanese are unable to utter a word in public concerning the emperor.

This writer, who calls himself "A Citizen of Tsuchiura City," demonstrates a considerable knowledge about the history of the imperial family. Their "luxury" was one thing, but few people knew about their lifestyles being colored with "promiscuity" and bloody power struggles. As one who knew about these things, it is perhaps natural that his criticism was directed toward the people. His words, "the foolish Japanese natives," ring with disdain at his own people. He is outraged about the spiritless Japanese, who even after the defeat could not speak openly about the emperor.

He is uncompromising in pointing to the responsibility of the emperor as the nation's top leader during wartime. His fear that MacArthur might leave the emperor in place echoes other letters that warn that the emperor could become the focal point for reactionaries in post-occupation Japan. But this writer goes on to elucidate a plan for action.

I am not a communist, but I am thinking of joining the Communist Party in order to bring down the emperor. The majority of Japanese people today think of the Communist Party as a great evil, so the power of the Communist Party is minuscule. I think you understand why the spineless leaders *of the Socialist Party make half-asleep remarks about democratic government under the emperor system.*

All of the previous letters in this chapter appealed to MacArthur to abolish the emperor system. This is the first letter expressing the writer's desire to take action himself, by joining the Communist Party, which was the only party calling for an end to the emperor system. As for the Socialist Party, one of its leaders, Kagawa Toyohiko, went so far as to shout "Banzai to the emperor!" at the founding convention of the party.

At the time this letter was written, presumably around the end of 1945, the Communist Party still considered the occupation forces a "liberation army." This was the party's honeymoon period with GHQ. The writer had no way of knowing how thoroughly MacArthur despised communism, so he spoke freely about his intentions. At the same time, he acknowledged the weakness of the Communist Party and bitterly concluded that the emperor and the emperor system were beyond the reach of the Japanese.

It is fair to say that it is absolutely impossible for the Japanese today to expel from Japan forever the emperor, who is the greatest sinner in Japan and the disrupter of world peace. Your Excellency, you may be satisfied as long as the emperor is not able to disturb world peace, but the Japanese people will not rest easy.

If Your Excellency truly loves the foolish Japanese, please punish with your own hands the emperor and his clan who have deceived the native Japanese for three thousand years. Please make sure they can never return to Japan. I believe that leaving the emperor in place will someday enable him to disturb world peace again, and our suffering will be many times worse than it is now.

Punishment and banishment of the emperor were not as extreme as the execution of the emperor as the number one war criminal, which was the outcome supported by public opinion in China at this time. The proposal, however, did echo that made by Owen Lattimore, a prominent Asia scholar based in the United States, who suggested that the emperor and all members of the imperial family who had rights of succession to the throne be interned in China. This writer felt it was hopeless to expect the Japanese people to abolish the imperial system, but this only raised the intensity of his complaints against the emperor:

> It has been proposed that the fate of the emperor system should be determined by Japanese public opinion. Twenty years from now it may be different, but at present public opinion is more than ninety percent in favor of the emperor system.
>
> The foolish Japanese natives are blindfolded and gagged, and they worship a vampire as a god. Your Excellency, from a humanitarian viewpoint, is it not a fearful thing to leave such deception on this earth? I ask you again, Where in the world can you find such absurdity as the worst scoundrel being worshipped as a god?
>
> If Your Excellency loves the foolish Japanese people and intends to save them from their slavish existence, please banish this ringleader of evil, the emperor, from Japan forever.

Written by pen in an easily legible style on seven pages of stationery, the letter abandons its harsh tone and ends with a hint of sympathy for the prospective exiles, the emperor and his clan. It concludes as follows:

> Despite what I have said, they too are human beings. As evil as they may be, when I see them as humans and think of the day they will be forced out of Japan, I cannot help but feel a bit sorry for them. Please allow every house throughout the land to drape their flag in black and sing the national anthem one the last time.
>
> I will not give my name nor my address. I do not wish to be charged with the crime of lese majesty.
>
> To the great apostle of humanitarian love, The Honorable MacArthur, I place this letter at your feet.

One wonders if it was Japanese tenderness that motivated the request for one last singing of the national anthem, whose lyrics glorify the emperor. Was it the nation's aesthetic sensibility? Or was it simply sentimentalism? In any case, it was unlikely that attitudes like this would lead to revolutionary change.

6

MACARTHUR AS FATHER FIGURE

 In the last two chapters we have seen letters filled with the raw emotions of the Japanese people regarding the emperor, but debate on the subject ended like a brief storm. The American decision to forgo pursuing the issue of the emperor's war responsibilities gave peace of mind to those who supported the emperor, and it silenced the small minority who were against him. The emperor's "declaration of humanity" on January 1, 1946, was like a sermon to the nation preaching acceptance of the new order under the occupation. Accordingly, the emperor assumed a symbolic status, with MacArthur's authority illuminating him from behind. If the emperor remained the leader in the people's hearts, MacArthur was indisputably the real power holder. In no time at all, as a natural matter of course, the new foreign ruler filled the vacuum of leadership created by defeat.

To many Japanese under the occupation, MacArthur represented above all a father figure. I do not think it is necessary to call upon Freud to make this case. The following letter is an example of how many families in Japan found a "father" in MacArthur. It was neatly handwritten with pen in English by a young mother, a schoolteacher.[1]

Mrs. S. Miura, Teacher at St. Margaret's Girls High School, (Rikkio Jo Gakko), 22nd Dec. 1946

To General Douglas MacArthur, Supreme Commander for Allied Powers, General Head Quarters

Mother's Word.

It was the middle of June, four of American pumpkin seeds were given to each home by neighbourhood association. Various vegetables were planted already at my garden, it was a little embarrassment to have another plant, but we decided to plant them and give attention. We planted those American pumpkin seeds between Japanese pumpkin and soy beans.

On the occasion my eldest son, Shigetaka was told by his teacher to observe nature and make the record on it. My husband suggested him to make observation on the American pumpkin. One of four seeds was selected to his object on the observation and was planted.

It was twenty first of June that the pumpkin diary was started. My son Shigetaka spent twenty or thirty minutes in the garden each day and continued to keep his record.

It was not only his surprise to find new bud but it became his joy to find the tiny leaves.

It seemed an important study to him that to watch the growth of pumpkin leaves. On that time the news paper reported the crisis of provision and our family lived with few pieces of bread and a kind of soup.

By the delay of delivering ration, we couldn't find any proper way to find food. The word "Starvation" became reality to us. All vegetables were picked up for the ration, but the American pumpkin was given special attention.

Without toys nor candies, my four little children devoted to observe the growth of pumpkin and at the dinner table, the conversation topic was "the brother's pumpkin." The conversation was cheerful and gave a good feeling even without dessert at the table.

At the end of August, when he started a short travel he greeted to the pumpkin as if it is his close friend.

Sometime September, father was reading news paper in the morning, and said that he read the news about the child who brought flower to General MacArthur as a return present of chocorate which was given to Japanese children. The picture was also seen on the news paper.

Four days ago of the time, American chocorate were given to children and it was a great concern of them.

"Shigetaka, how about to present your pumpkin diary to General MacArthur?" father suggested.

"My diary? does he like it? if it is possible I will be very glad" the son said.
"Why don't you present it? I will write a letter to the General and show
our gratitude", I told to him.

"I will draw a picture of the pumpkin" father said, for he is an artist.

Thus the opinions of our family decided to present the pumpkin diary to
General MacArthur. Until the fifth of November, the date of harvest, the observation record of pumpkin was enthusiastically continued. Five days after
he started to make a fair copy, and when he come back to home from the
school he spent his time to make the copy, till dinner every day. At holiday he
devoted to his work all day long.

This work was a big job on which he must put his all efforts, with the
boy of ten years old. Some occasion husband and I looked each other
and felt an embarrancement, but to my son, it became an joyful and hopeful work.

We came over the crisis of short provision hardly, and the optimistic reports on rice harvest cheer us, but unbalanced living expenses caused our
worries.

We sold our belongings one by one to get potatoes or some other foods, and
there was left only a few things to us, but I sold gladly my valuable sash to
get some papers and colours for my son. Father's picture was coming to its
end.

At the morning of twentyith of september, I asked to my son "When your
diary will be done?"

"To-day or to-morrow, oh yes, I will finish it up to-day". He answered with
cheerful voice.

I promised to my son that I will write a letter to General MacArthur on
this matter, but it seemed to me a venture. But friends of mine who teach
at St. Margaret's High School (Rikkio Jo-Gakko), Mr. I. Nakagawa,
Rev. Ken Imai, Mr. T. Hasegawa promised to help me out and gladly give
their hands.

My dear General MacArthur:
This is the story all about my son's diary and husband's picture.
We hope sincerely that these presents will show our feeling of gratitude.
We heard the botanist's opinion, who is the teacher at St. Margaret's and
she proved that this is outstanding work and encouraged us to publish it. It is
unexpected result of our work.

Here I like to express my gratitude toward your kindness and sympathy to our people and also show you that how the tiny seeds of American pumpkin gave joy last six months to my family.

Your very sincerely
Shigetaka's mother.

The title of the letter, "Mother's Word," refers to her part of the family project, the message to MacArthur that accompanied the diary and the painting. Is this not a touching letter? The mother lovingly watching her son's daily observance of the growth of a pumpkin plant, the young father adding a blossom to the diary with an oil painting. They joined together in a flow of gratitude to MacArthur. To this family, the general was truly a gentle father figure. (The painting is kept at the MacArthur Memorial. It is an oil painting, about two feet by three feet. The diary has not been found.)

In a similar vein, a letter was sent to General and Mrs. MacArthur on January 20, 1948, from a gathering called the Children's Thanksgiving Meeting, expressing thanks "from the bottom of our heart" for the gift of candy from the Allied forces. The letter is addressed, sweetly, to "MacArthur Ojisama and Obasama" (Uncle and Aunt MacArthur). It is signed by three children, evidently quite young given their poor penmanship, but it was obviously written in English by one of their teachers or mothers.

LET ME BE YOUR WIFE'S MAID

In a time of confusion, when a family looks to a foreign ruler for a strong father figure and a guide, it is not surprising that a woman might look to the same person for a man she can depend on. The writer of the next letter found in MacArthur the manliness lacking in Japanese men of that era, and she tried to cling to it:[2]

Photo 6.1   This illustration from a children's book published in May 1947 pictures a fatherly MacArthur gazing over the landscape of Japan. The accompanying text, entitled "Peace," extolled the general's famous reluctance to wear his military medals and explained, "The peace that has come at the cost of many lives cannot be called a good thing. Once a life is lost it can never be restored, so his sadness is deep. General MacArthur takes no pleasure in accumulating medals." Source: Makkāsā gensui, illustration by Yoshizawa Renzaburō, text by Satō Yoshimi (Tokyo: Fröbel-kan, 1947).

[October 20, 1945]
General MacArthur

Dear General MacArthur:

This is so sudden that it may anger you greatly, but my life depends on this request, so please forgive me. I have to bother you, busy general, with my request because there is nothing we Japanese can believe in. I even went to China before the war because I detested egoistic Japan and the ways of those in power. I had made up my mind to spend the rest of my life in China, but in 1931 my mother was taken ill, and regrettably I had to return to Tokyo. Not only I, but anyone who has a heart would abhor those in power right now. During the war and even now after the war, some high police officials and military officers live in my neighborhood, and police officials come home in cars and have their subordinates carry in case upon case of beer and sake, and the officers too get cases of food and drink brought to their homes.

The municipal government ordered us to evacuate our home, and the house we finally found was bombed within ten days. We lost our home and all our belongings in one night. My eighty-year-old mother was sick, we had no shelter and no food, we even contemplated suicide. Just at that time, my younger sister's home was burned during the bombing of May 25, and her husband was killed. The stress she went through must have affected her, for she fell ill while mourning her husband, and she is still sick. No one even feels sorry for our poor family of women; the local community leaders are that in name only and do not have any feeling for their fellow Japanese. . . .

It is inevitable in a war that one country must win. We women knew that your country would win. It was obvious you would win. I lost my home during the war, but I am not bitter or sad about that. What bothers me is that those in high positions use their power and money to have mistresses and buy expensive things on the black market and lead extravagant lives.

There are countless people in Japan who respect the general's great loving heart. I believe there are no more troubled hearts now. By losing the war, how much our minds have been eased. This is the truth. I hope you will believe me.

When I read an article in the newspaper about some general committing suicide, I even wish that they all would die. Those in power started a war on *their own and made us suffer. Now it is already getting cold, and we have not received one piece of warm clothing, and not a single piece of charcoal has come our way. Those Japanese in high positions went off and started a war, and they are to blame for us not having a place to live and not being able to feed my eighty-year-old mother and my sick sister. With your power, please do as you wish to the war criminals. I beg you.*

This letter rings with the resentment of an ordinary woman complaining about the hardships she suffered because of the war. The appeal may be addressed to a former enemy general, but he was a man who had power no Japanese man of that time had, and it seemed to her that he could be relied on. In saying it was better to have lost the war, this woman had found in the victor MacArthur a symbol of strength and righteousness. When she asks MacArthur to punish the former Japanese leaders, she seems convinced of his power, and one can almost hear her voice jump an octave in adulation.

General, you have become the number one leader in the world and we revere you. The weather in Japan is bad, so I pray you will please, please, please take good care of yourself and stay in Japan forever and ever and ever.

I think we are better off having been defeated. How sad to have been born in Japan. If I knew your country's language, at least I could work as your wife's maid, but unfortunately I cannot speak your language and it saddens me that I cannot be of use. Maybe I can at least help take care of your subordinates. Then the Japanese people will come to understand how much I respect you, and my mind will be at peace. I am not a bad person. I swear to God all I have said here, please believe me. For my rudeness, I apologize over and over. The weather in Japan is not the same as what you are accustomed to, how inconvenient it must be for you to live here. I pray to God that you will please, please, please take care of yourself.

In the history of occupations throughout the world, it may not be so unusual for the occupied to get on their knees and beg the foreign rulers to stay forever. However, it makes one sad to read it years later. This person says she is sad because she doesn't speak English and cannot work as a maid for MacArthur's wife, but what is really sad is her state of mind. In closing, this letter addressed to "Great General of the Army MacArthur" expresses absolute trust in the conqueror:

I believe that for a country like Japan, ministers are no longer necessary. Although you may be busy, you are the leader of the world, General MacArthur, please give orders for everything. Our minds will be more at peace if someone like the general who has a big heart handles matters for us. This is your country, so please take care of it. You are a very busy person; please forgive me for bothering you with my letter.

Sincerely,
H. K.
Setagaya-ku, Tokyo

TRYING ALL CONNECTIONS

Hundreds of letters like the one we have just seen were sent to MacArthur. Perhaps the reader will say one is enough. I myself do not much relish these songs of resentment and self-deprecation, so I will change direction here. After MacArthur established his popularity among the Japanese people and became the provider of "fatherly love," it was only natural that people would want to partake of it. The following, a letter typewritten in English, is just one example:[3]

No. 304, Nogemachi, Tamagawa,
Setagaya, Tokyo, Japan.
23 May 1950.

General of the Army Douglas McArthur;
Dear sir;
    Allow me to take this chance of approaching you and writing my personal problem.
    My name is Mrs. Haruko Goto, and the maiden name was Lady Kano. Forty-one years ago when I was attending to Peers' School, I was taught English conversation by a lady by the name of Miss McArthur. This is an old memory though, she was an American National, and was said that she came

to Japan as a tourist for the purpose of sight-seeing. And by the earnest desire of President General Nogi, she stayed in Japan one year and taught English course at the school.

I had very nice times by the invitations to her resident several times. And sometimes I invited her to my home at Ohmori, also. At the time Ohmori was a very quiet country, and had to take a steam-train from Shimbashi station. As she was away from her land and at the far-off country, we were desirous of showing her our appreciations, my parents and my brothers has some companies with her. One day in Winter, I remember that she called on us with a beautiful aqua-blue mantle, and told us, "This is an Italian material. My brother in Italy sent it to me".

When I heard General's name after the Occupation, I have been wondering if she might be one of your family. And if she happened to be your family, I would be very happy and sincerely appreciate you if you kindly give me her present address. I am sure that she remembers me, Miss Kano, as one of her students in the school.

If she is not in your family, I humbly apologize and hope that you kindly forgive me.

I want to express our sincere appreciation to your deep considerations to Japan in this chance, and God Bless You.

Sincerely Yours,
I remain,
[signed] Haruko Goto

Unless she felt a certain intimacy with the recipient, it is unlikely this writer would have sent such a friendly letter just because her English teacher of long ago was named "Miss McArthur." As would be expected from a person of her class, her signature is beautiful, and her style was elegant. I imagine that MacArthur, who had an aristocratic mien, might have been pleased with this letter, but unfortunately Miss McArthur was not related to the general at all. Douglas had two older brothers (Arthur, the eldest, died of natural causes while serving as a navy captain, and Malcolm died in childhood); he had no sisters. There is no record of anyone related to MacArthur residing in Japan during the time the hero of the Russo-Japanese War, General Nogi Maresuke, was president of the Peers' School. In addition to this letter, there is a similar inquiry from a fifty-six-year-old woman about a Gertrude MacArthur from whom she learned English at Tsuda English College.

If these women wrote letters simply because they once knew someone with the same name, it is not surprising that someone who believed he had an even stronger "connection" would write the following letter. This is also in English, written in pen, and is kept in the MacArthur Memorial archives.

Mr. HISAICHI OHKUBO
No. 102, UADERA-CHO
1 CHOME, SUMA-KU, KOBE
26th January 1951

General Douglas MacArthur Esqr.
My Dear General,
    Please allow me to send this letter to you in congraturation of your 71st, Birthday which you are going to cerebrate today in a very good health, amidst these busiest days in the Corean affairs. I am thus writing to you in consideration that it is my special duty to do so, as I was born on the 26th of January of 71 years ago, the same as your goodselves.
    Presenting herewith my heart-felt thanks to you for your continual kind guidance valuable to my country.

I remain, Dear Sir,
Yours faithfully,
[signed] H. Ohkubo

A LETTER FROM LIEUTENANT SHIRASE'S DAUGHTER

A different kind of appeal came from the second daughter of Lieutenant Shirase Nobu, a man who became famous for his expedition to the South Pole before the war. The letter, in the MacArthur Memorial archives, is written in beautiful calligraphy. It appears that it was written by someone else because another personal letter is attached that was written by the daughter herself.

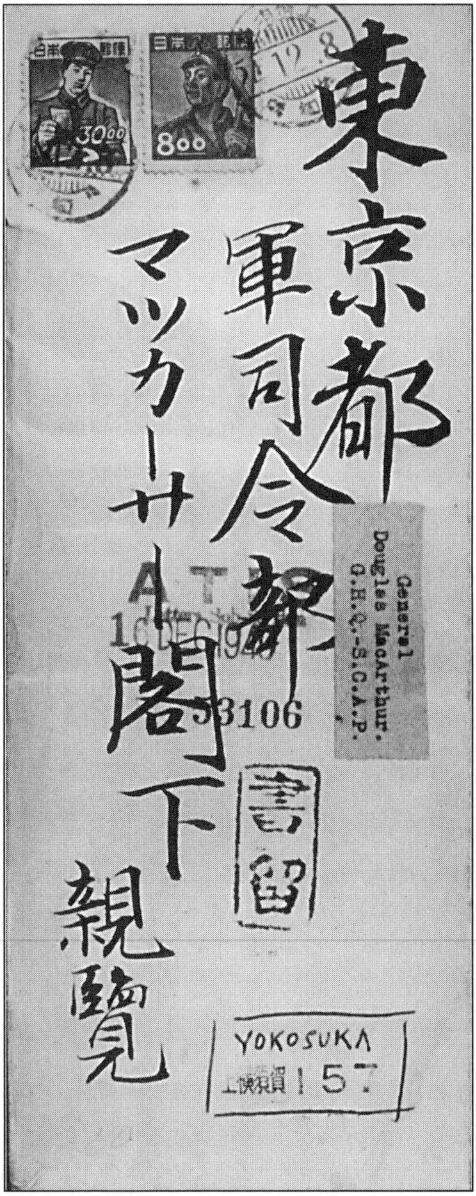

Photo 6.2   Shirase Takeko's letter came in this envelope, designated "personal" and addressed in beautiful calligraphy to "His Excellency MacArthur, General Headquarters, Tokyo."
Source: *National Archives*

December 8, 1949
The Honorable MacArthur
via His Secretary

Your Excellency has guided us, with your indomitable spirit, along the true and proper path for a considerable time. I am deeply grateful. Japanese women who have been oppressed for a long time are especially thankful. I hope you will continue to lead us for a long time to come.

I am Shirase Takeko, the second daughter of the leader of the Japanese expedition to the South Pole, Lieutenant Shirase. Despite the fact that I have never had an audience with Your Excellency, and with full realization that this is an inconsiderate thing to do, I have decided to write to Your Excellency with this request.

My letter concerns unfinished business, regarding the Antarctic Territory, of my late father Shirase Nobu who passed away four years ago on September 4, 1946. On behalf of my deceased father, I ask through Your Excellency's good offices that we be allowed to make a public announcement once peace is officially concluded. I imagine Your Excellency will remember my father sent a letter to you around the middle of June 1946, inquiring whether Shirase Nobu was to be considered a war criminal and be purged, and asking how the Antarctic Territory was to be treated thereafter. He also mentioned that he had been deprived of his monthly annuity of sixty-eight yen on which his livelihood depended, leaving him without any means for the next day, and that although he was eighty-six years old, he was still healthy and would like to work in some position. A reply was received soon afterwards, saying that Lieutenant Shirase was an explorer and not a war criminal, he would not be purged, and regarding the South Pole, the territory belonged to whomever discovered it. Reading your kind and sincere letter, my father wept his aged tears and immediately sent his record of the Japanese expedition to the South Pole, Nankyoku-ki, to you. Your Excellency responded by return mail and inquired whether this important document was on temporary loan or whether it was a gift. My father read your cordial letter over and over and often said that the Japanese people, himself included, are impolite and should learn from your example.

The correspondence between Lieutenant Shirase and MacArthur has not been found, but it would be surprising if MacArthur had actually written that Antarctica belonged to whomever discovered it. How-ever, what Shirase's daughter really wanted to convey appears in the latter half of the letter. It continues:

In May 1946, just two of us—my daughter who was eleven years old and I—were repatriated from Beijing in northern China. We went to live with my parents who were living in Katayama-mura, Kita Adachi-gun, Saitama Prefecture at that time. My father seemed to have developed dropsy from malnutrition, and he had difficulty walking. Despite these pathetic living conditions, my parents always said that we should fear God but not man. They felt that Japan had come to its current pass because we had a foolish spirit that did not fear God, and we were reaping what we sowed. My father would take out Your Excellency's letter, shed his aged tears and, choked with emotion, tell my mother and me and my daughter that we must never forget the great kindness of Your Excellency, acting directly, and indirectly [the kindness of] the people of the United States, who extended loving hands and saved us, as foolish and hard-headed as we were. My parents were leading a very lonely life without an heir, because thirty years ago they had moved away from their home after disinheriting his two sons—the older (now sixty-three years old) and the younger (now fifty years old)—who had evil beliefs incompatible with my father. I felt sorry for my parents and how sad they must have been. My parents and I believed in the same religion, and despite our wretched life, we were thankful for our blessings. With my father gone, my mother and I now lead lives of reflection and gratitude. When we were living in Saitama, my father's younger son had come to my father's room, and he asked to borrow Your Excellency's letter for a while. He took it and never returned it. My father was very angry and requested it be returned many times, but on one pretext or another he never returned it. My father called this son with bad ideas a devil and finally made up his mind to move to Koromo-chō, Nishi Kamo-gun, Aichi Prefecture on August 17, 1946. Seventeen days later, attended by my mother, my daughter, and myself, he passed away; he was eighty-six years old. His last words were for me to depend on Your Excellency. My father went to the Kuril Islands for three years from 1892; he went to the South Pole on November 28, 1910 for twenty months; and a year before the Great Kantō Earthquake [of 1923], he took my mother and went back to the Kuril Islands for three years. Thus he gave his whole life to exploration, and all this time he was unpaid. There are no words to express the hardships my surviving mother *endured. As a child, I can only feel great respect. She is seventy-eight years old now.*

I now teach home economics as an instructor at Yokosuka Middle School in Kami Yokosuka, Yokosuka-mura, Hazu-gun, Aichi Prefecture. I live in Sairinji, 13 Ōaza Seto, Hazu-gun, Aichi Prefecture.

I am afraid my long, long letter has taken time away from your busy schedule, but I beg you to hear to my request.

Finally, Your Excellency's health is of great importance, and since it is getting colder by the day, I pray you will take good care of yourself.

Sincerely,
Shirase Takeko

For this writer to expose herself and her family's story so openly, to confide in MacArthur and ask him to hear her plea, implies that MacArthur loomed even larger to her than her late father. The more personal the confession, the more it reflects the trust, respect, and love she felt for MacArthur. The intensity of the letter is a measure of how big a heart the writer imagined MacArthur to have. Perhaps many Japanese felt they could bury their faces in his chest and cry, putting MacArthur in the role of a Catholic priest hearing confession, for more than anything, the writer sought the comfort of being heard by MacArthur.

"A FACE ... INFINITE IN ASPECT"

So far we have seen how Japanese families identified with MacArthur as a father figure and women saw him as a man. What about the men? They had challenged the world in war and lost, losing their personal authority in the process. Did they simply stand in awe of MacArthur? Were they jealous of the adoration Japanese women felt for him? We have no way of knowing the feelings of those who despised MacArthur, since they generally did not write him letters. But we have seen many letters that embraced MacArthur's leadership, which is an indication that Japanese men found in MacArthur a symbol of manliness. I will present one extraordinary example.

The following is from a letter addressed to one of MacArthur's assistants from an obscure sculptor. He had made a plaster bust of MacArthur that had been accepted as a gift; now he was writing to suggest making a bronze version. The letter is written on a roll of stationery with brush strokes that can only be described as bold. The vigorous calligraphy reflects the writer's heightened emotion, and it also exudes the atmosphere of the time. The letter is dated November 23, 1949. At this point, the "reverse course" was in full swing, and the emphasis of occupation policy had shifted from liberalization and political reform toward anticommunism and economic reform. As a result, some Japanese were beginning to criticize the occupation, but Nakagaki Gengen dared to write the following letter:[4]

> . . . Looking back, I believed your fine statement to the people regarding "Class A" war criminals to be absolute, and I am not the only one who idolized you and continues to idolize you as a result.
>
> Fortunately, I brought my creativity as a sculptor into play. Unfortunately, to get a view of you, I could only wait as part of the crowd in front of your headquarters and catch a short glimpse of you in the distance through a pair of weak opera glasses. One might be able to paint a portrait with that, but a sculpture is not that easy. I jumped for joy when I finally obtained a great photograph taken by the Kyōdō News Service, and I was able to make the sculpture. I have never encountered, as far as I know, a face as infinite in aspect as this, which so universally satisfied all of the conditions for expression in relief.
>
> It is not a perfect square but a combination of a square and a circle, and in reproducing this state, I added some strong active elements of the general in contact with infinity, or, conversely, confronting the universe, securing his character, and leaving his mark on the universe. I am still very happy with it. I hope you will not be displeased.

MacArthur's good looks were recognized by himself as well as others, but it is virtually impossible to grasp the philosophical aspects of his looks that so impressed the sculptor. Perhaps he himself did not understand what he was writing, but it is fair to assume that the "infinity" he saw in MacArthur's face was at least one person's notion of the ideal man.

Photo 6.3   Japanese line the street outside GHQ in the Dai-Ichi Building to catch a glimpse of General MacArthur. The general kept a clockwork schedule, returning to his residence at the American embassy every day for lunch. Source: *U.S. Army*

Photo 6.4   MacArthur exits GHQ, accompanied by an aide. Source: U.S. Army

"A FATHER-CHILD RELATIONSHIP"

To the occupied Japanese, MacArthur personified the father, the ideal man, a confessor, even a god. I was especially curious about the many Japanese women who were infatuated with MacArthur. How could women not be captivated by such a remarkable man? That being the case, I would expect to find letters from women—love letters—confessing their feelings directly to MacArthur. I uncovered few such letters, however, and continued to wonder why.

Part of the answer came my way when I was writing the first draft of this chapter. It was the early part of December 1983, and a three-day symposium on the occupation took place at Hōsei University, where I was then a professor. One of the participants, University of Kansas historian Grant K. Goodman, had been a young language officer working at the ATIS during the occupation. Goodman heard about my series of letters to MacArthur that was then appearing in the journal *Shisō no kagaku,* and he told me he had translated letters from the Japanese at that time. He asked if I had come across letters from Japanese women who wanted "father–child relationships" with MacArthur. He explained that some letters plainly said to MacArthur, "I want to bear your child." I had never seen any such letters. "You know," Goodman added, "there were hundreds of them, and my colleagues and I had great fun translating them."

To many Japanese during the occupation, MacArthur was like a god who was too awesome to approach. However, the letters that Goodman translated suggest that there were many audacious Japanese women who wrote to MacArthur, the supreme man, asking him to father their child.

I have no contempt for these women. They only expressed their true feelings, honestly and bravely. What they did also vividly reflects an essential aspect of the occupation. I have often observed (sometimes to the shock of the more straitlaced among my audience) that the Japanese "went to bed with the occupation." The American occupation and its subsequent reforms were the equivalent of consensual sex, not rape, at least to the majority of the ordinary public. Consequently, many of those who were adults at the time have trouble resolving their memories of the occupation not because they feel resentment over a painful assault, but because of something closer to a guilty conscience for being seduced too easily.

We may never be able to see the letters to MacArthur from the audacious Japanese women who asked to bear his child, but it remains significant that considerable numbers of these letters were sent, which is why I have discussed them here, sight unseen.

7

GIFTS OF THANKS

GENUINE GRATITUDE

Japanese like to give gifts. Most people had lost their possessions during the war and were leading lives of great hardship, and yet there seemed to be no end to the number of people sending gifts of thanks to MacArthur and his administration. The letters that accompanied the presents elucidate the psychology of the times, as well as the feelings of the people who sent them. In this chapter, I will first introduce letters that simply convey gratitude and respect. They are the most numerous, and I believe they set the basic tone for this group of letters.

July 13 [1946]

Dear General MacArthur,
with your permission,

I offer best wishes for your health during this heat that could burn anything. Recently, fulfilling your heartfelt desire, you have sent us an abundance of food. This made me feel like a bright window had opened in my heart, and I cannot find adequate words to express my gratitude to you. I am sending you a set for assembling a Japanese lamp that is a favorite of mine. I would be greatly obliged if you would accept it.

Finally please take good care in the heat.

> *The words I slowly put together*
> *Do not flow easily, they only fill my heart.*

Sincerely,
Miyasaka Chiyo

The writer's gratitude seems to permeate the words of this sweet letter. It was written with a pen, but the occasional use of classic *kana* script and the closing poem suggest the writer's literary inclination. The address on the envelope says only "To Beloved General MacArthur," and the date on the back reads, "21-7-13" (July 13, Shōwa 21 [1946]), less than a year after the surrender. The sender lived in Ichikawa City in Chiba Prefecture.[1]

The next letter is from a well-meaning young girl.

February 16

General MacArthur:

I offer this letter to General MacArthur. I hear that you are diligently attending to your military affairs every day, and we congratulate you from our hearts.

About the doll I sent you out of the blue recently: Through the general's efforts, we are able to live in peace every day and every night, and I sent you the doll in the hope that our unlimited gratitude might give you some comfort during your busy days. Please accept it.

During this time of unpredictable weather, I pray you will take even greater care of yourself. It is my habit to pray every night to our Father in heaven for the health of the general and everyone. Please tell all who work at the general headquarters that a little Japanese girl prays for their health.

Good-bye,
Sakai Reiko

The year this letter was written is unknown. There is no return address on the envelope, but it is addressed to "My Most Beloved General Douglas MacArthur."

Gratitude to MacArthur also meant gratitude to the United States, and this sometimes had a long history. In 1891 a Japanese man was hired at the port of Yokohama as a "blacksmith-sailor" on an American battleship. He learned the latest metallurgy techniques on board and later established an ironworks back in Japan. After his death, the shop burned down in an American air raid, and MacArthur arrived shortly afterward. His son, who inherited the family business, wanted to express his gratitude to the United States for teaching his father the trade. He chose as his present a suit of black-threaded armor, a most splendid gift. The accompanying letter was written on ceremonial *hōsho* paper in a beautiful block style of calligraphy with an attached English translation (included here).

September 12, 1947
General of the Army Douglas MacArthur,
Supreme Commander of the Allied Forces,

Enlisting as a blacksmith sailor in 1891, fifty-six years ago, my father Tomikichi (alias Torakichi) boarded the Monokosi *[USS Monocacy] of the U.S. Chinese Squadron at Yokohama Harbor. He assiduously performed his duties as the sole Japanese sailor among the crew, finding favor with his senior officers and fellow sailors, until he left the service three years later, receiving a citation from the captain.*

The Japanese technical industry in those days was in a state of infancy, and his three years of service aboard the Monokosi *afforded him an excellent opportunity for gaining valuable experience in this direction. Equipped with further experience accumulated during the subsequent ten years he founded a steam-boiler manufacturing plant in Tokyo in May 1904. The plant was completely destroyed by an air raid on March 10, 1945, but was reconstructed with materials saved from the fire. Tomikichi died six years ago at the age of 78, and since then I have been managing the plant under the name of Kuroiwa Iron Works (limited partnership), employing 40 workers. It is with profound gratitude to America that I remember the fact that the foundation of the present prosperity of my plant was built by my father's three years of experience aboard the* Monokosi.

I hereby have the honor to present an armor of black-threaded plates to the Supreme Commander of the Allied Forces along with documents and photographs, reminders of my father's service aboard the said warship, partly in token of my heartfelt thanks and partly for the repose of the departed soul of my father. Acceptance of this humble gift would be highly appreciated not only by myself but by the plant.

Yours respectfully,
[signed] Sadashige Kuroiwa,

No. 55, Mama, Ichikawa City,
Chiba Prefecture.
Name of the plant under my management:
Kuroiwa Iron Works
Location:
No. 3, 3 chome, Minami-suna Machi,
Koto-ku, Tokyo.

The above present was sent in gratitude for the past, while the following carried hopes for the future. The sender, a doctor in Tochigi Prefecture, discovered a symbol of peace on a small bird and decided to send it as a guardian spirit for MacArthur and his family.

March 30, 1950
Commander MacArthur and his Family

Dear Sir:
I offer my congratulations on the health of Your Excellency, Commander MacArthur, and the members of your family.
I have brought a roller canary (band number 09-13535) to offer to Your Excellency's family. This bird miraculously has the symbol of peace, a black cross, on the middle of its forehead. I believe this is rare, and so I would like to offer this canary marked with the mystery of creation in the hope that it will long protect the health of the family of the respected commander. I beg that it be accepted.

Chikazono-mura, Nasu-gun, Tochigi Prefecture
Takahashi Yasuo, Doctor

A year later when MacArthur left Japan, this canary was given to Hayashi Tadaichi, the family's chief cook at the American embassy where MacArthur lived. When Hayashi retired to Tochigi Prefecture (people referred to his property as the "Otawara MacArthur Estate"), the canary was taken along, back to the prefecture it came from.

The gifts that VIPs of the time chose to send MacArthur were often luxurious. For example, the mayor of Kobe sent an outer kimono of silk brocade to General and Mrs. MacArthur, in the name of the city, on November 5, 1945. Mikimoto Kōkichi (the "pearl King") sent pearls to Mrs. Jean MacArthur on her birthday, December 28, 1949. Matsuoka Komakichi, Speaker of the Lower House of the Diet, sent gold brocade fabric to General and Mrs. MacArthur "in the name of international goodwill," and the industrialist Takasaki Tatsunosuke presented the first Japanese turkey produced from an American egg on November 20, 1950.

Some of those in high positions sent unusual gifts. On December 8, 1948, Shidehara Kijūrō, the second postwar prime minister, sent a copy

Photo 7.1 Hayashi Tadaichi, the chief cook at the American embassy (where MacArthur lived), with the canary that was passed on to him when MacArthur left Japan. This photograph appeared in the Yomiuri shimbun on April 17, 1951, the day after MacArthur's departure. Source: Yomiuri Shimbunsha

of a letter from President Grant to the Meiji emperor, which he said he had found at the imperial palace. Shirasu Jirō, a close associate of Prime Minister Yoshida Shigeru, designed a wooden chair, had it made at a studio in Tsurukawa-mura near Tokyo, and sent it "on the occasion of leaving the post of vice chairman of the Central Liaison Office" on June 22, 1947. However, for a person of high office to send a gift to someone in an even higher position is not unusual, and there is little worth noting in their letters. What ordinary citizens sent and what they said in their letters is far more illuminating.

Most of all people prayed for MacArthur's health. Although it was said that he was stronger than those in their prime, he was already sixty-five when he arrived in Japan. It was natural for those Japanese who wanted the benevolent conqueror to stay in Japan "forever and ever" to send him something that would contribute to his well-being. Noteworthy was the number of canes, many handmade with great care. One sent by a sculptor was described as "a cane made as his last remembrance by a sixty-eight-year-old living in Meguro," a section of Tokyo.[2] The following was sent by an old man who made canes for a hobby. The letter was handwritten in English, and although the penmanship looks like that of a junior high school student, the composition is as impressive as it is charming:

Wahichiro Tsuboi
Futagosho-mura
Tsukubo-gun, Okayama Prefecture
Jan. 1, 1949

Honorable Douglas MacArthur
General Headquarters of Allied Forces
Tokyo, Japan

Dear General MacArthur,

I am very happy to send this letter to you. I am an old farmer living in the country, working honestly from morning till night, hoping for the rehabilitation of Japan [as a] warless and peaceful country. I believe you are doing your best for Japan's revival and world peace. Every folks in the country do not suspect your success.

Now, today, I have the double pleasure to send you by post-parcel the walking-stick which I made myself, according to the Japanese custom New Year's present. It is my hobby of amusement to make stick of various trees which grow in my neighbouring hills. Once I presented it to Mr. Inukai, dead Japanese Prime Minister, and received a letter of thanks. The wood is so-called "moro" tree in my province which is not found in America or scarcely in Japan except my district.

This stick is made by firstly cutting off branches, barking, and secondly rubbing with sand-papers, polishing with cloth many times. The white stripe is the living, and others are dead one when the trunk is cut down. Please receive my humble present which will soon arrive at you by post and appreciate it.

Yours respectfully,
[signed] Wahichiro Tsuboi

Tsuboi's letter overflows with affection for MacArthur. There were others who wanted to send canes: The head of the Liaison Office in Kagoshima Prefecture sent an inquiry directly to MacArthur about someone in his prefecture who had found a rare forked stalk of bamboo ten years ago and had made a cane out of it. A photo of the cane as exhibited at the Kyūshū Industrial Exposition was enclosed, with a request that the cane be accepted as a gift. The initials of aide-de-camp Colonel Laurence E. Bunker are on the letter, showing that it was read, but MacArthur had abandoned the habit of using a cane during the war, so even if the forked bamboo cane was accepted, he would not have used it.

An "American-style belly band" was sent to MacArthur by Koyanagi Harukichi from Nakazato-machi, Kita-ku, Tokyo. The accompanying letter in English, dated March 3, 1950, was written in careful longhand. I will not quote the whole letter, but in it the writer introduces himself as a well-known specialist with fifty years experience in artificial limbs and surgical instruments, whose skill had been recognized by the best medical specialists in Japan. His most recent invention was an abdominal support he named the "American-style belly band." He wanted to offer his invention to MacArthur as a token of appreciation for enabling the Japanese to live happily. Whether MacArthur received this invention or not is unknown, but the sender added, in English, the following instructions for use:

Wearing this band will make the weak healthy, and the healthy healthier. I hope you would wear this and promote your health. If you wear this, please unfasten one of the front button, and then after fastening the button regulate and braid up the string so as to hold the stomach part upwards.

As long as he was governing such sweet people, the occupation of Japan must have been a very pleasant task for MacArthur. And this is only a small sample of the many ways the Japanese people expressed their gratitude and affection.

FLOWERS, FRESH FRUIT, TEA, AND DRIED PERSIMMON

To: Government Section

Dear Sirs:
I have sent some "lilies" to General MacArthur as a Christmas present, please handle them accordingly.
I do not know whether it is proper or not to send such a present. If you consider it improper, please discard them.

There is no date or signature on this letter, which seems to have been sent with some trepidation. This letter typifies one type of Japanese, kindhearted but timid. Sending a gift may not require as much pluck as writing a letter, but it is still an act of self-assertion that requires some confidence. I am sure that the number of people who wanted to send something to MacArthur but could not, out of shyness or for some other reason, far outnumbered those who actually took action.

The lilies were actually bulbs in this case, but many people sent fresh flowers. A Yokohama nursery, for example, sent along a request from one of their growers in Saga Prefecture, who wanted to send two dozen white lilies. He was willing to send them to the United States if necessary, and he was asking for guidance. The letter, dated December 2, 1947 was written in fine English, but the signature was so fancy it is illegible. Sending fresh flowers to the United States at this point, when military shipping was given priority, posed some unique problems. MacArthur's staff decided to ignore the offer.

Every occasion was seized as an opportunity to offer flowers. Hamamura Yoshio, a flower cultivator from Hiroshima Prefecture, sent Mrs. MacArthur "special carnations I have cultivated for twenty years" for Mother's Day in May 1948. Ueda Keikichi from Okayama Prefecture requested the honor of decorating the supreme commander's office with live flowers to commemorate Independence Day on July 4, 1947.

Others chose to send seasonal fruits. The following is a typical letter accompanying this kind of gift:

August 19, 1948
The Honorable General Douglas MacArthur
General Headquarters of the Allied Forces

Dear Sir:

Ever since the end of the war, Your Excellency the general has shown great concern for the reconstruction of Japan and the protection of the nations of the world, for which I am deeply moved and grateful. I am a simple farmer who works day and night without rest, hoping to respond to your noble deeds and repay even a tiny bit of our obligations to you. I worship Your Excellency's wise efforts and would like to show my appreciation for your continuing endeavors by sending you what I have harvested. (There are four kinds of oranges: Tosa orange, new summer orange, Valencia red, and large summer orange; they are last year's fruit but were protected through winter and harvested today.) I am sending you my humble gift, and I hope you will enjoy them. Please excuse my writing to you.

Very sincerely yours,

Morita Tokuhō
4577 Hage, Hage-mura
Takaoka-gun, Kōchi Prefecture
Empire of Japan

A waybill from the Higashi Yamanashi Trucking Company in Yamanashi Prefecture indicates that "a box of grapes" was sent to "General MacArthur, American Embassy" on November 1, 1950, by Ōbunsha, a publisher famous for its entrance examination reference books. Because Ōbunsha had promoted militaristic education during the war, it was branded a "war-criminal publisher" and president Akao Yoshio was purged. By the time the grapes were sent, Akao had been "depurged" for some time (he had been cleared in a letter from General Courtney Whitney, chief of GHQ's Government Section, to Prime Minister Ashida Hitoshi dated July 16, 1948). It could be that the box of grapes was an annual gift of appreciation for Akao's reinstatement.

Another shipment of grapes to MacArthur came with religious overtones. In November 1947, Takeshita Tameji, an ex-colonel in the Salvation Army, sent grapes harvested at his brother Ryōhei's orchard in the foothills of Mount Asama. In the accompanying letter, typewritten in beautiful English, Takeshita offers thanks to God for the bountiful harvest and extends his gratitude to MacArthur for his unselfish devotion to the rehabilitation of Japan. He adds that the name of his brother's orchard, Shinju-en ("true vine orchard"), comes from the Bible, John 15:1, "I am the true vine, and my Father is the gardener." To MacArthur, who was a devout Christian, these grapes must have been especially delicious.

Accompanied by a beautifully handwritten letter in English, "Dr. T. H. Kawashima" of Tokyo also sent Yamanashi Alexandria grapes to General and Mrs. MacArthur annually, and sometimes twice a year, beginning in October of 1945 and continuing at least through the fall of 1949. According to a thank-you note written by an aide to MacArthur, Dr. Kawashima had his office in the Marunouchi section of Tokyo and was the representative of the International Legal and Economic Agency. He was born in Ibaraki Prefecture, and he also sometimes sent beautiful chrysanthemums from Kasama (which he called "the city of peace").

Japan is blessed with an abundance of seasonal fruits, so the gifts were not limited to grapes. Ide Yasaku of Shizuoka Prefecture sent a box of pears on September 6, 1946. In his letter in English, he proudly explains that the "Kikusui" brand pears were being cultivated according to a "new botanical technology of nutrio-periodism." The handwriting is childish, but the writer had a notable command of English. Governor Hayashi Torao of Nagano Prefecture sent an inquiry in English on December 12, 1947, requesting that MacArthur accept an offer from a "G. Ōta" in his prefecture, who wished to send the general a crate of apples. And on January 28, 1947, Kidachi Rikizō of Aomori Prefecture wrote that he had sent, through his friend Hasegawa Saiji (the editor in chief of Jiji news agency), a crate of apples that were the fruit of thirty years of experimental cultivation.

For the most part, the gifts were intended, as one letter put it, "to express gratitude for Your Excellency's generous policies and spirit of leadership," but some had other agendas. A letter dated September 30, 1946, states that Suzuki Itarō and seven others representing the citizens of the town of Amori in Nagano Prefecture had visited GHQ in April to ask that the industrialist Fujiwara Ginjirō from their hometown be removed from the list of war crimes suspects. Shortly afterward, he was released "through your good offices," and to express their gratitude, they had sent three boxes of apples. Fujiwara, who was called the "king of paper manufacturing," served as minister of state in the Tōjō cabinet and minister of munitions in the Koiso cabinet during the war, which resulted in a warrant for his arrest, along with fifty-eight other business and political leaders, on December 2, 1945. It is not known how much MacArthur's influence had to do with Fujiwara's release. War crimes charges were not pursued against any of the many business leaders arrested, for reasons that have never been fully explained. Nonetheless, Fujiwara's hometown friends believed that his release was MacArthur's doing, so they sent apples in appreciation.

Shimoyamada Sadao, headman of a town in Ibaraki Prefecture, sent a box of persimmons, hoping that the General would take good care of himself with the onset of cold weather. His letter in English says, "I should be happy if my humble present would meet Your Excellency's taste," exhibiting a surprising mastery of nuance. The letter is not dated, but a GHQ staff note is marked December 2, 1949. It would appear that the Japanese were able to brush up on their English as the lengthy occupation continued.

Other seasonal produce was also sent to MacArthur. The following is a notice sent with a shipment of *matsutake* mushrooms:

> *To The Honorable General MacArthur*
> > *Offering*
> > *Item:* Matsutake, *one box*
>
> *October 19, 1950*
> *Nakagawa Kurakichi*
> *Rikutō-en*

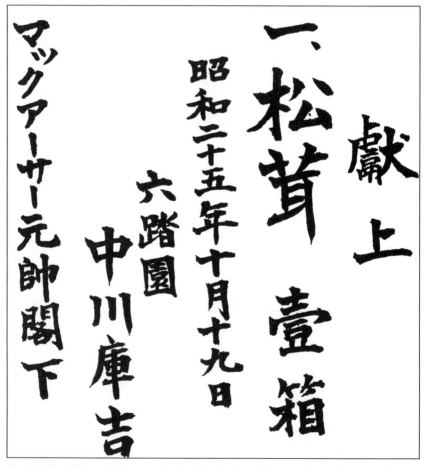

Photo 7.2   This note accompanied a gift of a box of matsutake *mushrooms.* Source: MacArthur Memorial

During the feudal period, farmers were customarily obliged to offer the first fruits of the harvest to their lord. Was the practice of presenting seasonal produce to MacArthur perhaps a carryover from this sense of obligation? I suppose it is more likely that most were expressing true feelings of gratitude. The following note from the governor of Ehime Prefecture, Aoki Shigeomi, was attached to a citizen's request for permission to send a gift; it was sent to Kimura Shirōshichi, head of the liaison section of the Japanese Foreign Ministry, on December 16, 1949:

As evident in the enclosed letter, Kurata Kitsu of Hirano-mura, Kita-gun of my prefecture has sent an inquiry hoping to present a can of tea and red beans to General MacArthur. I have deemed this to be an offering of genuine good faith, and I hope you will take the necessary measures to have this gift accepted.

Postscript: For your information, I would like to add that records show this person sent dried persimmons in December two years ago and tea and red beans a year ago, all of which were accepted. . . .

Motive for the present:

Since the defeat, this sixty-two-year old woman has been living with her husband, seventy-five, and a grandnephew, thirteen. They live by peddling ceramics and pottery. She was grateful that she is healthy and enjoying a completely untroubled life, and she hoped to make an offering to General MacArthur. In December two years ago, she sent some dried persimmons that were accepted [the rest of the letter is missing]. . . .

In the files at the MacArthur Memorial, there is a document that appears to be a translation of a letter from Kurata Kitsu, dated December 13, 1948. The letter says she is grateful to have received a note of thanks for what she sent the previous year and continues: "It is entirely owing to your kindness that I can keep on working every day in happiness, for which I thank you with all my heart. Recently I found and bought a story book about you, which I am reading to my children. Thank you very much again."

These presents were indeed "offerings of genuine good faith." People sincerely wanted to express their gratitude to MacArthur. Another example is the following, rather unusual gift. At a time when there were still severe shortages of food, Inagaki Gen'ichi, the managing director of the Imperial Vegetable Food Company, offered MacArthur a box of biscuits made by his company. The reason for this seemingly odd present is explained in his letter, typewritten in English as follows:

Dec. 23, 1947.
General of the Army Douglas MacArthur,

Dear Sir:

I beg to express my heartfelt gratitude for your most sincere guidance and kindest assistance which you have most generously afforded to the Japanese people who have highly admired the Christian spirit of your people.

It is my firm belief that in order to respond to your kindness, we, the Japanese people, must stand up on their feet in the first place in respect of the food problem, the solution of which is a vital momentum for the rehabilitation and democratization of Japan.

My company specializes in making a kind of biscuits made of fishes and flour, which are very much liked by our people.

I humbly present a box of the biscuits to you as a token of my gratitude, I should be most grateful if you would kindly accept it.

With the compliments of the season,

Yours faithfully,

[signed in Japanese]
(INAGAKI, Gen'ichi)
Managing Director
Imperial Vegetable Food Co.
(Teikoku Sairyoshoku
Kabushiki Kaisha)
67, Isshiki-cho, Banzu-gun,
Aichi-ken, Japan.

Inagaki's gift symbolized not only his gratitude but also his hopes for Japan's independence. Whether MacArthur tasted the fish-powder biscuits is doubtful. I have no doubt about the director's sincerity, but MacArthur probably did not like the smell of this gift.

A final letter on edible gifts follows:

The Honorable General MacArthur
and Mrs. MacArthur

I respectfully offer my gratitude at the end of the year. I thank you for enabling me to have a peaceful year.

I am happy and obliged to have received a kind letter from you for the humble gifts I sent you. Again this year, I am having the Takashimaya Department Store deliver rice cakes to you. Please accept them as a gift from my heart. I hope you will have a happy new year.

I pray for the health and happiness of Your Excellency, General MacArthur, Mrs. MacArthur, and the officers and soldiers of the occupation forces.

Prayers,
Kūkaku
Head of Jikōkai

There is no date on this letter, written horizontally on ordinary stationery with pen. It is inconceivable that rice cakes could have been delivered by department stores immediately after the defeat, so this must have been written after conditions had improved some. However, one must not interpret the words "humble gifts" literally; a list of her gifts, along with an explanation, was kept with her letter. The note explained that the "pacifist priestess, Miss Kashio Kukaku" had sent the following things "to show her appreciation to General and Mrs. MacArthur for the interest they have taken in the welfare of the Japanese people." They were delivered on December 15, 1945.

[The Gifts]
(1) Ancient wedding kimono. "Value of over 10,000 yen, immediately after the war."
(2) Fur-lined vest. "To keep General MacArthur warm."
(3) Hagoita [a battledore] with two shuttlecocks.
(4) Miniature hagoita.

(5) Ceremonial fan.
(6) Two trays.

It is not clear what kind of person the priestess Kūkaku was or what sort of organization Jikōkai was, but it is worth noting that her Tokyo contact address was c/o Kusano Masamitsu of Mitsui Mining Co., Ltd. in the central Marunouchi business district.

ALL KINDS OF WRITERS

Let me discuss some simpler gifts—books. Many people sent books to General MacArthur with hopes that he would read them. In general these were books they had written or helped publish. The following is a letter, in English, sent by a courageous woman writer:

1097, Sakurayama
Zushi, Yokosuka

August 17, 1949
General Douglas MacArthur
Dai Ichi Building Tokyo

Dear Sir:
    I present to you my book "Hiroshima". I had been a Hiroshima-citizen and a teacher until the year 1945. What I experienced there, you may read in this book, what I heard, seen and given, too. I think you may wonder why I dare to present this "Hiroshima" to you. But I have no rebellious intentions except the wish of being appreciated my true feelings as a Hiroshima-citizen. My intention is quite simple. I wish everyone, both Japanese and American, know the appeal of the citizens of Hiroshima.
    You may unlike to hear or tell about the atomic-bomb, and its miserable damage. I am unbearable to tell the story. But it is the fact, and no one can deny.
    I have written this report with all my heart without any exaggeration. I would hope and wish that in reading this book, there would be much more glory to your policy in Japan.

I am a teacher of Japanese language, so I can not speak or write English so well. My health is not quite well yet.
Please allow me this awkward writing.

Sincerely yours
[signed] (Miss) Kiyoko Koromogawa

The book was titled *Hiroshima—Genshibakudan no taiken o megurite* (Hiroshima: On the experience of the atomic bomb), and it had been published in July 1949 by Chōjiya Shoten. After four years of tight censorship of virtually all writing on the atomic bombing, in 1949 U.S. censorship relaxed enough to allow the publication of some works on the bomb. MacArthur's feelings on receiving this book are not known. He was one who would order the ATIS to translate and read every Japanese biography of himself, but it is unlikely that he would have had a book on Hiroshima translated in order to read it.

A copy of *Bei-So tatakawaba?* (The outlook for an American-Soviet war) was sent to MacArthur upon publication in March 1949 by Kuwabara Tadao, president of the publishing house Nichibei Tsūshinsha. The author, Kawakami Kiyoshi, was living in the United States, and the book's preface was in English. Kawakami hailed from Yamagata Prefecture, and in 1901, along with Abe Isoo and Sakai Toshihiko, he organized the Socialist Democratic Party, the first socialist political party in Japan. The party was banned immediately, and Kawakami moved to the United States to became the first Japanese journalist to write for an international audience. In 1923 he became the Washington editor of the *Mainichi shimbun*. He moved steadily to the right and after the war became fervently anti-Soviet and anticommunist. He died in October 1949 in Washington. Kuwabara's letter to MacArthur includes the following note:

. . . When you discover, as related in the preface, that he was very close to Japanese revolutionaries like Kōtoku Shūsui and Sakai Kosen, you will understand that Kawakami's conversion to American democracy is the result of his thorough understanding of and trust in the United States that came from his long experience of living there.

His son, Clark Kawakami, remembered that toward the end of his life Kiyoshi would often remark, "All my ideals were realized by Franklin Roosevelt." Whether MacArthur, who deferred to no one in his anticommunism, had anything to learn from this book is hard to tell, but he must have been pleased to discover an ideological comrade.

Ishii Saburō of Itabashi-ku in Tokyo sent his own work, with an accompanying letter dated October 26 (the year is unknown, but it was probably not long after the end of the war). The letter begins, in error-ridden English, by declaring how the Japanese were misled by the military and how American democracy would save them; it ends with the request that MacArthur accept his book, *Nihon wa doko e* (Whither Japan?).

There is also a letter dated May 21, 1950, from Hanayama Shinshō, the Buddhist chaplain for "Class A" war criminals in Sugamo Prison. He reports that the English translation of his book, *Discovery of Peace*, had been published in New York and he would like to present a copy. He quotes his writings on MacArthur and requests that he be allowed to present the book in person, but MacArthur, through his aide, Lieutenant Kan Tagami, replied that he was too busy to meet him. In general, it appeared that MacArthur was not greatly impressed when people sent copies of their books.

Flowers, fruits, books—the gifts sent to MacArthur were varied indeed. The following was attached to a New Year's greeting in flowing, delicate calligraphy:

To General MacArthur:

One set, porcelain candy containers.
The above has been sent to you in celebration of the season. I would be obliged if you would accept it.
My New Year's greetings to you.

Anzaka Teruko

For this person, sending a gift to MacArthur had become a relatively routine matter. As we have seen, she was not alone in this. The priestess Komatsu Chikō of Jakkōin in Ōhara, Kyoto, sent a letter on April 8, 1948 saying, "On this auspicious birthday of Buddha, who blessed the dry hearts of humans with the sweet rain of teaching and caused the flowers of peace to bloom, I wish to present a humble gift," but there is no mention of what the gift was. Another letter says, "I practice acupuncture and moxibustion for my living and work on crafts during my spare time. . . . I would be greatly obliged if you saw it as something made by a blind man." It is dated October 15, 1949, from Kamiya Katsumi from the city of Ōmuta in Fukuoka Prefecture, but again details of the gift are not provided.

THE PSYCHOLOGY OF SENDING A HIDE

Noteworthy among the many gifts were the large number of animal skins. In a note dated February 1950, Takiura Bunshirō from the village of Shinokubi in Hyōgo Prefecture addressed aide-de-camp Bunker, "Recently I obtained the hide of a fox caught in my village and I wanted to offer it to General MacArthur. . . . I sent it to your attention." He asked if it had arrived safely. From Obihiro in Hokkaidō, Takahashi Makoto of the *Ainu shimbun* sent a deer skin and antlers via Daniel Imboden, chief of the CI&E press division, with a cover letter (dated autumn 1947) to MacArthur, "the great hero of the present world who has shown generosity in the occupation of Japan, with prayers for Your Excellency's good fortune and long-lasting military success, on behalf of all the Ainu of Hokkaidō."

Some of the thinking behind sending a hide to MacArthur is revealed in the following letter. Toda Kōsaburō wrote that he owned a small factory in Tokyo that burned during the bombing, and he evacuated to the countryside (there is no envelope, so it is not clear where he was staying). In fourteen pages written on October 21, 1945, he condemns the cruelty of the Japanese military and police and describes his own experience of being brutalized by the special police, adding, "I eagerly await Your Sublime Excellency's guidance and pray for your and Mrs. MacArthur's health." A postscript follows:

I have a large bear skin about five and a half feet long. A bear skin is an essential decoration in the living room of a high-class Japanese house. We have no hope of being able to relax and sit on a bear skin for some time to come. Therefore, since it makes the best possible gift, I would like to offer it as a memento from a citizen to honor Your Excellency the general, whom I revere. If you will pardon my rudeness and accept it, I would be much obliged. I hope you will let me know.

To this request, MacArthur replied, "Will gladly accept," through his senior aide, Colonel Herbert B. Wheeler. MacArthur also accepted a different kind of honor, one that came from Tokyo Governor Yasui. In a letter dated April 17, 1950, the governor explained that he planned to mark Arbor Week by planting two hundred cherry trees as symbols of peace along the Tsukiji River. He inquired whether he could name the trees to be planted at the foot of the Mannen Bridge in front of Tokyo Theater "General MacArthur Cherry" and "Mrs. MacArthur Cherry." Naturally, MacArthur agreed, according to a letter from Colonel Bunker to Governor Yasui dated April 23. The cherry trees must have been planted in May of that year, but they did not survive, for there are no MacArthur cherries near the Mannen Bridge today.

On January 26, 1950, citizens of Toyama celebrated MacArthur's seventieth birthday at a "Celebration for General Douglas MacArthur's Birthday." The present they sent was a pair of large Imari plates. The following year, a congratulatory flag was sent from Toyama "to celebrate General MacArthur's birthday and expand friendly relations between the United States and Japan." Okamoto Seizō, a representative of the group, sent letters along with the gifts, and a letter of thanks from MacArthur was sent by Colonel Bunker.

While flattery was the motivation for some gift givers, others simply expressed genuine feelings of admiration for MacArthur by offering generous gifts. The following is an example:

March 24, 1946
The Honorable General MacArthur

Dear Sir:

Ever since Your Excellency arrived in Japan, you have guided the Japanese people, and I thank you sincerely for your efforts. The enclosed poems are by Motoori Norinaga, a famous poet and scholar of the history of Japanese thought. For your health, I hope Your Excellency will appreciate these poems. This collection has been in my family from the time of my ancestors. I am offering it to Your Excellency, and I hope you will treasure it as an heirloom forever.

I am also sending a bonsai that I have cultivated from a small tree for sixteen years. It is an oak. Please put it on your table, and when your eyes are tired rest them by enjoying the green of its leaves. I pray to god for your family's health and for the health of your subordinates.

Irisawa Minekichi
Age 66 Years
662 Yoyogi Hatsudai-machi
Shibuya-ku [Tokyo]

The sender offered a family heirloom and a bonsai cultivated for sixteen years but asked for nothing in return. This type of generosity is perhaps characteristically Japanese and was not limited to this gentleman. Horikoshi Shimakichi from the town of Yaita in Ibaraki Prefecture sent a letter inquiring whether he could send a seven-piece tea set (teapot, five tea cups, and a water-cooling pot) signed by Ogata Kenzan (a famous Edo period potter and painter). The letter, dated "an auspicious day of February 1946," is written in flowing calligraphy and says, "I am an uncultured farmer living in the countryside with neither status nor title nor fortune. I have no ambition or desires, except to live out my allotted days enjoying nature, as I turn sixty-five this year." He expresses appreciation for the general's "ceaseless efforts" and adds, "I shed tears of gratitude and offer a poor man's lantern" (a reference to a Buddhist saying that a poor man's offering of one lantern is equal to ten thousand offered by a rich man).

It must be said that this kind of humility is highly valued in Japanese culture. Another example is a letter, dated December 11, 1945, requesting a meeting with MacArthur to present him with Christmas gifts: a thirty-eight-inch Japanese sword and a set of twelve *daruma* dolls, ranging from three and a half inches to twenty-four inches in height. The sender is Kawamura Tairyō, sixty years old and living in the town of Kanuma Nakata in Tochigi Prefecture, and he refers to himself as "a refugee from the war." He might have been repatriated from overseas or an evacuee from the air raids, but it is clear from his letter that he is actually a company president. How else could a "refugee" make such a generous present?

The last letter in this chapter is another example of a splendid gift. On MacArthur's seventieth birthday, an elderly man sent ten old documents that he had collected over the years. He was not asking for any favors in return. With his letter, he enclosed a list of the documents, which included the seals of Lord Matsudaira of Noto and twelve other feudal lords from the Edo period. His letter reads:

January 26, 1950
The Honorable General MacArthur

Dear Sir:

Your Excellency General MacArthur is a general of a democratic nation, so I beg you to pardon my offering you a letter this day to congratulate you on your seventieth birthday. Through Your Excellency's godly benevolence, we Japanese are most fortunate to be able to prosper today as a peaceful country even though we were citizens of an immoral militarist nation.

Your Excellency is truly a living savior, and I am deeply grateful.

I have served as a member of my city council for many years and since middle age have enjoyed collecting old Japanese documents. Rest assured that I am an anticommunist, and in the past have offered swords to imperial princes and to Count Ōkuma.

What will become of Japan when Your Excellency returns home? It will be unforgivable toward you if communists become a majority and disrupt the fortunes of the country.

I pray Your Excellency will take good care of yourself and assist us as long as you can. Today, because I did not know the proper procedures, I have sent by parcel post a package of ten old documents with authentic handwritten seals of daimyō of the seventeenth- and eighteenth-century Edo period. When you return home, perhaps these old documents written by leaders of the feudal era will be of some interest to the American people. That would be my greatest happiness, so I ask you to accept my gift.

Most humbly yours,

Sekine Jūhei
Seventy-one years old

In short, all kinds of people sent every kind of gift. We shall see in the following chapter, as the stories become ever more intriguing, that there was an even broader range of mentalities reflected in the gifts given to MacArthur.

8

CRAFTED FROM THE HEART

HANDMADE WITH GREAT CARE AND EFFORT

 One way people expressed their feelings toward MacArthur was by producing handcrafted gifts, often investing extraordinary amounts of time and painstaking effort in their production. An embroidered portrait of the general was sent by the families of Japanese still detained overseas, with the following letter:[1]

April 6, 1950
The Honorable General MacArthur

Since the war, several million of our overseas countrymen have been able to return home, through the immense compassion of Your Excellency, General MacArthur. We, the families of those who have yet to be repatriated, offer our deep gratitude and plead for Your Excellency's further assistance in expediting the return of all those still detained overseas.

Today, the families of detainees from the entire country were able to gather, and to express our gratitude we are sending via Mrs. MacArthur this gift that we families produced, stitch by stitch with complete sincerity. We earnestly request your continued endeavors on our behalf.

Ōtsuka Kyōjun, Shiga Prefecture
National Representative, Families of Detainees

The embroidered portrait and this letter, written on a roll of traditional paper in outstanding calligraphy, were delivered to GHQ by the Central Liaison Office of the Japanese government. A "Memo to the Supreme Commander" was prepared the same day (with the initials K. T., probably those of Lieutenant Kan Tagami, MacArthur's interpreter), which reported that "it took eight months to complete this portrait; 120,000 family members of those not yet repatriated embroidered it stitch by stitch." This information probably came directly from the organization, but even if the figures were somewhat inflated, it is clear that a tremendous number of people were mobilized for the project.

There were some individuals whose painstaking efforts even exceeded the monumental labor of the families of the overseas detainees. The evidence we have for the following example is not a letter but the English translation of a prayer made at Ise Jingū, an ancient Shinto Shrine where the gift was given a ritual purification. Judging from the peculiar style and the numerous errors in the typewritten document, the translation seems to have been prepared by the sender and delivered to MacArthur along with the finished piece.

PRAYER: REPORTING OF FINISHING THE EMBROIDERY AT ISE SHRINE

I revelently report to the Great God, AMATERASU [ancestral goddess of Japan] omniscient who art in TAKAMAGAHARA [the legendary abode of the gods].

It has passed four years already since we deserted weapons and converted to peaceful country. It is because of the outcome of Japanese Spirit or "Yamato Gokoro", but it is because of General McArthor SCAP's right and meet policy. Everybody admire him.

Tenshu Nakajima, living in the old Kyoto City and famous in embroidery work, revelent gentleman and has pure heart, looking up the august virtue of Their Emperors Ancestor and anxious to have sound and righteous country, have been trying very hard to calm rough mind of Japanese and execute devine providence to secure peaceful country.

I have devouted myself to exress Japanese real pure and meek heart in ganuine Japanese embroidery or Yamato Nishiki, secluding myself in Shimogamo

Photo 8.1   A painting of MacArthur, one of many such portraits presented to the general during the occupation. Source: MacArthur Memorial

shrine from the very morning of Nov 1st, 1946 for whole three years from morn till night, concentrating my all energy in every needle for 70,000,000 times and completed a beautiful coal and sash. Going up to Tokyo, I want to present them to General McArthor.

On a glorious cherry day, I offer them in front of the shrine, I offer them preparing holy rice, wine and others, playing holy orchestra.

May God accept my player and grant that I may go up to Tokyo without any hindrance and present these coat and sash to General McArthor on behalf of 70 million pure hearts of my countrymen.

May God bless Tonshu's unselfish desire that our people be ever peaceful and friendly people and be a corver stone Peaceful World, I ask thee from the bottom of my heart.

An auspicious day March 1949.

After this prayer was offered, Holy Orchestra was played. As the orchestra was so mystic and sublime, I felt as if I united with God. So naturally there came out following poems. (Originally they were of 31 lettered poems and the meaning was as follows)

> *What will be the heart of God?*
> *In the heart there must filled with world peace.*
> *The nobleness of Japanese God*
> *Guides the way of peaceful order.*
> *The true heart to present McArthor*
> *Must be the symbol of world peace.*
> *The figured brocade that offered God*
> *Is the pledge of peace and trustworthiness.*

The idea was to personally represent the entire Japanese population of that time, one stitch per person, in an embroidered robe and obi, but it is incredible to imagine the patience required to spend three years making seventy million stitches.

Another example is a fan with the entire Japanese constitution written out in small characters on both sides. The accompanying letter was typewritten in English:

Tokyo, April 28, 1947
General of the Army Douglas MacArthur
Supreme Allied Commander for Japan

Dear Sir:

On the occasion of the proclamation of the new Japanese constitution, on May 3rd, 1947, the basic principles of which will bring us true freedom and happiness in Japan in the future, I wish to express my opinion that it is true, that all Japanese people have been deeply impressed with your guidance and courtesy, by which brightness has been brought to the whole land of Japan.

I, myself, also have great pleasure in the fortune given by our God in Heaven for such an opportunity in my long life of 69 years; and an emotion has naturally sprung up to express my thanks for it from the bottom of my heart.

I have herewith a Japanese paper fan, upon which all sentences of the new constitution have been written by myself in the Japanese way.

It will be my great honor, if you will kindly accept this as the symbol of my appreciation for your excellency.

Your most obedient servant,

[signed] Kozo Sawa
Address: 82 Jiyugaoka, Meguro-ku, Tokyo

This fan has been on display at the MacArthur Memorial. The front side has the constitution from the prologue through Article 52, and the other side has the rest, all written in very small characters.[2]

A final example is two hanging scrolls, on which the entire Bible was written in tiny English and Japanese lettering. The writer is Yoshikawa Mototake from the town of Fujine near Mount Fuji in Shizuoka Prefecture. That he sent a letter to MacArthur dated November 22, 1948, along with a photo of himself with the scrolls, is evident from an acknowledgment from Colonel Bunker, but I have not seen the original letter. Bunker's note

Photo 8.2   The entire text of the "MacArthur constitution" was written on this fan in extraordinary, minute calligraphy. Source: *MacArthur Memorial*

says that MacArthur gladly received the gift and, at the suggestion of CI&E chief Lieutenant Colonel D. R. Nugent, he had the scrolls sent to the Library of Congress in Washington, to make them accessible to as many people as possible. The scrolls were kept at the library as material of unknown origin until I inquired about them in 1984 and the source was clarified. That same year the Library of Congress sponsored a calligraphy exhibit, and the scrolls were made public for the first time.

The incredible craft involved in writing the whole Bible in tiny script on a single scroll is hard to imagine without seeing it. The scrolls were actually not completed at the time the letter was written, but years before, on May 25, 1935. Thirteen years later Yoshikawa must have felt he had found, in MacArthur, someone worthy of receiving his scrolls as a gift.

GIFTS AS A MEANS OF SELF-PROMOTION

It was sometimes hard to tell where sending a gift as an expression of gratitude ended, and where the gift giving was an excuse for voicing opinions and tooting one's own horn. The following are some letters that fall increasingly into the latter category. The first example was sent at the end of 1945 by a goldsmith living in Chiba Prefecture. It was written by hand in English. The penmanship looks like that of a middle school student, but the structure is sound and easy to understand.

Now it is Christmas week and I wish you to enjoy it in good health.

Lately a soldier of my kindred has come back from your country, who had been sent there after the Saipan defeat, and told me with gratitude about the kind treatment of your people. I think it owes to the deep sympathy of Your Excellency, and I as Japanese, sincerely thank for it.

I am a humble goldsmith, and have devoted my life for it these fifty years.

I should like to dedicate my work as a Christmas Present in token of my hearty gratitude.

Please give me the pleasure of it being accepted.

December 23, 1945
Chibaken Sanbugun Otomimura
Yoshitake Maebashi

This letter is intended, of course, to convey gratitude to MacArthur, but the writer's mention of his fifty years of work as a goldsmith suggests a desire to show off his workmanship. The next letter has a stronger tinge of self-promotion. It is also in English, two pages typewritten, and the composition is so good that one suspects it was translated by someone who knew English well.

No. 3 Tsukudajima, Chuo-ku, Tokyo,
November 24th, 1950

General Douglas MacArthur,
Supreme Commander for Allied Powers.

Dear General,
   Allow me the liberty of addressing this letter to Your Excellency. I am a retired fisherman, 71 years old, residing at No. 3 Tsukudajima, Chuo-ku, Tokyo. My remotest ancestor when the Tokugawa Shogunate Government was established in Yedo (now Tokyo), settled in this city together with 34 other fishermen from Tsukuda Village in Settsu Province (now part of Osaka Prefecture) at the call of the Shogunate Government. These people were the pioneers of fishing industry in Yedo. I am the 17th generation of Magoemon Miichi who headed that group of fishermen.
   I have since my childhood been engaged in fishing trade and have lived through the Meiji, Taisho and Showa Eras. During those dismal days immediately following the termination of the war Japan had embarked upon so foolishly I was thrown into indescribable terror, the like of which I had never experienced, dreading what would become of us Japanese faced with the terrible shortage of foodstuff. With the arrival of the Armed Forces under your command, however, the whole nation felt as if they had been resuscitated, being shown such magnanimity and benevolence by those military personnel as our countrymen had never dreamed of. It is solely due to Your Excellency's fatherly guidance and benevolent administration that the Japanese, young and old, could embark upon a new start in their life with hopes for the future, for which we cannot be too thankful.
   Particularly at the time when our food situation was in a critical condition you showed profound interest in the expansion of our country's fishing industry. Again you permitted a further expansion of our fishing area in 1949, thus bestowing a boon of untold magnitude upon the life, health and economy of

the Japanese nation. I, as a man having a life-long interest in fishing, feel grateful more deeply than anybody else for the benefit you have extended to our fishing industry.

As I grow older I have found my hobby in miniature landscapes and have now made one which represents Fujiyama, the symbol of Japan, for presentation to Your Excellency as a token of my heart-felt gratitude for your benevolence. I shall deem it a great honor if you will kindly accept this present.

I have the honor to be,
Your most obedient servant,
[signed in Japanese with seal] Kamakichi Miichi

Again the note struck by this letter is gratitude to MacArthur, but it is quite self-involved. As the seventeenth-generation descendant of Miichi Magoemon, "the founder of Edo fishing," the writer almost seems to feel that he embodies Japan's fishing industry. His simple gift of a miniature landscape of Mount Fuji thus becomes a means for announcing his existence.

The writer of the next letter happened to possess an ancient clay shield, and since a shield symbolizes defense, he offered it as a pretext for presenting his rather unique interpretation of geopolitics and a pet theory of peace between Japan and the United States.

March 5, 1950
General MacArthur

Offering
One haniwa [prehistoric clay burial] shield, height 1 meter.

With this letter I am requesting permission to present a shield to General MacArthur.

All Japanese have deep, deep admiration for the general, who has endeavored for five long years on behalf of world peace and the happiness of the Japanese people.

The general's efforts have resulted in the peace of the Japanese today. With gratitude in mind I looked at the United States and Japan on a map and dis-

covered the reason why we cannot fight each other until the earth is destroyed. The reason is the Pacific Ocean. This body of water is embraced in the far east by Japan and in the west by America, the two countries guarding it so that not even a drop of water will escape.

For this reason, I hope there will be everlasting peace and friendship with your country. Japan will gladly become the bulwark of East Asia.

With this in mind, I am offering my treasure, a haniwa shield. I hope you will understand the ancient culture of more than a thousand years and accept the shield that protected the warriors of ancient times.

Tomioka Ushimatsu
60 years old

Around the time this letter was written, MacArthur had begun to emphasize Japan's right to self-defense in response to the growing sense of crisis in East Asia. Ushimatsu endorses MacArthur's stance and naively vows that "Japan will gladly become the bulwark of East Asia."

There must have been no response to this letter because Ushimatsu wrote another letter dated April 5. A synopsis of his letter, prepared by the ATIS, reports that Ushimatsu lived in Ōta City in Gunma Prefecture and had written, "If this could be of any cultural value to the American people, I would like to offer my clay shield to the United States." He asked that extreme care be taken: "Clay is breakable, so someone from the closest American military unit should come and pick it up with a car, and the driver should have a document of proof that GHQ would accept the shield." However, MacArthur did not accept the shield after all. He instructed Colonel Bunker to write back and suggest that Ushimatsu keep the shield as a family treasure and pass it on to his descendants.

The next letter begins as a follow-up to confirm that a gift presented through an aide-de-camp had been received by MacArthur. However, that is only the preamble, and the rest of the letter presents a theory on the building of a new Japan. Written in pen on three sheets of stationery, the words carry a certain force. The whole letter is quoted below:

May 1 [1949]
Your Excellency General MacArthur

Most respected General MacArthur:
 On April 5 I traveled to Tokyo to visit General Headquarters to present you with a painting of the goddess Kannon (a representation of the goddess of peace) by Deguchi Wanisaburō (the late head of Aizen-en). Your aide-de-camp met me and promised that the gift would be passed on to you, saying that you would probably be happy to receive it. I assume it is in your hands by now.
 The Republic of Israel that God promised is nearing the first anniversary of its declaration of independence, which makes me appreciate the importance of Your Excellency's mission. This is because I hope you will make Japan into a republic too. I wish you would please stipulate in the first article of the constitution that the people should hold love in their hearts and pray day and night to thank God the creator and father of our soul. I have an inspiration that numerous angels are guarding and guiding you so that Your Excellency may create a paradise on earth according to God's will.
 Recently, a plan for a world state has been announced in the United States. To make the world into a paradise with no war or economic conflict, I would like Your Excellency to experiment with this plan on Japan first. I believe that unless each individual nation becomes a paradise, a world state will end in failure, just as the League of Nations ended in failure in the past. By making the Republic of Japan into a paradise, the world state will succeed and world war and economic conflict will end. Everlasting peace on earth will be established, and mankind will say, "Heaven has come," and forever applaud the accomplishments of Your Excellency and of the United States. The day has come for Your Excellency to fulfill the mission given to you by God with your honorable authority, duty, and responsibility. I congratulate you from the bottom of my heart.
 In order to cooperate with Your Excellency's execution of this mission, if necessary I am willing to change the movement to build Yamato Japan, which I have previously mentioned, into whatever you may desire and develop it according to your appropriate guidance. As in olden times when Lincoln built

the foundation of the United States under God, I hope and believe that Your Excellency will establish the Republic of Japan centered on God and with God's love as its life. I thank you for your efforts.

Yours most respectfully,
Yamaguchi Toshitaka
90 Ueno, Ayabe-chō, Kyoto

The writer of this letter was undoubtedly a follower of Ōmoto-kyō, a sect of Shinto that was suppressed during the war and regrouped after defeat as Aizen-en. The year the letter was written is not noted, but it must have been 1949 because it mentions the first anniversary of Israel's independence. Deguchi Wanisaburō, the head of Ōmoto-kyō, had passed away a year earlier in January. Yamaguchi hopes to carry forward Deguchi's plan for a republic of "Yamato Japan" by following MacArthur's lead, but unless he intended to make MacArthur the first president of the Republic of Japan, he had no apparent plan for abolishing the emperor system and establishing a republic. He only suggests that the first article of the constitution stipulate that the people pray day and night to "God the creator and father of our soul." This man seems to believe that God's love would make everything possible, including the creation of paradise on earth. It is not known whether this letter was translated into English and read by MacArthur, but if it was, it must have satisfied the supreme commander's huge ego.

As we have seen, many people sent presents as an excuse to make MacArthur aware of their existence and their opinions. The following is an extreme example.

Amano Tatsutarō, stationmaster of Tokyo Station, sent an inquiry to MacArthur on November 29, 1945, typewritten in English on Transportation Ministry letterhead. According to the letter, Sunakawa Genroku had sent a box of *matsutake* mushrooms from the Seto station on the Sanyō Line on October 26, but due to some mishap the mushrooms did not reach Tokyo until November 14. By then the mushrooms were rotten, so delivery was suspended and a letter mailed to the sender asking for his direction. The reply was to go ahead and deliver the package, since there was a letter addressed to General MacArthur inside. What would you like us to do? was the inquiry to MacArthur. One can almost picture the misery of the Tokyo stationmaster. This "rotten mushroom" incident illustrates how the primary goal of the sender was to have MacArthur read his letter, and the gift was only a means to that end. It is interesting to note that MacArthur sent a message through Colonel Wheeler, dated the following day: "Thank you for the fresh *matsutake*."

PAINTINGS AS GIFTS

More than a few people sent MacArthur paintings, especially portraits of the general himself. Whatever the subject of the paintings, the accompanying letters were consistently self-involved. The original of the following letter was in Japanese, but I could only locate the English translation. MacArthur must have liked the letter a great deal since he had two copies typed and archived.

c/o Imurakan hotel, No. 120, Shoan Kita-machi, Suginami-ku [Tokyo]
Aug. 14, 1946.

His Excellency General MacArthur
SCAP
Daiichi Sogo Building
Marunouchi, Kojimachi-ku, Tokyo

Your Excellency:
I take great pleasure in presenting you with a Japanese painting from the brush of Mr. Rokyu Yugami, a well-known artist, which I hope you will kindly accept.
The theme of the painting, let me call your attention, Your Excellency, is to be found in my waka—a 31-syllabled Japanese poem—which you will remember was extemporaneously translated and interpreted for me to you by Mr. Keiichi Kitagawa, a Nisei, at our meeting on January 7 last.
My Japanese poem was as follows:—

> *Ake-gane wa ima Shikishima ni nari-wataru,*
> *Mezame yo tami to tsuku hito ya tare.*

(A liberal prose translation: The bell tolling the hour of dawn rings throughout the Land of the Nipponese / Who is the man that strikes the bell arousing the people of the Land from their slumber?)

"The bell tolling the hour of dawn . . . " refers to issuance of the Order of banishment or expulsion of war criminals and other similar suspects from public office. "Who is the man that strikes the bell . . . ?" is of course a poetical euphemistic way of putting "Your Excellency General MacArthur."

We Japanese can never thank you too much, Your Excellency, for your great services rendered in the cause of democratizing Japan. This presentation of the Japanese painting to you is but a slight manifestation of my sincere appreciation of your indefatigable worthy efforts made by your good self in the above-stated cause.

Accept, then, please, Your Excellency, this present of mine from a peace-loving, democratic Japanese citizen, in your friendly spirit, for you have invariably and consistently proved yourself to be a true friend of Japan and the Japanese. Your very act of accepting the present will gladden my heart more than anything else.

Mr. Yugami, the artist, who has executed the painting work hails from Toyokawa village near Kitakata, Aizu, Fukushima prefecture. He is now 42. He is an able pupil of Mr. Gengetsu Yazawa, a leading artist of the Japanese school of painting. He has thus far had the honor of having his art works accepted four times by the Imperial Academy's art exhibition.

Yours truly,
Sayuri Miyama

This person's name is Sayuri, which is a woman's name, but he is not a woman. The letter has a long postscript that clarifies his background, but first it is worth noting his "meeting on January 7" with MacArthur. MacArthur only rarely met ordinary Japanese citizens. What kind of connection did this person have to make the meeting possible? Sheer determination, tenacity, and waiting for an opportunity while staying at an inn in Tokyo's Suginami ward must have all contributed to his success. As to his background, I will let the following postscript speak for itself:

1. Theme of the Painting: Morn of Banishment (cf. 2nd and 3rd paragraphs of my letter).
2. Mounter of the Painting: Mr. Masujiro Kobayashi, of Kitakata-machi, Yama-gun, Fukushima prefecture.

3. Frame-maker: Mr. Seiki Watanabe, of Iwatsuki-mura, Yama-gun, Fukushima prefecture.

4. Frame-painter: Mr. Bunji Inomata, of Kitakata-machi, Yama-gun, Fukushima prefecture.

5. I, Sayuri Miyama, hails from Aizu, Fukushima prefecture, which is noted for its scenic beauty. I am now 54 years of age. I have at my country house my wife, Matsuyo, 53 years old; my daughter-in-law, Matsumi 32 years old, (who is the wife of my son, Shigeru, 36 years old, who is now an internee away at Leyte, the Philippines); my daughter, Kiyoshi, 25 years old; my grandson, Akira, 11 years old; and three granddaughters. Thus it will be seen that my family consists of 8 members with my son, Shigeru, now at Leyte, inclusive. My family occupation is farming, but I myself also take to calligraphy vocationally. I have had no school career to be proud of. After finishing my elementary school course, I have tried continuously to be self-taught or self-educated. This reminds me of your Lincoln who, under all manner of difficulties and hardships, tried so courageously to be self-educated.

From about the middle of the Pacific war period up to the present, I have consistently urged the Tojo, Koiso, Suzuki, Higashikuni, and Yoshida Governments to enforce responsible, democratic administration.

S. M.

This short self-introduction clearly captures several aspects of the psychology and character of people who sent letters and presents to MacArthur. First, by elaborating on details about family, they attempt to create an intimacy with the ruler and win his sympathy. Second, by bragging about career and accomplishments, they satisfy their own egos. A third feature is the attempt to align themselves with something American, such as a self-made man comparing himself to Lincoln. Last, it can be said that the sort of people who wrote to MacArthur might also have written to their own rulers during and after the war. While some people opened their hearts in their letters because the recipient was foreign, many of those who like to send gifts and write to famous people would do so regardless of who was in power. However, if this writer had actually urged the wartime prime ministers Tōjō and Koiso to "enforce responsible, democratic administration," he would not have survived. So perhaps we can add one more characteristic of this type of writer: Not everything they say is reliable.

One surprising point is that he waited until his postscript to mention that his only son was a prisoner of war on Leyte. If this letter came from a westerner, he probably would mention this first, then offer thanks for the treatment being received and ask for further consideration. But for the writer of this letter, to make such a request directly would have violated his sense of propriety.

INNER MEANINGS IN A PORTRAIT

There is a rather potent symbolism in the act of painting a portrait and presenting it to a ruler. It could be called the artistic expression of subservience, although the artist often respects the subject and freely chooses to revere him. On March 19, 1947, Prime Minister Yoshida Shigeru wrote to Courtney Whitney, chief of Government Section of GHQ, that the artist Kajiwara Kango, who had painted portraits of many of the speakers of the Diet, had done a portrait of General MacArthur in gratitude and would like to have it presented to the supreme commander. (The letter was typewritten in English on Foreign Ministry stationery.) It also stated, "Artist Kajiwara was greatly moved by MacArthur's intervention regarding the February 1st strike." (A general strike planned for February 1, 1947, was prevented by General MacArthur's intervention the day before.)

Kojima Michikata from the town of Ichinose in Iwate Prefecture, calling himself "an unknown artist," sent a portrait of MacArthur to GHQ through Brigadier General Frayne Baker. In his letter two years later (November 3, 1949) he expressed thanks that the painting had been accepted and said he would not forget the honor for the rest of his life. He also enclosed a photograph of his family, sent hopes for friendly relations between Japan and the United States, and closed his letter, "I hope the U.S. occupation forces will be stationed in Japan semi-permanently. This is the desire of the majority of the Japanese people." (The original letter is in Japanese; this synopsis is from the English translation made by the ATIS.)

A portrait was also sent by another rural artist, in this case a woman. Amari Chiyo of the village of Shinonome in Yamanashi Prefecture believed that her husband's early repatriation from mainland China was due to General MacArthur's generosity. To "repay this immeasurable debt," she painted his portrait, and after displaying it at a cultural festival in her village, she sent it via the 441st Counter Intelligence Corps based in Yamanashi. I have not seen the original letter, but the English translation conveys the genuine gratitude of the artist.

The paintings we have discussed to this point were done at the artist's own initiative, but the next case involves a rural cultural group that revered MacArthur and commissioned an artist to paint an image of Jesus. The following letter in English explained the gift:

May 14, 1948

DEDICATION
of
The Image of Jesus
Painted in Japanese Colours

To General Douglas MacArthur
Commander in Chief
Of the Allied Forces in Japan

We the Japanese people had in recent years committed a grave blunder in misguiding ourselves and causing a great war whereby we were outlawed from the Grace of God and experienced our due chastisement in the form of a dire disaster unprecedented in our history. The world's history tells us that a defeated nation in many cases is destined to decline and finally lose her integrity and vitality as an independent state. But in our case it is otherwise. Instead, our nation is now filled with a new joy, energy and aspiration to see ourselves reborn as a peace-loving democratic nation.

The Allied Forces under your command have not only shown us the magnanimity we little deserved from the conquering army, but further given us the needed guidance, advice and leadership in transforming us into a democratic people, thus reinstating us in the Grace of God. Our gratitude to you and the Allied Forces under you is therefore boundless. Your leadership among our people reminds me of Jesus teaching his disciples through His Sermon on the Mount.

The Motoyama Bunka Kyokai (Motoyama Cultural Society) is a small group of the educated and cultured people residing in a village of Motoyama near Kobe, whose earnest purpose is to foster general culture among its members and broaden its influence over the people around, thus helping to elevate

Photo 8.3 This portrait of Jesus, "painted in Japanese colours," *was presented to General MacArthur by the Motoyama Cultural* *Society. The general was often compared with Jesus in letters from* *the Japanese.* Source: *MacArthur Memorial*

the status of the entire population as a peace-loving and cultured member of the world's family of nations.

Our Society has long cherished the desire to express our gratitude to you and through you to the Armed Forces in token of the nation-wide thanksgiving, which has finally taken shape in presenting to you the image of Jesus in the famous scene of the Sermon on the Mount, rendered in Japanese colours by a noted Japanese artist. We shall be most happy, if you will kindly accept this gift not only of theirs, but also the entire population of our country embodied.

Very respectfully yours,
Kunijiro Tanida
President
Motoyama Bunka Kyokai
297 Nayori, Motoyama-mura
near Kobe

Here MacArthur is clearly compared with Jesus Christ. It is well known that the general himself thought of his mission along these lines, so the painting of "The Sermon on the Mount" was truly an appropriate gift. Colonel Bunker's response, "The General says he will gladly accept," was probably not an exaggeration. The *Gekkan Motoyama* (Monthly Motoyama) of January 1949 reprinted the letter to MacArthur and described the presentation. The painting—a mounted scroll thirty-eight inches wide and seventy-nine inches long—was presented in a wooden box to aide-de-camp Colonel Bunker at GHQ on October 13, 1948. Enclosed with the gift was an endorsement in English from Kanzaki Kiichi, president of Kwansei Gakuin University, who described the artist Sadakata Taikai as "the only Japanese artist still living who takes up no other subject but Jesus for his art of painting . . . who for the last fifty years has wholly devoted himself to portraying Jesus in various Biblical scenes in Japanese colours." (Painting in Japanese colors was apparently another way of saying that the artist painted in the Japanese style.)

There was another artist who painted two pictures and sent them as gifts. According to his letter in English (dated December 24, 1946), his name was Toya Banzan from the hot spring spa of Yudanaka in Nagano Prefecture. The first of the two paintings, he explained, depicted Jesus meditating on the Mount for the salvation of mankind, where his mother finds him and is struck by his nobility. When the artist writes, "The Lord has a great hope for Japan, for which you are sent over to this country," it is clear that he too was portraying MacArthur as a Christ figure.

His explanation of the second painting, "Goddess of the Loo-Choo [Ryūkyū] Islands," is impossible to fathom. The location of the island and the shrine to this goddess are unknown, but the artist makes an odd request for permission to investigate the shrine. The oddity was only enhanced when he sent another painting with an explanation two years later, again on Christmas Eve. I think the letter in English is worth quoting:

Bozansho, No. 2,
Yudanaka-Onsen, Nagano-ken
Dec. 24, 1948

General Douglas MacArthur,
General Headquarters, Tokyo

Dear General,

Most respectfully a humble painter addresses this letter to you. In the year before last, I trespassed upon your generosity by offering you a scroll of my humble painting, for which I was much honoured by Col. Wheeler, who favoured me with a letter of acknowledgment.

I had another inspiration this year, with which I began painting another picture, which, being just completed, I make bold to offer as a humble Christmas present to you.

I told you before that Jesus Christ had special relations with Japan, which, according to our archaeic records, he visited. I have made very careful and extensive studies of his visits to Japan. I am sure that this fact will prove great help in your administration of Japan, although I have as yet had no opportunity to tell it in detail. This needs of course a careful study of scholars.

The picture I present you with represents Santa Claus, who, according to our archaeic records, is identical with Christ himself. He is an aerial being on the Cross, called Tengu in the Japanese language, who visited holy lands and holy mountains. The chaotic and threatening conditions of the world require His second Advent, in order to bring peace on earth.

I take liberty of presenting you with this humble picture of mine without undergoing your regulations and I must ask for your generous pardon for my breach of decorum.

Most respectfully yours
Banzan Toya, 74 years old

The story that Jesus died in Japan is a deeply held belief among some Japanese, but to identify him with Santa Claus and even go as far as to imply he is the flying Tengu of Japanese myth is truly outlandish. However, the effort to blend the Western God (or a similar deity) with Japanese deities was not at all rare during the occupation. Perhaps it was one way for people to soften the culture shock and come to terms with being under American rule. The following letter is a final example of that kind of effort. It is also in English.

No. 1401 Tatebayashi City
Gunma Prefecture
August 24, 1949

To the General Douglas MacArthur,
Supreme Commander for the Allied Powers.

Sir:
Seeing the fact I am deeply impressed that a certain American Military Soldier, on July 4th at the front yard of Ueno Station, salutes priously to the damaged Japanese Flag. In reciplocating to the above I have sent to the Supreme Commander for the Allied Powers the goddess "Heiwa Kanzeon Onaibutsu", and also on August 16th "Santa Maria", in which body the former goddess can be put in.

All members of "Seibokai" prayed to the "Santa Maria" for your health and long life and the happiness of all your family.

I would like to know whether you have received my presents or not, and I am,

Yours respectfully,
[signed] Taiken Kashima.

An *onaibutsu* is a small Buddhist sculpture that is placed inside a larger sculpture. To have Kannon, the Buddhist goddess of mercy, placed within the body of Mary must have seemed, for some Japanese under the American occupation, to be the ideal image of the U.S.–Japanese relationship.

SEEKING SOMETHING IN RETURN

The gifts we have examined thus far have been expressions of gratitude toward MacArthur, some of which were used as a platform for self-promotion, at times bordering on the outlandish. None of these asked for anything in return, but, not unexpectedly, there were some among the many letters that did carry a request. I will present several of these to close out this chapter.

The first example accompanied a basket sent by a bamboo weaver, Maeda Chikuhōsai from the town of Kuse in Osaka Prefecture. The letter in English was typewritten on the letterhead of Japan Industrial Art Company, Ltd., c/o Mitsukoshi Department Store, Nihonbashi, Tokyo. It explains that he was engaged in producing bamboo articles for export in prewar times and had recently resumed his work at the encouragement of the company. With hope of exporting his work to the United States, he had sent some pieces to GHQ so that they might be presented to the most respected supreme commander. He clearly hoped to have MacArthur put in a few words on his behalf.

Of course, this is a modest request. Another example is from Amamiya Junji, head of the International Friendship Society in the village of Mutsuai in Yamanashi Prefecture. The gift he sent was a wild boar shot in his village and with it a long letter (typewritten in English on three pages, dated November 29, 1945) explaining the difficulty of wild boar hunting. After going into some detail about local efforts to promote international friendship, he finally comes to his request: to borrow a bulldozer (called a "carry-all" at the time) to use in clearing a mountainous area in his village. It was a typically Japanese approach to bring up the most important matter at the very end of the letter.

The next message seems to have come from a rather impatient person: he sent a telegram instead of a letter, and he sent it urgent special

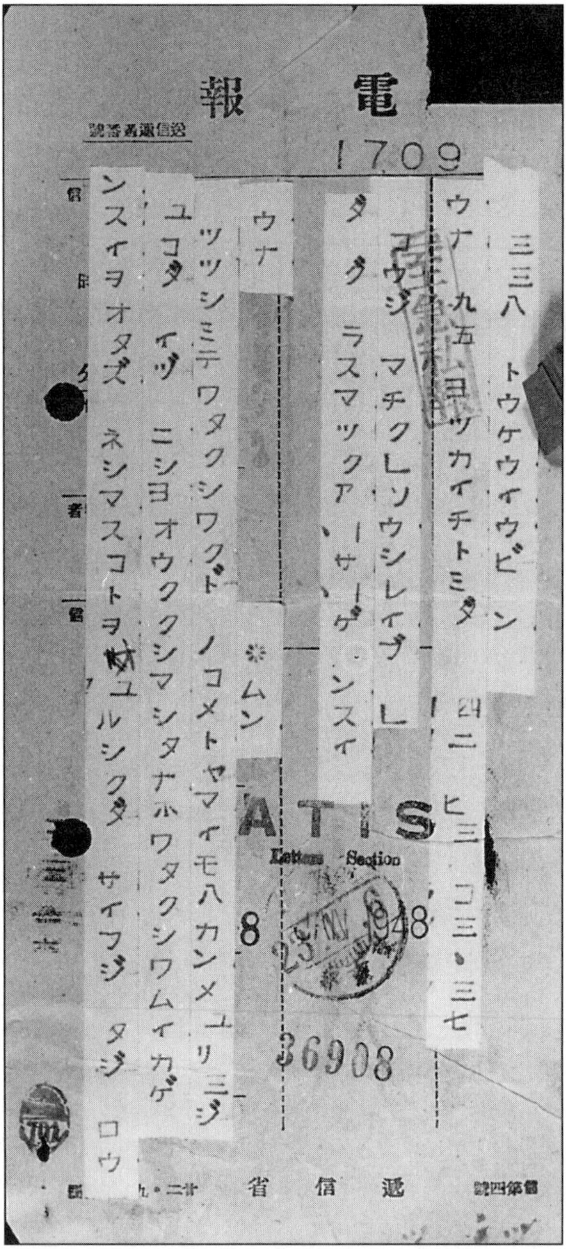

Photo 8.4   A telegram announced the delivery of rice and vegetables to the general. Source: MacArthur Memorial

delivery. It is dated January 6, 1948, and was wired from the city of Yokkaichi in Mie Prefecture:

Respectfully, I have sent 9 to [about 4.6 bushels] of rice, 8 kan [about 66 pounds] of mountain potatoes, 30 lily bulbs, and 2 shō [about 4 quarts] of soybeans. Please permit me to visit the general on the 6th.

What this person wanted in return was an audience with MacArthur, but I doubt it was granted. Disposing of this abundant gift of food must have caused the GHQ staff some consternation.

The next letter, dated July 1, 1948, was sent to Colonel Bunker with a request that the message be passed on to MacArthur. The original letter was not found, but a synopsis in English by Lieutenant Kan Tagami is in the files. I will give the writer's name as H. M. from the village of Ōzumi in Niigata Prefecture. He had sent a woodblock print of Commodore Perry earlier in the year, and in the July letter he generously offered part or all of his house for use as a Christian cultural center. But in this letter the request appears first: H. M. wanted to be appointed a regional intelligence agent, reporting directly to the general, without any compensation whatsoever. Put bluntly, he was asking to be a spy, although he did not say so explicitly. He described the job as investigating the ownership of famous art objects throughout Japan, so his idea must have been to work for MacArthur to uncover hoarded art. H. M. attached a detailed ground plan of the layout of his house, including the positions of stone lanterns and the rocks in his garden, so it seems he was quite serious about making his home available.

The next letter also seems innocent enough at first glance. It was written in English and is not dated, but it seems to have been sent quite early in the occupation.

The International Christian Body,
near Yoyogi Station
President Tosen Yoshimoto

To Gen. MacArthur.
Dear Sir,
   I earnestly pray that God's Grace be abundant on Your Excellency, Lady MacArthur and Mr. Arthur [MacArthur's son].

Would you please accept my sincere thanks for your kindly regards towards our enterprise of our Christian Association for which my family and all members of the Association feel profoundly grateful?

May I add that on the last Xmas day early in the morning 5 A.M. our young members of eleven boys and girls made a chorus of Christmas Carol in front of your residence, wishing all the good for your family.

Please kindly accept this parcel as a token of the best wishes of our Sunday School to be presented to Lady MacArthur and Mr. Arthur.

May God's protection and guidance be graciously on Your Excellency, Lady MacArthur and all your family, at the present time when the world is going on for a great turning point.

Wishing a happy New Year I may cite 16. and 17. Chapt. 19 St. Luke.

With the most reverend regards,
I remain
humble servant.
[signed] Tosen Yoshimoto

The parcel, according to an aide's note on top of the letter, was a "lacquer bowl with top." The passage from Luke 19 he referred to is "The first came and said, 'Your money, sir, has increased tenfold.' 'Well done,' he replied; 'you are a good servant. Because you have shown yourself trustworthy in a very small matter, you shall have charge of ten cities.'" The gift was modest, but the reference to money increasing is a bit unsettling, even if it does come from the Bible.

As one might expect, another letter came from Yoshimoto, dated July 27, 1948. It somewhat abruptly raises a secular matter: He offers to give the general 50,000 *tsubo* (about 41 acres) of land in Chiba Prefecture. MacArthur did not reply, and the writer sent another letter on December 31 of the next year. The two letters cover similar points, so I will quote only the second letter here. It reads in English:

838, 5 chome, Sendagaya, Shibuya-ku, Tokyo
International Christian Order
Principal Minister, Tosen Yoshimoto

General MacArthur
Dear Sir:
   1. I pray that God's blessing will be bestowed upon Your Excellency and your family members.

2. Around December 1947, our religious order promised a contribution of 50,000,000 yen to the International Christian University now under construction at Mitaka; I offer my congratulations to Your Excellency for assuming its presidency.

3. Dated July 27th of last year, I sent a letter to Your Excellency, but from printing errors it seems it was not understood, so I am repeating what I mentioned previously. The land (woodland) which our church owns—current approx. price, 20,000,000 yen—is offered to Your Excellency and Mrs. MacArthur to be used for U.S.–Japan and international charity enterprises.

4. On the 11th of this month, there was a complication; we received a notice from Chiba Agricultural Land Commission informing us of forced sale to buy up the land (woodland). I called up Chiba prefectural office and informed them about my plan for the land and was told that if it is true then it may be possible if within several days to have the notice withdrawn.

5. Please somehow accept my proposition, and I pray that Your Excellency and Mrs. MacArthur could use it for a commemorating enterprise that would be noted in history.

MacArthur did not reply to this letter either, but he did not ignore it. He assigned the appropriate sections of GHQ to investigate the background of this seemingly extraordinary gift. Lieutenant Colonel Nugent, chief of the CI&E Section, submitted a report to Colonel Bunker regarding "Petition from Tosen Yoshimoto" on February 15, 1950, which read as follows:

1. Reference is made to . . . a petition brought orally to Col. Bunker by one Tosen Yoshimoto who desired to contribute to the Supreme Commander for educational or social welfare purposes a plot of land in Chiba Prefecture to which Yoshimoto claimed to hold title.

2. In view of previous experience in dealing with Yoshimoto, he was asked by CIE to reduce his plan to writing in order that it might be given more careful consideration. He accordingly submitted two petitions on 31 Dec 49 and 5 Jan 50 respectively . . . His petition of 5 Jan 50 requested special action to secure the payment of wartime insurance claims amounting to 58,559,111.70 yen which he has been advancing for several years without success. In the latter petition Yoshimoto promised, if the CinC [commander in chief] would order the release of these funds, to give the bulk of the money, 50,000,000 yen, to the International Christian University, retaining only the remainder of 8,559,111.70 yen to finance the project of his property.

3. An inquiry made of ESS [Economic and Scientific Section] revealed that there is no basis for Yoshimoto's claims. The funds in question were never the property of, nor in the possession of, Yoshimoto or the organization he represents.

They represented assignments to Yoshimoto of numerous individual bank accounts at the time bank deposits were written off due to the cancellation of War Indemnities, Yoshimoto having persuaded the owners to transfer their rights to him in the hope that certain substantial exemptions from the Indemnity cancellation would be granted to charitable, religious and educational juridical persons. Moreover, actual transfers of these accounts to Yoshimoto were never consummated and the accounts remained in the various banks concerned in the names of the individuals concerned. Even if the actual transfers had been effected, there would be no means of granting Yoshimoto's request since such balances were subsequently cancelled and there remains no source of funds to meet such demands.

4. . . . . What he apparently hoped to do was to get control of the subject balances by some device and salvage a portion of them. In this connection it should be noted that Yoshimoto was sentenced to three years of imprisonment at hard labor by the Tokyo District Court in Dec 47 on charges of fraud in connection with the raising of funds for an international university (not to be confused with the International Christian University to which he now proposes to give the bulk of the insurance funds). He appealed the case to a higher court, and this appeal is still pending.

5. . . . . Experience with him to date has inspired *distrust* and revealed a need for caution in dealing with him.[3]

On February 13, two days before the date on this memo, Nugent wrote to Yoshimoto informing him that there were no grounds for his request for the insurance funds and that the matter was closed. The letter also informed Yoshimoto that "existing policy precludes the holding of title to Japanese land in the name of any Occupation authority" and suggested that he contribute the land in Chiba to some other organization engaged in educational and social welfare purposes.

Nonetheless, Yoshimoto's gifts continued, although they were quite humble. On May 13, 1950, he sent some honey produced in Hokkaidō to MacArthur's family for Mother's Day, the next day. In the accompanying letter he says that his group's office is located near the headquarters of the Communist Party, but they have suffered no adverse consequences, and their peaceful existence is due to the protection of MacArthur and Almighty God. And once the Korean War began, the gifts carried an additional layer of meaning. The following letter, written in English in flowing longhand, is also worth quoting:

Tosen Yoshimoto,
Representative of
International Christian Body,
No. 838, 5 chome, Sendagaya
Shibuya-ku, Tokyo
31st Dec., 1950

To General Douglas MacArthur,
Dear Excellency,
   Now that we are about to welcome New Year, 1951, I fervently pray for
Your Excellency called forth to perform the highest and grandest mission for
all democratic nations for the whole world, together with Lady MacArthur
and Mr. Arthur that the Almighty God's grace be abounding upon you all.
   This is a humble present of mine that may be good at this moment for the
significance it implies:—lst Aramaki, a salmon seasoned with salt, that means
to go ahead with increasing and invincible energy to reach up the river and
attain the end, and 2nd Kachiguri, dried chestnuts that means to overcome
and conquer the enemy or all the temptation.
   The salted salmon may be served by frying with butter, after being freed
from salt, putting in the water for some while and the dried chestnuts may be
used by boiling half an hour or so and then adding sugar.
   Symbolizing the complete and crowning triumph in the coming year 1951,
I offer these things, trusting in your greatest success God will confer, and hop-
ing you will taste them with pleasure.

With the most respectful and sincerest regards,
Yours faithfully,
[signed] Tosen Yoshimoto

   The letter certainly seems straightforward, though it is impossible to
tell what might lurk behind his reasoning. Certainly these last few letters have contained heavy doses of self-interest along with their adulation of MacArthur.

9

UNSOLICITED ADVICE

A BIT OF ADVICE

 The period of fearful darkness that lasted so long is passing, and it is truly heartening that gigantic steps are steadily being taken toward a democratic nation where modern thought and social organization will be permitted. Those of us who are true believers in liberalism can hardly find a way to express this joy. From my heart, truly from my heart I offer to America, the goddess of world peace, a prayer, Long live the Stars and Stripes! I have learned from the newspaper that reasonable and freedom-loving General MacArthur and his advisers give ample consideration even to the opinions sent in by ordinary citizens, so I have decided to offer some advice. I believe this is the only contribution I can make to a free Japan at this time. . . .[1]

The newspaper story to which this letter refers is probably the October 15, 1945, United Press wire story I mentioned in the introduction, which described the correspondence MacArthur had received during the first weeks of the occupation. This article certainly encouraged people to believe that their letters to MacArthur would be read and their opinions heeded. In the above letter, undated but probably written immediately after the article appeared, the writer develops his numerous suggestions at a leisurely pace. He begins with preliminaries describing the spiritual environment during the war:

First, regarding the indictment and punishment of war criminals:
To create a society of free discussion and activity free from threats by anyone, the most important thing for our country at present is to

completely uproot the fanatic Shintoists and the militarists. Simply remov-
ing them from important posts would not only leave the evil roots in place,
but it would also leave liberals, most of whom are delicate and not very
bold, subject to constant fear. However, the most important thing that I
want the Americans to understand is that 99 percent of the Japanese peo-
ple, at least until now, were absolute fanatics and militarists. The history
of Japan that begins with the descent to earth of the descendants of the Sun
Goddess . . . [sic] a series of poems beautifully crafted by cursed fanatic
scholars and bureaucrats . . . [sic] based on this the Japanese people were
thoroughly indoctrinated to believe in Japan as the divine land. The poetry
and the people's intoxication interacted with each other, resulting in the be-
lief in a national polity superior to all other nations. This was the basis for
all of Japan's invasions and atrocities.

Please examine carefully the Ministry of Education publications Shimin
no michi *[The way of the subject] and* Kokutai no hongi *[Cardinal princi-*
ples of the national polity]. These books were published in quantity, all of the
people were forced to read them, and they were indispensable in preparing for
entrance examinations for all schools. The forced indoctrination of such prim-
itive thought, something modern foreigners cannot even imagine, was imple-
mented with fanatic energy. . . .

The writer reaches the conclusion that "those who forced this ideology on the people and those who aroused support for the ideology are
the top war criminals," and he condemns educators for being in the
front line of this activity. But these are not the only ones who should be
named as war criminals:

After the crazy fanatics, the next important war criminals are those who
committed atrocities. In general the American military lacks thoroughness in
punishing those responsible for the war. From what I have gathered, those
who treated prisoners of war cruelly; the perpetrators of atrocities at the front;
the oppressors and torturers of liberals, socialists, communists, and those
connected to Christian churches; the kempei *[military police] and police*
who treated the ordinary people, especially students, with hideous cruelty;
the kempei *and the people who shot or brutally killed American pilots*
who came down in parachutes . . . [sic] their numbers must reach several
hundred thousand.

The punishment for war criminals should be the death penalty. Those of us who remember how viciously they crushed our awakened spirits, and how they guided awakening spirits in the wrong direction under the veil of military training, cannot help recognize that at least up until now the American authorities lack thoroughness. Let me offer my suggestions in locating the above war criminals:

- *The press, the radio, and other communications media should be mobilized to request that the people identify war criminals by confidentially reporting their names to the American authorities.*
- *Carefully monitor the media for reports of those who committed atrocities and other war criminals, and arrest them immediately. . . .*
- *Study old newspapers, weeklies, books, and correspondence courses and examine the authors to find and punish as many war criminals as possible.*
- *Almost all the* kempei *were frightful oppressors of the people. All* kempei *and police should be thoroughly investigated. It is awful that the* kempei *are being demobilized and returned to the general population.*

The writer's suggestion that the Japanese people identify war criminals is interesting. During this time, the Intelligence Section of GHQ was fully engaged in drawing up lists of suspected war criminals, but there is no evidence that Japanese cooperation was solicited. The designation of war criminals was considered the prerogative of the Allied authorities. The generalized advice offered by this writer, as opposed to actually naming war criminals, was already within the grasp of GHQ. Nevertheless, the writer continues with his advice, turning to the issue of new leadership:

Second, concerning the identification of true liberals and support for them: There are astonishingly few genuine liberals in Japan. Even during more than ten years of my school life, I could only find a few. Genuine liberals certainly cannot be found among the present bureaucrats. The bureaucrats are unprincipled, to the extent that they even allowed a fascist and a war criminal like Yamazaki [Iwao], the former home minister, to keep his office. Even if there were a liberal among them, he would be timid and passive.

When I say " genuine," I mean that someone meets these conditions: Even if the person's ideology is a deeply held conviction, he should have a solid education, he should have an abundant spirit of Christian love, and be learned in philosophy, literature, languages, art, music, sports, social problems, and politics. Besides, he must have sharp and fresh senses like that of a first-class reporter. . . .

Koizumi Shinzō, Watsuji Tetsurō, Miki Kiyoshi, etc. are impressive as true liberals. In particular, Koizumi Shinzō is truly a great man. I would hope the American military authorities meet him and talk with him. Of course, he is fluent in English. There are other people who love liberty, both famous and unknown, who are the treasures of a new Japan as well as soldiers for world peace. The American authorities should use all means to identify these people and place them in all the important posts, including cabinet ministers, government officials, presidents of universities, newspaper reporters, presidents and directors of large companies, and others. These are the necessary steps as a prelude to building a society where those with pure spirits may rise to better positions. With America's vast wealth, I do not think it will be difficult for you to give necessary and sufficient economic support to the few true liberals of Japan.

The United States had compiled a list of "friendly Japanese" during the war but did not need to use it. Most Japanese were very friendly toward the occupation and did not hesitate to cooperate. As it happened, the writer's advice addressed issues that MacArthur was already well aware of. Still, there is no doubt about the writer's sincerity, evidence of the great expectations many Japanese had for the occupation forces.

Miki Kiyoshi, one of those mentioned as a prominent liberal, was imprisoned during the war and had not been released despite the surrender. He died on September 26 in Tokyo Prison from aggravation of the scabies he suffered. This news was reported widely in all the newspapers on October 5, but perhaps the writer did not notice. Instead of dispensing general advice about identifying and supporting liberals, one wishes he had more pointedly criticized the lethargy of those in power. However, when it comes to viewing his own countrymen, he is quite objective and unforgiving in his assessment of Japan's democratization:

The Japanese are really an interesting people who should be studied. At least in Asia, they are the tops in anthropological capabilities. With such capabilities and with such a large population, if the nation's ideology could be directed toward a bright and pure love of peace, the world would benefit to no small extent. . . .

As a person who experienced with truly terrifying depth the era of ideological darkness that held sway over this country for twenty-plus years, I feel that the American military's judgment regarding democratization is extremely optimistic and lacking in thoroughness. Therefore, although I have some doubts and fears about our postal authorities, translators, and other dubious people who cooperate with the American armed forces, for the sake of "liberty" and righteousness, I have dared to send my opinion. I was burned out in Tokyo and evacuated to the present address. . . . I was discharged after the war, but the present food condition in Tokyo prevents me from going back to college, so I am thinking of seeking a job. . . .

Clearly this person was a student during the war, and he had enough vision to grasp the implications of the postwar occupation. One senses a certain good grace in his complaints. He signed his name as Asai Takashi and gave his address in Kagawa Prefecture on the island of Shikoku.

People who thought they had a worthy idea spared no effort in writing to MacArthur and GHQ. The scope of their suggestions was extraordinarily wide, and the contents of their letters provide a window on the convulsive changes that were rocking Japanese society. The date of the next letter is unclear, but it was probably sent on December 21, 1949. The writer filled a postcard with his suggestions, written in ink in tiny characters small enough to require a magnifying glass to read. Some of the thoughts are requests and others are appeals, reflecting the fact that he was writing to someone far superior in rank. As we will see later, in this type of letter the distinction between recommendations, appeals, and sometimes compromising information is often unclear.

A. The prefectures, cities, towns, and villages of the country go to great expense to establish offices in Tokyo and staff them with high-paid bureaucrats. Then, many governors, mayors, etc., go up to Tokyo every month to engage in so-called lobbying. This is one of the remnants of the centralized feudal authority of the Edo period. For the sake of democratization, please abolish the centralization of power. It is impossible for the Japanese to do this, so please issue orders to revise the prefectural boundaries into ten new prefectures and to implement the same state system as the United States. If we leave things as they are, a second Tōjō will emerge again.

B. A million babies are born each year. People are unconcerned about this. Foreigners do not trust Japanese, so emigration is probably impossible. Please order the government to encourage birth control in the farming and fishing villages. If the rural areas practice birth control, there will be fewer people migrating to the city and Japan will improve. Until now the government has not issued a single circular in the farming villages.

C. According to the constitution, the government grants land to shrines and temples, but to require that they obtain permits each time they give or lease that land to others is interference and against the constitution; it should be stopped. All grants to shrines built after the 5th year of Meiji [1872] for militaristic and nationalistic purposes should be stopped (with the exception of the Meiji, Heian, and Kashiwara shrines). Unless there is a reliable guarantee, grants should be prohibited to shrines and temples that have no prospect of reconstruction. Please decrease the size of the land grant when it is deemed unnecessary. When city planning calls for the land of shrines and temples to be used for other purposes, suspend the grant and give them land in exchange somewhere else.

This writer's first proposal was right on target. Local self-government, one of the pillars of the occupation reforms, was already becoming a hollow promise, and lobbying for the central government to get a bigger share of government funds was intensifying. It is not likely, however, that adopting the plan to divide the country into ten states would have corrected the situation. The strength of the bureaucrats from the old Home Ministry, who at the time were reasserting central control over local governments, was such that even MacArthur's power was no match for it. Reading the second proposal today makes one aware of how quickly things change. No other country has achieved population control as rapidly as Japan, even though it meant legitimizing such methods as abortion. The migration of the rural population to the cities continued in increasing numbers in the years that followed. The letter continues, interweaving its many layers of recommendations and appeals:

D. *I wonder if foreigners think that Japan has been democratized. I want to say no. Please have CI&E make constant visits to local elementary and middle schools to give lectures, and show* kami-shibai *[picture plays] and movies to teach democracy. If you keep quiet, the Japanese will do nothing on their own.*

E. *Please distribute American fire extinguishers to fire stations throughout the country. Please prohibit the building of inflammable houses in cities.*

Japanese who were old enough during the occupation remember education officers from the local military government (their home base was CI&E, the Civil Information and Education Section) coming to their schools to give lectures on democracy. During this time before television, great entertainment was provided by the simple picture-card shows *(kami-shibai)* produced under the guidance of the CI&E, and by touring groups that showed movies in rural villages.

F. *The Communist Party around here says that reports of the number of Japanese detained [in the Soviet Union] is American anti-Soviet propaganda. Can't we get the true figure by asking for reports from the families of those who still have not been repatriated?*

G. *Please hold a conference of American principals operating schools in Japan to set a uniform educational policy. Some Japanese teachers and staff take actions that undercut the intentions of the American principal. Especially, to suspend or expel a student because he can not pay his monthly fees and to spread the word to others causes the student despair and turns him into a delinquent, which Jesus will not like. Please lend him the amount he owes and collect it after he graduates.*

The back of the postcard contains this astonishing array of proposals, covering everything from fire prevention in the cities to the problem of unpaid fees at Christian schools. The front has the sender's name and address as Hideo Sakaguchi, c/o Minami Tanegashima Post Office, Kagoshima Prefecture. Was he really from

Tanegashima, a small island in the Pacific south of Kyūshū? The letters to MacArthur truly came from every corner of Japan. This card was buried in the CI&E files in the archives, suggesting that among its many proposals, GHQ may have picked up on the ones concerning education.

PLEASE REVISE THE LAND REFORM

While some of the letters contained general, all-embracing proposals, many others focused on specific problems. The latter doubtless carried a great deal more weight. The next letter was written immediately after the general election of 1949, which the Democratic Liberal Party won decisively, providing a vote of confidence for prime minister Yoshida Shigeru and ushering in a period of stable conservative administration. The letter, filling five pages of lined paper, is a "statement of opinion" aimed at a rollback of the sweeping land reform, implemented early in the occupation, that had taken much of the land owned by rural landlords and distributed it among tenant farmers. It is archived in the files of the Economic and Scientific Section of GHQ. The writer's impassioned and detailed criticism of land reform, together with the accomplished calligraphy, suggests that he was (or had been) a landowner.

January 28, 1949
General Headquarters, Occupation Army
The Honorable General MacArthur

Following on the completion of the general election, please allow me to offer Your Excellency my opinion.

Since the war, Japan has suffered ideological confusion, and villains have taken advantage of the situation, leading the people into even more confusion. Numerous political parties have formed, with their leaders simply fighting for political power, ignoring the nation and the people. This has resulted in frequent changes in the cabinet and the inability to pursue fixed political policies. As a result, the government's power is weak and does not reach the lower strata of the people. There is no national or social order, villains are rampant, and honest people suffer endlessly. The people have lost faith in the Socialist Party's unjust social policies and the Democratic Party's middle-of-the-road politics. This is why we placed our hopes in the Yoshida cabinet and elected many members of the ruling Democratic Liberal Party. We were able to take the weak Yoshida cabinet and replace it with a strong Yoshida cabinet. Therefore, for at least the next four years, this cabinet must govern to bring order back to Japan and peace to the people. Furthermore, may I ask Your Excellency to guide the Yoshida cabinet and assist it in rebuilding Japan.

A government with fair social policies should be established to expedite the reconstruction of Japan.

After the collapse of two coalition governments, the incompetent Socialist-led Katayama cabinet in February 1948 and the corrupt Democratic-led Ashida cabinet the following October, it was not only conservatives like this writer who celebrated the advent of a strong, stable Yoshida administration. MacArthur himself commented to William J. Sebald, the chief of the diplomatic section, "The elections were a great victory for the conservatives and will stabilize Japanese politics for four years."[2] On the other hand, the Japan Communist Party, which had only four seats in the Diet before the election, increased its share to thirty-five seats, and political confrontation between conservatives and reformists was expected to heat up. The letter continues by touching on this point:

There are several reasons for the increase in Communist Party members in the recent elections. In the countryside, in addition to tax struggles there has been the problem of the sudden land reform. Although the new constitution stipulates that property rights will not be violated, an evil new land adjustment law was put into effect that disregarded property rights and recognized absolute tenant rights. The result is the middle-class landowners' poverty, which is worse than words can describe. It has made it impossible for lower- and middle-class landowners to grow their own food, and they weep over the difficulty of their lives. The farmers' quota rice is bought up at close to 40 yen per shō [about two quarts], plus in-kind compensation, while the lower- and middle-class landowners can only collect 0.75 yen per shō from a tenant farmer. With such a huge discrepancy, the amount collected is insufficient to pay the cost of irrigation, to say nothing of land taxes. Moreover, landowners have to pay 51.50 yen per shō for rationed rice, while they could not be paid more than 1,000 yen in cash for land that was bought up from them. How could a policy of such great inequity be called a social plan! It is only natural that political ideology has suffered. If democracy means peace, freedom, and happiness for each person in society, I would like to see fairer policies for the common people.

This is a straightforward criticism of land reform. MacArthur had attacked the feudalistic character of land ownership in Japan with a vehemence that even surpassed Japanese Marxist scholars. He made the liberation of tenant farmers through land reform a pillar of his plan for the democratic reform of Japan. Even if the consequences were severe for a relatively small number of nonresident landowners (the writer of this letter most probably among them), MacArthur did not heed their complaints. Among the many reforms introduced by the occupation, none took root as firmly as land reform. Even the "reverse course" that

Photo 9.1 GHQ representatives discuss land reform with farmers in Chiba Prefecture, June 10, 1948. Source: Mainichi Shimbunsha

rolled back a number of reforms beginning in the summer of 1948 did not undermine land reform. Notwithstanding, this letter makes its appeal and warns that, if these policies continue, even former landowners will join the Communist Party.

Where the middle class in the countryside is suffering hardship, members of the Communist Party used the recent general election to call for a reduction in taxes, the overthrow of the rich, and help for the poor, and as a result of their organizing efforts they have gained many new members. During the recent general election, the village chief of Kibe-mura came to our village to campaign for Kimura Sakae, a Communist Party member, and declared in a fiery speech that everyone in his village office belonged to the party. The rural upper and middle classes, to say nothing of the ignorant masses, have to resort to crimes like burglary because of the harsh living conditions, and they are turning communist in reaction to current politics. The Yoshida cabinet must be made to correct these unfair policies to enable the people to enjoy the true peace and liberty and happiness of democracy. That is, the present 0.75 yen per shō collected from tenant farmers should be raised to 20 yen per shō, which is half of the price paid for the growers' quota rice. I hear that land reform will be completed this spring. In the future, the land adjustment law should be more lenient, and landowners should be able to reclaim up to two tan [about half an acre] of their land (with ownership protected) to farm on their own. I beg of you deeply and many times over that you stabilize the livelihood of the middle and lower classes in the rural areas. Please pardon this long letter.

Please pass on the main objectives of this letter to Prime Minister Yoshida.

Kado Katsuyuki
Muikaichi-chō, Kanoashi-gun
Shimane Prefecture

Of course, no matter how elaborate an appeal this writer put together, there was no chance that a tenant farmer's land would be returned to its former owner. Later that year, on October 21, MacArthur sent an open letter to Prime Minister Yoshida marking the third anniversary of land reform: "This achievement," MacArthur declared, "stands as one of the most important single demonstrations of [Japan's] approaching maturity as a democratic nation." He cautioned that "any possibility of a gradual reversion to the land tenure system as it existed before the reform must be forestalled."³ It was clear that appeals from former landowners were futile.

Naturally, some of the many suggestions actually did come to fruition. An example is the following appeal for the return to Japanese control of Amami Ōshima, the largest of the Amami group of islands south of Kyūshū, written by a native of the island. The Amami islands were under direct American military control, as was all of Okinawa. There were quite visible, repeated appeals for reversion to Japan by organizations of citizens from Okinawa and the "northern territories" (the islands north of Hokkaidō occupied by the Soviet Union), but the following letter commands our attention because it is an individual's courageous appeal for the return of the island, and it reflects the determined spirit that some Japanese displayed during the occupation. Covering three small pages of stationery, the writing is neat and dignified.⁴

February 1 [1950]
To General MacArthur:

I respectfully address General MacArthur.
I come from Amami Ōshima in Kagoshima Prefecture.
As you know, under orders from General Headquarters, the Japanese government has been prohibited from exercising general political jurisdiction over Amami Ōshima, and we cannot even travel there freely.
Why not return it to Japan without waiting for a peace treaty?
Amami Ōshima was not attacked during the war, and it is an original Japanese territory from ancient times.
I fear I am being impolite, but I do not think that Amami Ōshima should bear more of the sacrifice of war than mainland Japan.
Okinawa was invaded by the American military during the war, so Amami Ōshima should not be treated the same way as Okinawa.
It should be returned to the Japanese government as soon as possible. Would it not be prudent policy to show more sympathy and win over the Japanese hearts forever?

*I am aware of my rudeness, but relying on the spirit of democracy, I have
dared to offer my advice.*

Respectfully yours,
Satō Seiichi
Maehara-chō 1-5, Nagata-ku, Kobe

The Amami islands were returned about three years later, under a
U.S.–Japanese agreement in December 1953. According to the leading scholar on the occupation of Okinawa, Miyasato Seigen, the
United States returned the Amami islands because they had little
strategic value, and because returning the islands where there was a
strong movement for reversion partially satisfied Japan's demands,
while exacting acquiescence of the Japanese government in the long-
term U.S. administration of Okinawa in exchange.[5] It might have appeared to the writer of the letter that his request had been granted,
but of course the reversion resulted from U.S. global strategic
considerations.

A NUMBER OF SUGGESTIONS ON EDUCATION

All sorts of suggestions were sent directly to MacArthur, many of which
concerned minutely detailed matters. What follows are several letters
concerning education, from the CI&E files.[6]

February 11 [1946]
To the Supreme Commander for the Allied Powers

Honorable Sir:
    *As one citizen I offer you my deep, deep and honest gratitude for your
tremendous efforts day and night for the democratization of Japan.*
    *I hereby submit to you some of my thoughts and wishes, and I will be
pleased if they are of some use to you.*
    *1. There are huge differentials among teachers depending on whether they
are graduates of public or private schools. I would like to see this corrected soon.*
    *Those who graduate from a [public] normal-school specialist course re-
ceive a ten-yen raise upon graduation, but no special compensation is granted*

to teachers graduating from a private university higher normal school. The city of Tokyo also gave a special raise to the specialist-course graduates in 1944.

Based on the above, I would like to see special raises given to those graduating from private schools (elementary-school teachers with middle-school teaching certificates). I would like to see some kind of favor shown to those who obtained a national elementary-school teaching certificate by strenuous study at night and who also have a certificate for teaching middle school. I beg your consideration.

2. Among the current principals of elementary schools, there are many who detest democracy and instead prefer the totalitarian ways of the past. They are not happy with democratization among the teachers, and some even favor suppressing such moves. Is it not necessary to have some policies regarding principals of national elementary schools?

3. There is no hope for democratizing schools without first improving the system of school commissioners. There are many commissioners who are opposed to treating teachers according to their individuality, and they try to unite teachers under their own ideology.

Many commissioners also build local factions with the aim of expanding their own power.

There are many commissioners who inspect schools and try to oppress the teachers.

The above three points are in outline only, and they mostly concern what happens in the elementary schools. I hope you will make an effort on our behalf.

Respectfully,
Taira Toyoichi

The back of the envelope lists the teacher's address in Tokyo's Yodobashi ward. I was impressed that the writer included a complete handwritten translation in English, apparently done by his own hand. His English was quite good (the translation included here is based on the original Japanese). But according to the notes attached by the Education Office of CI&E, nothing was done to respond to his concerns.

The next letter contains a laudable suggestion from a female middle school student.

Photo 9.2 The caption on this International News photo read, "No red schoolhouse—but school goes on; Tokyo: Using makeshift benches and desks, Tokyo schoolchildren attend open-air classes as their studies, with jingo deleted, are resumed. Their schoolhouse was burned down during a B-29 fire-bomb raid before Japan tossed in the sponge." April 29, 1946. Source: MacArthur Memorial

We entered school in April and have been studying with our teacher since then, but I would like to have different teachers teaching the variety of different subjects.

Also if every class could have its own homeroom teacher, our school would advance, it would be very convenient, and our desire to study would increase. During the three years we will be coming to school here and for the new students who will enter, we will all think it is a more convenient way to study. As long as the number of teachers is not decreased, we will be able to study our subjects fully. Please do whatever you can for us.

Good-bye.

The addressee on the front of the two-yen government postcard is "General MacArthur, Tokyo." The card is dated August 12, and the writer is identified as Kurashige Keiko of Ōmine First Middle School in the town of Ōmine in Yamaguchi Prefecture. From the ATIS stamp, it is clear that the card was received in 1949.

The next, anonymous letter denounces the Ministry of Education. After the war, a ceiling was set on the number of former students of the army and navy academies at 10 percent of the entering class at any university. This letter claims that the Ministry of Education is not enforcing the quota.[7]

MacArthur General Headquarters should take decisive action on the stance of the Ministry of Education and force them to keep their promise. They should be ordered to revoke admission of military-academy students beyond the ten-percent level and to redo the selection. The limitless power of the MacArthur General Headquarters should be made known to the conservative, reactionary Ministry of Education.

The envelope for this letter was handmade from an entrance-examination application form. I suppose the writer believed that he was not accepted to a university because of the military-academy students.

The last of the letters related to education was a recommendation, dated January 13, 1950, that groups of students be formed in each prefecture to provide disaster relief. The writer notes the work would guarantee student livelihood, provide practical training, and contribute to forest conservation and flood control, thereby killing three birds with one stone. However, since he already has gathered 170 students, he pleads, "Is there any construction work for the occupation forces? Something for about 100 people a day, even outside of Tokyo would be fine. I hope you can help us, and if possible could we have something before March?" So this is what the letter was actually getting at. I am tempted to quote the entire letter, but I will just note that it was written by Yoshida Shizuichi of Suginami ward in Tokyo.

A DIAMOND IN THE SOIL TO REVEAL TO THE WORLD

Many letters were sent to MacArthur from people trying to sell themselves or their ideas, but the following letter passes on the story of someone who was quietly doing good deeds.

To General MacArthur:

I respectfully make a request. I am a student in Chiba Prefecture, and I would like to introduce to you our mentor, Mr. Itō, a true democrat. Some time ago one of your soldiers, a member of the U.S. Air Force, met his death in the town of Sawara in Chiba Prefecture, and his grave is hidden among others in the town cemetery. There is a person who comes once in a while to clean the grave and offer flowers. When I asked his name and address, he simply smiled and went home. I thought it was odd that he would continue to come four years after the war, and on Christmas Day when I passed by he was there, so I asked him why. He smiled and said that Japanese and American soldiers are the same. The other graves have many flowers, but there are none on the American grave, the grass has overgrown it, and no one even offers a stick of incense. I believe, he said, that we should be very grateful to His Excellency, Supreme Commander General MacArthur for extending his deep love to the former enemy Japan and for the tremendous effort he is making daily to build a peaceful nation. On top of this, we should be grateful for the deep love of the American people, who are helping us with food and other things. He had tears in his eyes.

Since then, I found out his name and address, so I visited him. He told me that since the Meiji era, Japan has been helped by the people of the civilized countries England and the United States in all aspects of politics and culture. He is honest and suited to democracy, but he lives in poverty. In our feudalistic region, no one pays any attention to a person who does not have money. With Your Excellency's sole discretion, please interview this man who is like a god and give him the capability to be a leader. In Japan today, even if a person is pro-American, no one will pay attention to him if he does not have money.

His background is as follows:

Age: 42 years

Address: 294 Yoshihara, Katori-chō, Katori-gun, Chiba Prefecture

[Name:] Itō Tokuji

He is a graduate of engineering school and runs a blueprint shop. After the beginning of the Japan–United States war, he expressed opposition, so he had to leave Tokyo and move to the country. I could not get more details.

I request again that with Your Excellency's sympathy, I would like to reveal to the world this diamond hidden in the soil.

[signed] A WRITER

There is no date on the letter, but the envelope was postmarked February 13, 1950; the back reads "Sasaki [first name illegible], A High School Student, Katori-gun, Chiba Prefecture." It is not known how GHQ responded to this suggestion.

The next letter expresses opposition to the proposed abolition of reign names (the Japanese practice of counting the years from the beginning of each emperor's reign). I will quote the whole letter (the first two lines were in English, the rest of the letter in Japanese).

Gen. Macarthar [sic]
A Japanese Yuji Wada [sic]

Japan's Reign Names
The movement to abolish Article 12 of Japan's old Imperial Household Law—one reign name to one ruler—is meaningless to the nation's democratization, and it destroys our honorable tradition in a negative, crazy, and useless manner. The deep significance of Japan's reign name is that it is a gentle and natural symbol of the emperor system; it is a distinguishing feature of the emperor system. However, the various newspapers carry reports that public opinion considers this symbol of the emperor system to be useless. I can only view this as the intelligentsia's "toadyism" toward the occupation forces. This general opinion must have been formed because the revised Imperial Household Law does not mention Article 12 of the old law. Not having a reign name as part of the emperor system absolutely does not mean the abolition of imperialism. This is because the ideology of Japanese imperialism in the past was not that of a monarchy that existed for a reign name, or monetary gain, or totalitarian repression, or for discriminatory one-sided purposes. It existed on the principle of universal brotherhood for the purpose of world peace. The basic idea is no different from the principles of today's UNESCO, except that we used military power as the final method of legitimate self-defense. The Emperor Meiji did not bring about the prosperity of the Meiji era for the purpose of aggression. There is no benefit to Japan to be had from abolishing the reign name. It will not be evidence that we have rid Japan of imperialism. It is just a passing fancy of shallow novelty seekers who consider themselves to be the only progressive reformers. It is an anti-Japanese policy that inter-

feres with the emotion between the people and their most revered emperor. I cannot see it as a policy of anti-imperialism. On the contrary, it is a method of severing the ties between the emperor and the Japanese people. This effort will result in weakening Japan's determination to contribute to world peace. Some stupid Japanese cater to the current trends and forget their true nature. That's one way of living, but just as true Americans will never forget the spirit of American independence, true Japanese will not forget the sincerity of the Japanese tradition. The education committee of the House of Councilors of the Diet is discussing the abolition of the reign name, and they are trying hard to do it. These useless people act smart and carelessly enjoy a novelty that cannot be undone. It is one of the largest failures of the year.

Sincerely,
February 22, 1950

The discussion before the education committee in the House of Councilors centered on the testimony of twenty-six people summoned to give their opinions on the reign name. The large majority favored abolition of the reign name, and outside of the Diet, the *Asahi shimbun* published an editorial calling for abolition on March 2, 1950. It appeared as though the conditions for abolition were ripe.

However, this writer—Wada Yūji from the city of Takasaki in Gunma Prefecture—need not have worried. The reign name survived, although it was only legally sanctioned in 1979, almost thirty years later. A core constituency behind doing away with the reign name never emerged. This is not the time to theorize on the issue, and it is easy enough to point out the shortcomings in this writer's logic, but it is worth noting how rare it was for a Japanese under the occupation to so boldly accuse the press of toadying to the occupation forces.

SUGGESTING BY WAY OF INFORMING

In stark contrast to this kind of courage are letters involving compromising information. Quite a few of the letters of this type sent to

MacArthur had the sender's name and address, so they certainly cannot be considered irresponsible slander. In this chapter, I present them as evidence of the depth of confidence that people had in the supreme commander. The first letter suggests that a candidate should not be allowed to refer to MacArthur as "Mac" in his campaign speeches. The letter was typewritten in English.[8]

January 13, 1949.
To: General Douglas McAurther,
From: Kenzo Kato, No. 57 Honmuracho, Azabu,
Minato-ku, Tokyo.
Subject: Concerning the control of the contents of election speech of evil nature.

Dear Sir,
  On January 3rd 6 P.M. at the personal lecture forum hold at the [Ō]miya Primary School in the city of Fujimiya, Fuji-gun, YASUSHI MIYAHATA, the official candidate of Democratic Liberal Party, after having explained the general movements of the party, his personal situation, and the present economic problems, refered to the importance of the coming election and relation and development between U.S. Army and the two preceding cabinets and also the present one. In his speech, he touched on following important points.
  1. The opinion of General Head Quarters on the result of the two preceding combined cabinets of three parties ends in a word of "dissatisfaction." As its result, they are now rather favourably inclined toward Democratic Liberal Party lead by Mr. Yoshida; The coming general election is going to be executed with the object to prove of this and also to prove of the national approval toward the party. As its result, if Democratic Liberal Party could secure more than half of the seats in National Congress, it is possible to realize its policy, which the Party already made public. In this speech, he strongly expressed that "Mac is wholly supporting Mr. Yoshida."
  2. He continued his speech and now turned to attack the two preceding cabinets, saying that the nation was entirely betrayed by them. In this speech, he firmly expressed that both cabinets of Katayama and Ashida had relation with Mr. C. Whitney, the head of Government Section, Mr. C. L. Kades & Mr. J. Williams of the same department, and tried their best to win support of U.S. Army.

Such words & deeds clearly show that he has the intention of alluding how he is familiar with the inner workings of political circles and that he plays an important part in the negotiation between U.S. Army. Especially such words instigate the voters to hold the feeling of kind of worship as to think that "he is a great man; he speaks out boldly what ordinary people cannot speak." Above all he thus tried to hit their psychological feeling such as to instigate the sense of superiority by calling MacArthur without any courtesy.

It may be a trifle, if the audience took no notice to his speech, but when we well think of it, the psychological influence this speech may give to Japanese nation, who are on the stand point of economic restauration with great & various help from U.S. Army, is a matter of great importance. Accordingly, if we leave such words & deeds of abusing the occupying army, the influence is clear and we cannot overlook such traitor who tries to flatter the public with such speech & action of evil nature.

We herewith inform you to arouse your attention and at the same time we beg for your apposite dealing.

Very truly yours,
[signed] Kenzo Kato.

This impassioned denunciation failed to persuade GHQ to take action. Miyahata Yasushi, from the second district of Shizuoka Prefecture (with an allocation of five seats in the Diet), came in third at the polls and won reelection. It is true that MacArthur did not like to be called "Mac," and even the most reckless person would not dare call him that in his presence, but MacArthur's staff was not so narrow-minded as to take action based on this letter, and in reality, they probably could not have interfered with the election.

The next letter reports on fraud at the Hachiōji Derby, on the outskirts of Tokyo. The writer begs General MacArthur to do something because the gangsters were in control of horse racing in the countryside.

To General MacArthur:
I entreat you. Please do something about the bosses [i.e., gangsters]. It seems the Japanese police are unable to do anything. Please read through this letter. I am a jockey in nearby prefectures. Late last year a friend of

mine earned a thousand yen from betting at the Hachiōji Derby sponsored by the Tokyo Federation of Horse Breeders. Two hoodlums followed him and banged into him, and after being knocked about he was dragged to a nearby forest. He was beaten, and he had to give up the thousand yen and apologize before they would let him go. Hachiōji and Saitama are the two places with so many hoodlums. He said a policeman passed by but acted as though he had not seen anything and went away. I hear that there were many similar incidents last spring. Others have told me that it happens often in Hachiōji . The vice chairman of the federation, U [initials only in the original], is a boss and a former hoodlum with a criminal record. He does not know anything about horses but is the vice chairman of the federation. It seems to have been a shady appointment, and he is pretty bad. The chairman, I, is a greedy man, and the manager, S, is also a crook. They say that the three are filling their pockets, and to do that they have bribed most of the officials of the Ministry of Agriculture and Forestry and the Tokyo metropolitan government. The derby has been held more than ten times since October of the year before last, yet its account is in the red because they have apparently embezzled six or seven million yen. That is why, even though the race is held in the Tokyo Metropolis, the prize money is rather small, and among us jockeys there are some who are dishonest. But when the bosses who come to the derby tell us that all the fans are predicting that a certain horse is bound to win, so that we should hold that horse back to make it finish third or fourth, we are on the spot and sometimes have to do as told. Still, it is only a horse, so even if the reins are checked it may finish first. Then the bosses chase us and beat us, because they bought a lot of tickets for the horse they decided would finish first, and they lost a lot of money.

I could not help but laugh when I read "it is only a horse," but this whole letter has a sort of humorous cast to it. Of course one can also sense the writer's absolute seriousness in informing on "the enemies of the people" and the tension this involves. His neat writing fills each page of stationery. The letter continues:

The bosses tend to be arrogant about other matters too. Because Vice Chairman U is a boss, naturally many hoodlums gather around Hachiōji . The racing ground at Tozuka is closely patrolled by the police, but at Ha-

chiōji   the hoodlums do it. They say that hoodlums were recruited for the job. After all, U controls the whole place, and no one dares to stand up to him. He is also good at bribery and is said to have bribed more than half of the heads of the associations in the federation. Therefore, his staff members do not have any backbone and are yes men to their superiors. I hear that there were two or three upstanding people, but they were fired for forming labor unions or insubordination. There is no hope because everyone is afraid and works to protect themselves. For a long time, the judging of races at Hachiōji has been strange, and trouble occurs frequently. First the crowd will surround the judge and complain that the start of a race was flawed. Then the leading hoodlums will come and appease the crowd and send them back to their seats. These men get rewarded tens of thousands of yen for pacifying the crowd, but it is said that they have to split part of the reward with the chairman and vice chairman. This is how awful the situation is. The people of Hachiōji are all laughing. However, a recent ordinance will dissolve existing federations, and it is said that the metropolitan government is going to control racing. Of course, being good at bribery, Chairman I and Vice Chairman U have already secured positions on the new committee. The jockeys at Hachiōji all wish there was a way to get these men out. As long as these people are in control, there is no way to make money at the races, and there can be no clean racing. We jockeys come to this derby often, so I request that you investigate, fire the crooks, and allow us to ride in a clean derby. It would be so good if we could ride with peace of mind and the fans could bet without worrying. After all, it is Hachiōji of Tokyo Metropolis, and Hachiōji actually has one of the better regional race tracks, so it is a shame. At any rate, please control the bosses at all of the race tracks.

A Certain Jockey
(Please forgive me for using a false
name because of my weak position.)

It might seem unimportant, but events in Tokyo affect federations all over the country, and I think this is rather important, so please inform your subordinates to do something about it.

This letter is not dated, but the date of receipt at the ATIS is July 26, 1948. The following month the town of Honjō in Saitama Prefecture was named by the military government as a gangster-controlled "town of violence," and around the same time, Japanese police all over the country began a crackdown on bosses and gangsters.

There were many other letters from informers. One reported that bureaucrats were bribed during the construction of the Jinsei-za Theater (now called Bungei-za) built by the novelist Misumi Kan.[9] Another claimed that Takushoku University was a school of ultranationalism so it should be closed and all present students and alumni should be purged.[10] Still another argued that the correspondence courses of Shuchiin University were equivalent to fraud. The contents of these letters were severe. Needless to say, there were many letters pointing to politicians, educators, chiefs of police and others, requesting they be purged for their activities during the war. I will introduce one letter from this group to close the chapter. The content is predictable, but what is interesting is the writer's attitude. When I hand-copied the letter, I omitted most of the first half, which argued in essence that it was right for Hatoyama Ichirō to be purged from public office.[11] The rest of the letter went as follows:[12]

> Diet member Ōno Banboku, who was elected from Gifu Prefecture, is a trusted protégé of the boss Hatoyama, and he has been boasting that he is a direct political descendant of Hatoyama. He was elected by waving Hatoyama's name all the way, leading the uneducated rural people, who still worship greatness and are not free from feudal thinking, to believe in him. . . . We believe that he, Ōno, should also be purged.
>
> In our Gifu Prefecture, this boss of reactionary power was grandly elected, and ironically the Socialist Hiraku Kiichi, who has fought for the liberation of farmers for thirty years, was the runner-up. This is extremely lamentable for Japan's democratization. I await Your Excellency General MacArthur's wise judgment.
>
> Ishizuka Chōmatsu
> Member of Gifu Prefecture Communist Party
> May 8, 1946

There is no doubt that this person still regarded MacArthur as the supreme commander of the "liberation army." Hiraku Kiichi was a leader of the Central Japan Farmers' Union, and as mentioned in the letter, he was an activist in Socialist Party politics. At least in the mind of this writer, the democratic united front of the Socialist and Communist parties, which in fact was facing difficulty, had already been achieved. The letter reflects the depth of his confidence in MacArthur, but does it not also show a sparkle of the spirit of the times?

10

TO THE RIGHT OR TO THE LEFT?

A UNITED FRONT WITH THE "LIBERATION ARMY"

 At the end of the last chapter, Ishizuka Chōmatsu clearly identified himself as a member of the Communist Party in Gifu Prefecture. The letter was dated May 8, 1946, a time when the Japan Communist Party and the "liberation army" were still enjoying their honeymoon. Many Communist Party members and supporters wrote to MacArthur and GHQ, proposing a united front for a Japanese democratic revolution. They undoubtedly thought this was a realistic possibility. The following letter also illustrates the high expectations of veteran Communist Party members for cooperation with GHQ.[1]

> . . . I am a member of the Japan Communist Party and also the secretary of our village farmers' union. During the war, I was thrown into jail twice on the grounds that I was a pacifist. . . . No one but we Communist Party members can crush the obstinate believers in the emperor system, the imperialists, and the thieving war-lovers, and truly lead Japan to democratic nationhood. I look to the headquarters of the Allied powers for your support and determination that we should be allowed to hold power.

Kumaō Tokuhei
Yamanashi Prefecture
December 2, 1945

Clearly these members of the Communist Party did not know that MacArthur had a visceral antipathy toward communism. Apparently, few people realized that GHQ had freed the long-imprisoned leaders of the Communist Party, not as a sign of support for communism, but as a tactic of mobilizing "the enemy of my enemy" to help finish off the militarist forces that the Allies had finally toppled. The occupation forces were fighting a bloodless war to achieve peace on Japanese soil. What appeared to be support for the Communist Party was part of this strategy.

Of course many Japanese, alarmed by this apparent support for the Communist Party, sent appeals to MacArthur. It was undeniable that the influence of the Communist Party had spread rapidly, especially in the labor unions, and conservatives were dismayed. The following letter conveyed this concern in a most straightforward manner. (The date and the writer's name and address are missing, but the letter was received by the ATIS on May 12, 1947.)

To His Excellency MacArthur:

The Japanese people today are grateful for Your Excellency's immeasurable benevolence. This treatment is contrary to what we had expected from defeat, and I am utterly filled with gratitude. I firmly believe that, given the generosity and kindness from you and America, happiness will come in Japan's future and everlasting peace will also come. However, the biggest fear of the Japanese people is the spread of communism. Moreover, communism hinders the peaceful development of the world. True peace cannot be maintained with two ideologies confronting each other throughout the world. In Europe [Asia?] the most direct evidence of this is China, at the root of which is the Soviet Union. Without restraining the Soviet Union, it is absolutely impossible to check the spread of communism in Japan, as well as the communists in China, and also in Europe.

Your Excellency! Except for the Communist Party, all of the Japanese people believe in you and America and denounce communism. Please suppress the Communist Party for the sake of peace in Japan and the world. . . . Please be firm in doing this. The Japanese people will absolutely support you. This is the true feeling of the Japanese. I beseech you.

Please take care of yourself.

Sincerely,
A Patriot

This letter was probably written by an ordinary citizen who just happened to possess the daring to write to MacArthur. In contrast to its simple anticommunist sentiment, the next letter is a well-argued anticommunist thesis written by someone with intellectual leanings. There is no name or address on the letter, which was signed "A Citizen of Kyoto."

September 22, 1946
The Honorable General MacArthur

Dear Sir:

I convey to you my deep admiration for the wisdom and virtue of America represented by your policies. I firmly believe that the democratization of Japan can develop only with the pro-American sentiment of the Japanese people, so I am always concerned about the appearance of the slightest anti-American feelings among the people as a hindrance to Japan's democratization.

From this point of view, I believe the primary object of concern at present is the activity of the Communist Party. I am absolutely not a supporter of capitalism. I believe that as the people's enlightenment advances, production should be socialized, but this should only be done democratically with the people's full understanding. However, the Communist Party is trying to achieve this goal without the people's understanding, through secrecy and radicalism. Moreover, they are trying to achieve this under the guidance of the Soviet Union. For the sake of Japan's democratization, this requires our closest attention. I can summarize this under the following three points:

(1) Even if at times Communist Party members pretend to be pro-American, this is only because it happens to benefit their development, or it coincides with the Soviet Union's interests. In other words, being pro-American is not the priority, being pro-Soviet comes first. That is why over the past several months Communists have secretly turned anti-American. At present, Japanese people everywhere are hearing criticism of America from Communists.

(2) The Communists' criticism of America seems to concentrate on the argument that the present American government is conservative and reactionary, and that progressive elements in America are repressed. They describe conservatives as reactionaries, communism as the most ideal form of democracy, and they argue that being pro-Soviet is most progressive. As a

noteworthy example of this trend, I present to you an article from the Asahi
shimbun *dated September 22. . . .*

The enclosed clipping was a seven-column analysis of the resignation
of commerce secretary Henry Wallace, the former vice president, following a speech on foreign relations. The headline, "Taking a Shot at
the Anti-Soviet Faction," indicated the article was favorable toward
Wallace, who had advocated reconciliation with the Soviet Union.

The Asahi shimbun *has often printed such tactically Communist analysis and commentary, and I have secretly admired your headquarters' toler-
ance in allowing it. However, I absolutely do not believe that it has a good influence on the true democratization of Japan.*

*(3) Beginning with the railway general strike, numerous vicious strikes
have occurred under the leadership of the Communist Party. There is a real
danger that the arrogance of the extreme left will cause the extreme right to
rise in reaction. As long as your headquarters is in Tokyo, the extreme right
may not rise up, but once you leave Tokyo, Japan may become a major bat-
tleground between the extreme right and extreme left. This is because the
"tyranny of the masses" aroused under the leadership of the extreme left will
eventually threaten the existence of Japan, and there is a possibility that the
extreme right will rise in reaction to this. In such a case, it goes without saying that both the extreme left and the extreme right are anti-American and
anti-democratic. Therefore, I would like to ask your headquarters to halt the
communist conspiracy to turn democracy into the "tyranny of the masses."
The present Japanese government does not have the ability to stop it.*

*At a time like this, newspapers play the most important role. However,
with the exception of the* Yomiuri shimbun, *all employees of newspapers,
wire services, and radio stations throughout Japan belong to something called
the All Japan Union of Newspaper, Wire Service, and Broadcast Workers.
The chairman of this union is Kikunami of the* Asahi shimbun *editorial staff,
and the vice chairmen are Suzuki (Tōmin), who was at the* Yomiuri shimbun *until recently, and Makino of the* Mainichi shimbun. *These three are
all secret members of the Communist Party. Kikunami is simultaneously head
of the Congress of Industrial Labor Unions of Japan. In this way, the Communist Party controls the newspapers, wire services, and radio throughout
Japan. Through very clever methods of expression, they strive to stupefy and*

drive the people beyond the bounds of common sense. The one that is most clever at this is the Asahi shimbun.

However, most of the Japanese people do not respect or trust their newspapers very much, so the efforts of this newspaper have not had much effect, but still, one has to rely on newspapers to know current affairs, so, before you know it, you are influenced by the press. At present those who are affected the most are ignorant scholars and immature young people. Moreover, in the future of Japan's economy, there will be numerous opportunities for the Communist Party to advance its conspiracy through the press.

Having lingered here with this self-confident anticommunist intellectual, one wonders whether there was any point in communicating this kind of information about communist activities to MacArthur in the context of occupied Japan. MacArthur's right-hand man, Major General Charles Willoughby, was the head of G-II, the Military Intelligence Section whose responsibilities included civil and counter intelligence, and he had informants placed deep inside the Communist Party. The record shows that detailed reports of important secret meetings of the party were passed on to G-II and to MacArthur the very day they occurred. It was also hardly necessary to alert the anticommunist MacArthur to the dangers of the Communist Party. Of course, the writer sent the letter believing it was necessary because he was the one who best understood the danger. So please bear with him a little longer.

I am one who holds a somewhat favorable attitude towards the Socialist Party. However, within this party, there are secret members of the Communist Party and quite a few opportunists who may turn communist any time. The present battle plan of the Communist Party is to first help bring about a socialist government and then to extend it to the next stage of revolution. Whether consciously or unconsciously, most of the newspapers in Japan seem to fall in line with this strategy of the Communist Party. It is most desirable for Japan to have our Socialist Party become a healthy party like the Labor Party of Great Britain. The establishment of a counter force to the Communist Party is the most pressing problem facing Japan, and it is also the last and largest task for the American democratization of Japan. They are planning to brainwash judges, attorneys, policemen, teachers, and bureaucrats. It is my firm belief that America's goal of democratizing Japan may lie in a victory over communism. If so, I must appeal to you that now is the time for drastic measures.

In conclusion, from the bottom of my heart I pray to God for Your Excellency's health, the success of your occupation, and the sound recovery of Japan.

Respectfully yours,
A Citizen of Kyoto

Regardless of whether it was of any use to MacArthur, the urge to notify him of the dangers of the Communist Party and its activities took many forms. Among them was a secret report that the personnel office of NHK's central broadcasting station in Nagoya had been taken over by the Communist Party, and a firsthand account of an ongoing strike at the *Yomiuri shimbun*.

SUPPORT FOR THE COMMUNIST PARTY

Surprisingly, along with the letters warning of the activities of the Communist Party, letters in support of the party came to MacArthur's office from ordinary citizens who were not communists. The following letter, for example, was from a seventy-four-year-old man who had been evacuated from Tokyo to the countryside in Miyagi Prefecture. It was written by brush in dark black ink. The style is old-fashioned, but the flexibility of thought is amazing for a man his age.

February 1946
The Honorable Supreme Commander for the Allied Powers,
General MacArthur

With great esteem, I offer my letter to Your Excellency, supreme commander for the Allied powers, General MacArthur.

Under our constitution, the emperor as commander in chief holds total military authority over the army, navy, and air force, and by this absolute authority declarations of war and mobilization of the army and navy, etc., are issued. Therefore, in theory, even if only formally, it is obvious that the emperor bears the ultimate responsibility for war. Groups such as the Liberal

Party and the Progressive Party, who support the emperor and the emperor system in the spirit of guarding the national polity, are only wearing a mask of democracy to fool the people; in reality they still support the emperor's absolute power, the zaibatsu, and the privileged class. They are the people's enemies who obstruct the people's rights, and under these conservative Liberal and Progressive Parties, to hope for true democracy and people's rights is comparable to looking for fish in a tree; it is absolutely impossible.

To insist on the emperor's war responsibility so clearly was a very rare thing among this man's generation at that time. Moreover, he calls the parties that support this "war criminal" the people's enemies, under whom there is no possibility that democracy can be achieved. If so, what party can steer Japan's future?

The Communist Party stands at the top, because with impartial judgment they discarded the empty promises of the national polity, and they continued to pursue democracy, people's rights, and freedom for many years, and persevered under oppression by bureaucrats and militarists, without bending their ideology. I think that the people under the absolute monarchy became submissive slaves and do not have the ability to understand the true meaning of the Communist Party and socialism. They are unable, on their own, to fight the emperor worshipers of the present government and the Liberal and Progressive Parties, or to build the foundation for people's rights and welfare. But, if today's opportunity is lost, I feel there will never be any hope for democracy, liberty, and liberation.

Your Excellency, Commander MacArthur, I beseech you to completely eliminate the former militarists, and in the general election for representatives who will be the motivating force for the cultural revival of a peaceful Japan, to eradicate the conservative and obstinate Progressive and Liberal Parties. I sincerely hope for your great and holy assistance for the triumphant victory of the revolutionary reformism of the Communist Party.

In conclusion I offer my prayers for Your Great Excellency's health and happiness.

I am definitely not a member of the Communist Party.

Iwabuchi Daisō
Seventy-four years old

Photo 10.1   Some 250,000 people gathered on the grounds of the imperial palace for Food May Day on May 19, 1946, following quickly on the heels of the first postwar May Day demonstration. Among the banners were many calling for the restoration of the school lunch program. The Dai-Ichi Building, headquarters for the occupation, is visible in the background. Source: Kyōdō News Service

It makes one smile to see that this old man, who asked His Excellency for holy assistance for the victory of the Communist Party, has added in small characters at the very end, "I am definitely not a member of the Communist Party." Among the various strata of the people there must have been quite a few like this man, who supported and were sympathetic to the Communist Party but were not members. The next letter, undated, also asks MacArthur, in a simple manner, to "protect" the Communist Party as the driving force for democracy.

I believe that the Socialist Party and the Communist Party should be strongly protected so that they may be able to promote the movement for democratization without being harassed by reactionary elements. Under present social conditions, the people of the Communist Party are treated as traitors and are battered with violence. How can anyone seriously think of the de-mocratization of Japan?

Sugiyama Ichirō
Shimane Prefecture

PRO-AMERICAN FEVER VERSUS PRO-SOVIET FEVER

The logic of the next letter seems strange, but if read with an under-standing of the situation described so far, perhaps it will be easier to comprehend.

March 11, 1946
The Honorable General MacArthur

Your Excellency, General MacArthur:
    The present cabinet has announced its epoch-making, progressive con-stitutional revision bill, and having received Your Excellency's overall sup-port, this constitution clarifies Japan's future. It is my observation that the adoption of an American form of democracy under the emperor system is a decision to establish a Japanese-style democracy. I express my full sup-port and the support of the Japanese people. This will mean an end to de-bates on the emperor system, the rejection of communism, and the import-ing of American-style democracy. Japan will benefit from American culture in general, and movies will likely be imported in large numbers. The question of whether Japan should be Americanized or Sovietized has been resolved. This is natural, since the United States sacrificed the most during the war against Japan.

This writer notes that Japan has chosen the road to Americanization, and yet he feels that the danger of communism has not passed and rec-ommends to MacArthur a number of anticommunist measures.

Nihilistic young Japanese are fascinated by communism and are joining the Communist Party in great numbers. Oh motherland Japan, how dangerous!

(a) General MacArthur, you have supported the emperor system in the draft constitution, so please prohibit political activities against the emperor system.

(b) Please prohibit political activities advocating the negation of private property.

(c) Please prohibit democracies other than American democracy.

I await Your Excellency's proclamation regarding the above three points. Children are very fond of American troops, and the streets are filled with their voices shouting hello, hello. I am certain that if prowar materials are eliminated from school texts, future Americanization will not be far off.

Viewing American movies is most effective for reeducating Japanese youth. Before the war, Mr. Smith Goes to Washington *and* The Citadel *were the last American movies before they were cut off. After the war, the first time they were exposed to dazzling American movies like* His Butler's Sister *and* Madame Curie, *young men and women quickly began praising American culture and gossiping about American stars.*

Will pro-American fever win out through movies, or will pro-Soviet fever win through propaganda? Future developments will be watched closely.

I pray for Your Excellency's happiness and health.

Respectfully,
Yamada Ryōnosuke
Ichikawa City

Despite the writer's apparent optimism regarding the new constitution and the power of American cinema to win over Japan's youth, he remains concerned about the latent influence of communism. His concluding remark, "Future developments will be watched closely," reminds one of a weak-kneed news commentary, but he's not actually a fence-sitter. He is concerned about the strength of pro-Soviet sentiment: "Oh motherland Japan, how dangerous!" Because of the latent influence of the Communist Party, he implies that Japan will inevitably follow the road to communism, unless the United States steps in to rescue the country. This message is a form of intimidation by the weaker party. This tendency is also evident in the following postscript, which was appended to the February 1946 letter from Yagi Chōsaburō, the enthusiastic supporter of U.S.–Japanese union introduced in chapter 1. It is something like a frightening mask worn by a coward.

Postscript

If by any chance Japan were to suffer the bad fortune of not being rescued by your country, Japan's movement toward the communist system would probably become inevitable. Japan stands at a crossroads and must choose either to be rescued by the compassion of your country through Japanese–U.S. annexation, or if not, to reconstruct under the communist system. Rather than poor Japan reviving under communism, I firmly believe that being rescued in liberalism by your country's hand will bring the greatest happiness and prosperity. However, if Japan is to maintain its independence, I regret that the communist system may be the only way we can manage. I am sure of this. I must cry out for U.S.–Japanese annexation and raise public awareness before the coming peace treaty is concluded.

PLEASE PURGE UNWORTHY PARTY MEMBERS

We opened this chapter with a letter from a communist appealing to General Headquarters for a united front, and we return here to another urgent request, this time from a local committee of the Communist Party. It was dated June 25, 1946, and came from the West Kure district committee in the city of Takaoka in Toyama Prefecture. Soizumi Tomonori, perhaps the committee's representative, is listed as the return addressee.

We offer our congratulations on the recent establishment of the remarkable popular front by the party headquarters. We were quite astonished to see the name of K. N. [I will use only his initials] among the members of the Toyama Regional Committee of the Communist Party. Actually he did join the Communist Youth League and we were comrades in the same cell, but long before the war in about 1933, he converted and started a business, displaying extreme Jewish-type managerial individualism. The townspeople gossiped about him, amazed at his complete turnaround. When the war started, he moved to the extreme right and became a student at the Tateyama Juku (headed by Mr. Daidō, who was later purged). After two months of indoctrination, he became an enthusiastic nationalist, and he advocated unity with the emperor to everyone he met. He became chief secretary of the Society to Serve the Nation through Commerce and

*was also a leader of the Imperial Rule Assistance Association. He used to
exclaim that he would offer everything to the emperor.*

*In 1944, when fierce fighting began on Guadalcanal between Japan and
the United States, he made contact with Yukawa Shigeo (Kiyokawa Shigeo),
a survivor of the February 26th incident of 1936 [an attempted military
coup], in the city of Kumamoto, Kumamoto Prefecture, and advocated imperial-way economics. He then proposed building a branch aircraft factory in
accord with the imperial-way economics prescribed by Yukawa in order to
win the war. He screamed with the most extreme nationalism, and by saying
that those who did not join the Demachi branch of the Tōhi Society [a nationalist organization] are not human beings, he was able to recruit members,
collect their thumbprints in blood, force members to go through* misogi *[a
Shinto purification ritual using cold water], collect money that was as precious as blood to the poor masses, and through daily meditation promote the
society's ideology. And when the aircraft factory fell through from lack of capital, he led a hundred and thirty of his colleagues and joined the Kureha aircraft company.*

*His activities during that time were violations of the Potsdam Declaration.
He is the very model of an activist in the leadership of antidemocratic organizations and the local leadership of nationalist organizations, which GHQ
considers undesirable, and as such he should have come under the Purge Directive. At a time when the Communist Party is considered the true democratic organization, if someone like K. N., who should be a "Category G" war
criminal [sic, actually a reference to the purge directive], is allowed to be on
the Toyama Regional Committee, the committee members will be considered
opportunist corrupt officials and the loss of trust in the region will be great. It
is our hope that you will investigate in his hometown, where there are many
former members of the Tōhi Society who worked with him who can attest to
the truth. We would like to have him expelled. If you do not purge him, the
Communist Party itself will be doubted and people will move further away
day by day, until the people will come to harbor extreme hatred and opposition to the party, so for the future activity of the party please take action.*

Representatives,
West Kure District Committee
Communist Party

The content of this letter would be great material for a tragicomedy, and it also brings into the open some of the problems the Japan Communist Party was facing during that time. Stories of prewar Communists who converted and then became fervent, sometimes fanatic ultranationalists were not unusual. The political cartoonist Katō Etsuro is a famous example.[2] The problem was that some of these enthusiastic collaborators in the war effort reconverted and returned to the Communist Party after the war. Aside from some notorious converts like Sano Manabu and Nabeyama Sadachika, it seems that the party in most cases did not question the wartime activities of these "born-again former comrades" and allowed them back into the party. This was what lead to the tragicomedy of the letter above. However, what was more serious to the Japan Communist Party of that period was the fact that the party organization was not able to deal with the expulsion of problem members on its own, and that members would secretly turn to MacArthur's headquarters to do it for them. Perhaps it goes without saying that communists are also human, and that turning to the one with the most authority was a natural human tendency.

RECORD OF A TURNCOAT

The final letter in this chapter is a report to MacArthur from a young man who joined the Communist Party full of hope but quickly changed his mind after exposure to American culture. It is an amusing account of conversion.

July 4, 1947
To General MacArthur

Dear Sir:
  Please forgive me for this poor paper and the impolite form I am using.
  I have been active as a cell member of the Japan Communist Party from April of last year to the present, but I have been reading Your Excellency's clear and appropriate directives and statements issued from time to time, and I was so moved that I could not help but have a change of heart.

One also learns the meaning of liberty by viewing movies like Boys Town and Going My Way.

Another thing that thoroughly affected my mind is that after August 15 a portion of foreign trade will be reopened. (August 15 is the anniversary of surrender, and it is also the anniversary of my liberation. I say this because during the war I endured a suffocating life for three years and two months at the former Sasebo Naval Arsenal and the former Hikari Naval Arsenal. At that time, the tyranny of the militarists was manifested as clubs that were used to instill the military spirit, and we had to put more effort into escaping beatings than into manufacturing weapons. This resulted in long-term absence and desertion. We endured the unendurable, both economically and spiritually, and fervently waited for the day when we would be liberated. On August 14, B-29s bombed Hikari Arsenal. Burning black smoke, total destruction of the factory, the death of comrades, and my rebirth. The next day, August 15, Japan's surrender, the loss of face of the military and bureaucracy, confusion all around, our liberation and ecstasy. I cannot forget the B-29s. I love Japan. I thought, we should make Japan into a country of liberty, Fuji, and cherry blossoms.)

Together with your permission for the reopening of trade you are allowing Antarctic whaling, mining of phosphate ore on Angaur Island, etc., etc., For today's Japan this timely permission has the effect of welcome rain in a time of drought.

Japan has little land, a growing population, and few raw materials. I thought that to build a new Japan, we had to adopt socialism, so I joined the Communist Party. But what do you think I learned there? Behind the principle of gaining fundamental human rights, I found the trampling of human rights. Under the beautiful name of liberation there was oppression, and while saying it was for the people's sake, it was for the benefit of a foreign country. What the Communist Party called "liberty" was actually destruction, sacrifice, and tyranny. Described in a formula, it would become:

Destruction + sacrifice + tyranny = Communist Party's liberty.

I am against such liberty.

I admire the supreme commander of the Allied powers, General MacArthur. I support the United States.

By the time this letter reaches the general, I probably will have left the Communist Party.

In closing, I pray for the General's health and praise forever his distinguished service of bringing good tidings to East Asia.

From Okumura Kazunori

This young man poured out his feelings over three pages of "poor paper," which I discovered upon turning them over were mimeographed applications for membership, addressed to the Kagawa Regional Committee of the Communist Party. The writer had discarded the party both in body and in spirit.

GRAND PLANS

Throughout the course of the occupation, Japanese continued to send letters with all kinds of requests to MacArthur. What did the recipient, the supreme commander, think when he read them? He had a far more complex personality than the Japanese people of that time could have imagined. For example, two high officials at GHQ who observed him at close hand offered totally opposite interpretations of his character.

Major Faubion Bowers, who was the general's aide and interpreter during the early stages of the occupation, remarked that "MacArthur never listened to others; he was a monologist and when he spoke, he held an emotional confidence in himself."[1] In other words, he was extremely self-confident and never sought other perspectives. In sharp contrast, Colonel Charles L. Kades, the deputy chief of the Government Section who served as a trusted adviser to the general, had this to say: "MacArthur was not arrogant and unapproachable as often reported. He knew his limitations and was thoughtful, and he welcomed opinions from others."[2]

It is likely that MacArthur's personality included both sides. He may not have listened to most opinions, but I am sure he paid attention to worthwhile ideas. One wonders how many of the innumerable thoughts and suggestions offered by the Japanese were considered worthy of his attention. What kinds of ideas were these? Let us begin here with a letter written in English:[3]

Suggestion: Dedication of Non-Sectarian Church in Memory of American war Dead in Token of Crowning Consummation of Service of General MacArthur.

113, 3-chome, Kugayama,
Suginami-ku, Tokyo-to.
1st September 1947.

Sir:

I beg to state that this country was undoubtly on the verge of being collapsed for ever on the eve of the ending of hostility. It is due entirely to your
providential and statesmanship occupation policies which saved her from
eternal ruin. Subsequently the essential framework for political, social and
economical democracy has been founded. Meanwhile, the new constitution
was proclaimed on the 5th of May while the first session of two houses of
representatives and councillors were opened on the 1st of July respectively.
I believe that your men whose blood has been shed for redemption of this
country held under the iron heel of merciless feudalistic militarism for centuries, are following every process and change from heaven above with
cheer and satisfaction.

Speaking of these heroic sacrifices of your nation for the freedom of the
world, there is the following statement in the article "Plain Facts About
Bringing the Bodies Home" in "The Reader's Digest" of past month relative
to the conveyance of 6500 caskets containing the remains of American war
dead:

"The Government expense will be $700 per body returned. The program,
which is to go on for five years will require a total of about $200,000,000.

Many who have attacked the reburial project have asked this question:
"Could not these vast sums be used instead to do good for the living?"
The Social Service Commission of the Protestant Episcopal Church in
New York has asked bitterly, "With millions of people in the world suffering and dying from lack of food, clothing and shelter, would it not be
more truly Christian to feed the hungry, clothe the naked, and minister to
the living, rather than to have the bodies of our beloved dead brought
home?"

I fully endorse the import expressed above. Meanwhile, the General has asserted now and then that Christianity is the foundation of democracy. I entirely agree with you on this point. Accordingly, I would like to make my humble suggestion to you regarding the dedication of a non-sectarian church in
memory of those men whose blood has been shed for redemption of Japan and
crowing consummation of your brilliant service rendered freely in connection

with the resuscitation of this country. As to the site, I should like to suggest a part of the Imperial Palace compound as most fitting and the St. John's Cathedral Church in New York city as a model style of architecture of the church suggested. Finally, I beg to avail myself of this opportunity, Sir, to express my highest esteem.

I have the honour to be,
Sir,
your obedient servant.
[signed] S. Momikura

To General Douglas MacArthur,
Supreme Commander for Allied Forces,
General Headquarters.

Copies of this letter are being sent to the Prime Minister, Governor of Tokyo Metropolis and Editor of "The Nippon Times".

There are two initials—W and B—on the top of the letter, indicating that MacArthur aides Wheeler and Bunker both read it. At the bottom of the letter is "C in C," an abbreviation of commander in chief that MacArthur often used as a short signature, along with "MacA." This indicates that MacArthur also read the letter. One can only guess at his reaction, but he must not have been displeased to read about a plan that would commemorate both the soldiers who gave their lives in the war with Japan and his "brilliant service" to Japan.

Of course no church was ever built on the grounds of the imperial palace, and I am sure the remains of the war dead were returned regardless of the expense. Japanese people have quite an attachment to the ashes of the dead, and Westerners have a likewise strong desire to identify the bodies of their beloved. Besides, no matter how brimful of confidence MacArthur might have been, he was not so thick-skinned as to endorse a plan to build a church in his honor.

In a similar vein, there were many proposals to erect statues of MacArthur. I will introduce a few here. The first was typewritten horizontally on a Japanese typewriter, with the address added by hand, and a large seal pressed next to the writer's name.

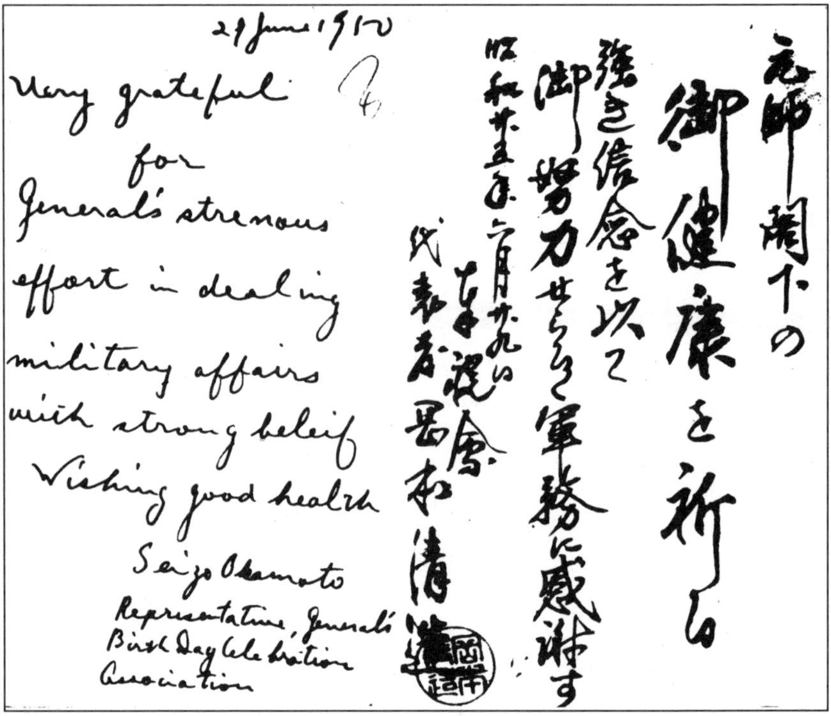

Photo 11.1   A thank-you note to General MacArthur. Source: MacArthur Memorial

April 28, 1948

The Honorable General MacArthur, whom I esteem:

Your Excellency's speeches and activities are the foundation of a peaceful Japan, your footsteps are carving great history, and Your Excellency's deeds are worthy of the respect of the entire world.

At a time when we were liberated from a war that was like a terrible nightmare, and when the light of peace had begun to shine, like a messenger from God you offered us your hand in love and sympathy.

For the unexpected treatment we received, we offer you our gratitude and pledge everlasting friendship to the American people who stand behind you.

I am one who eagerly awaits the conclusion of peace in the near future. I have made a proposal to the Japanese government.

It is a small personal desire of mine, but I am filled with thoughts of realizing it. My hope is to build a peace monument in a prominent place to commemorate the spirits of all the Americans and Japanese who died during the war and to erect a bronze statue of you to be unveiled on the day of the peace treaty as a symbol of lasting friendship between the United States and Japan.

If there were a country that would invade us in front of this peace monument, it would be the enemy of mankind. If there were a country that would invade Japan, a country that declared to the world that it will renounce war for the peace of mankind, that country would be a destroyer of human morality. If such a thing were to happen, I think we would give up on the world and destroy ourselves.

I firmly believe that my proposal is most appropriate for promoting mutual trust and love among the people of the world. In the hope that I may realize the building of the peace monument, I have petitioned the necessary officials of the Japanese government. I would like to ask Your Excellency's favorable disposition and a letter of support in this matter.

I pray for Your Excellency's happiness and for the light of prosperity to fall upon you.

A Japanese who feels friendly to you,
From Yamaura Yasukichi [seal]
664 Narutaki-chō, Nagasaki City

This man's proposal is similar to the previous one: a peace memorial for the war dead of both the United States and Japan, with a bronze statue of the general in front. Although his proposal would be submitted to the Japanese government, he believed his plan could not be realized without MacArthur's support. He enclosed ten yen with a note saying, "This is how much each Japanese person would be required to contribute." He also wrote that a friend from his days in Shanghai had contributed fifty yen to the military government for the building fund. It appears that the writer assumed that GHQ would be the main vehicle for building the peace monument and the statue. There is evidence that MacArthur read this letter, but he probably took no action. The contribution was returned through Colonel Bunker in a letter dated June 5, 1948.

"I WANT TO ERECT A STATUE OF YOUR EXCELLENCY"

The next letter makes a similar proposal, but it includes plans for organizing a "peace memorial society," and the writer includes an appeal to MacArthur for his support. The letter is yet another indication of how brightly MacArthur shone as a symbol of peace in the minds of many Japanese.

March 7, 1948
The Honorable General MacArthur

Dear Sir:

I worship the figure of the general who exerts himself in strenuous efforts to guide Japan's reconstruction, and I convey my deep gratitude, renew my self-reflection, and with deep respect make this request of Your Excellency, the supreme commander for the Allied powers.

With Japan's defeat and the holy Tokyo trials that followed, we were shown for the first time the true picture of Japan's past education, politics, and diplomacy. Belatedly the general public came to realize and reflect on the effects of militaristic education and how militaristic, autocratic politics and diplomacy had deceived the innocent people and dragged them into a reckless and doomed war. The Japanese people deeply apologize for our sins against the people of the world, and vow to God to henceforth actively pursue the democratization of Japan and, in building a peaceful and cultural nation, to seek from the bottom of our hearts the everlasting peace that humanity yearns for. We are eager to be the first among all nations in putting our hearts and minds to the task of building a peaceful world. However, there is nothing that suggests domestic stability in the politics, economics, and culture of present-day Japan, nothing for the people to believe in. It is truly a chaotic situation. Public order is especially in disarray, morality has declined, and the general public is confused about their future.

Therefore we should, with the enthusiasm of the people, erect as a symbol of peace a memorial and a bronze statue of the general for whom the Japanese people have the ultimate respect. Under this symbol, Japan should free itself from the evil roots of its past and plan the reconstruction of a future, blessed Japan. To develop an active moral movement to build a cultural nation that will win the love and respect of the world, I am enclosing a prospec-

tus and offering it to the general. The society for this purpose hereby reverently seeks your permission.

Respectfully yours,
Ōyama Namio [seal], Representative
Peace Memorial Society (temporary name)
5, 188 Ōihara-machi
Shinagawa-ku, Tokyo

According to the brief biography that was enclosed, Ōyama served as secretary to Ōtani Kōen, chief abbot of Higashi Honganji, a major temple in Kyoto. He was a devout Buddhist, and he later started a successful business. It is interesting that the prospectus he enclosed was in his own name; it mentioned only the statue and the peace memorial and was dated August 15 of the previous year, 1947. Most probably it was a private endeavor that made little progress, so he designed a "peace memorial society" and tried to obtain MacArthur's approval for it. Let me quote a part of the prospectus:

First, through the enthusiasm of the Japanese public, erect a statue of the saintly General MacArthur and a peace memorial as symbols of peace that the people would emulate as their goals in life. Standing under the memorial, the people will pledge from the bottom of their hearts not to repeat the horrors of war. Based on the grand laws of the new constitution and a broad perspective of the nation's present condition, the people would put their minds and energy together and strive to overcome the difficult situation with a spirit of self-reliance. We would solemnly vow to the Allied forces that we will build a democratic and righteous Japan, and ring the bell of peace and righteousness from the peace memorial, thus contributing to the active movement for world peace. . . .

I am often impressed by how earnest the Japanese people of that period were. Looking back today, one senses an obsequiousness toward the occupation rulers. However, those who were involved in these efforts sincerely regarded MacArthur as a symbol of peace and were genuinely grateful for the outcome of the occupation. These people were not an exceptional minority but rather represented the main thrust of national sentiment.

There were other requests for permission to form international peace organizations, with the placement of a MacArthur statue as one part of the program, while others proposed to go it alone but wrote to MacArthur, seeking his approval. The following letter came from a remote corner of the Tsugaru district of Aomori Prefecture in northern Japan. The original Japanese letter has not been located, but the English translation by ATIS has survived:

#132 1 January 1950
SUBJECT: Establishment of a Monument and Memorial Statue in General MacArthur's Honor.
TO: General MacArthur, Supreme Commander of the Allied Powers.
FROM: SOMA Koso, teacher of the Nakamura Middle School, Nishitsugaru-gun, Aomori Prefecture.

I wish you a happy new year.

Eighty million people of Japan, hailing the 5th New Year since the end of the war, are deeply grateful to you for kindness which could not be expressed by any great writer or any eloquent speaker.

In old days we worshiped, morning and evening, before a portrait of the Emperor as if he were a god but now-a-days we do so before that of General MacArthur.

Japanese people though they are a defeated nation, are enjoying happy days without any pain and trouble. This is quite attributable to your kindness. Everytime we receive food rations, we are grateful for your kindness with tears in our eyes.

Whenever a meeting of public bodies is held, we are always stressing that we must continue our present pains-taking livings in order to reduce the heavy burden of the American people. School boys and girls also are investigating the same subject at their meetings of school self-governing parties [bodies]. I believe that when these boys and girls become grown-ups they will repay the America's kindness.

Japanese people are, in nature, very simple and submissive to their traditions and therefore if guided well they could be developed to any extent. Now-a-days there may be some boys and girls who do not know the Emperor but I am sure that there is no one who does not know General MacArthur throughout the nation. Even old men living the heart of a

*mountain knows him well. I believe that the Japanese race will appreciate
your kindness forever.*

What a lofty paean to MacArthur! And the writer is the very embodiment of seriousness. It is quite surprising that this letter was written not during the early phase of the occupation but in 1950, when
problems with the occupation were becoming increasingly evident.
Once the shining image of MacArthur was established in a place like a
farming village in the northern Tohoku region, it was not easily erased.
It was natural that a desire to build a statue honoring MacArthur would
flow from such adulation, and it is difficult to label it toadying. The letter continues:

*Now I want to propose a plan of erecting a monument and memorial
statue in General MacArthur's honor somewhere in the Imperial plaza in order to commemorate the establishment of a peaceful country.*

*If Japan realizes a peaceful country, abandoning a war, I am sure that not-
a-few countries will follow this example.*

*I, SOMA Koso (real name SOMA Toyojiro), teacher of the Nakamura
Middle School, Aomori Prefecture, am burning with the desire of launching
the above drive.*

*If the understanding for the drive is given, I will make my utmost efforts
together with SASAMORI Junzo, diet-man, and SATO Naotake, president
of the House of Councillors.*

*This drive does not need an approval nor decision of the diet. I want to
erect a monument and statue with donations to be collected from boys and
girls, young people, women and local public bodies.*

*I hope to be instructed whether or not you will accept the whole-hearted
desire of boys and girls and whether or not this attempt is permitted as an act
of the Japanese people who are under the occupation.*

Note

*1. If there is a violation of a law or discourtesy in this letter, please forgive
it as an act of an old man living in the country.*

*In the old days in Japan, a man who appealed directly to the authority was
put to death. But now in Japan so democratized, such a thing can not be
dreamt of.*

1. *I enclosed herewith a ten yen note as I have no stamp (the post office is very distant).*

1. *If unable to get directly your instruction, please let me know it on the newspaper "Asahi Shimbun".*

Translated by [signed] Y. Ito
dtd, 16 Jan. 50

Sasamori and Satō were both members of the Diet representing Aomori Prefecture, and it is easy to see why the writer would want to ally with them. But one wonders if the writer, living in a rural area without even a post office nearby, had any idea of the kind of organization that would be necessary to carry out his plan. Still, that a rural middle school teacher of Japanese or classic Chinese (one can infer this because he uses a pseudonym) wanted to write to MacArthur is another measure of the general's towering presence. On the top of the letter in Colonel Bunker's handwriting was the note "File, No action. B." "No action" probably meant "no way," which was undoubtedly Bunker's actual assessment. Like many similar proposals, this one was dealt with by MacArthur's aides before it reached him. For a proposal to grab the attention of the busy general, it had to be somehow extraordinary. Let us turn to the next letter, which was written in English.

BEHIND THE DESIRE FOR PEACE

Feb. 17, 1950

To: Commander In Chief
Far East
General of The Army
Douglas MacArthur

PETITION

All the honest and thoughtful citizens of Japan have one and only desire, and that is to realize a lasting peace on this earth as soon as possible.

These citizens with the express desire for peace have been inspired by the deeds and teachings of the Holy Buddha who has never even once uttered or acted to destroy peace throughout his 80 years of life. These citizens have fought against class conflict and avoided any utterance or action that will be detrimental to peace.

The birthday of Holy Buddha, which is on April 8th, has been observed year after year with deep significance and with much celebration. This birthday celebration has resulted in a "Flower Festival" liked and welcomed by all the people of Japan. April 8th is coming again soon.

Thinking of the many brethren today who have lost hope from the sufferings of defeated war and sacrificed for the sake of war leaders inspired by wrong ideas, we would like to take the lead in celebrating the "Flower Festival" to foster a happy peace in heaven and on earth.

We deeply appreciate your great effort in realizing world peace and in this respect we humbly request the use of your aircraft in dropping flowers from the sky to mark an unprecedented desire of peace in the history of Japan.

If by your good offices and special permission we are permitted to carry out his "Flower Dropping Flight" or "Peace Flight" we firmly believe the impression will be extremely great.

We humbly request your special permission to carry out this peace loving project.

[signed] Rosen Takashina
Chief Abbot of Buddhist Sodo Sect

To scatter flowers of peace from the sky to celebrate the Flower Festival! The petition asks MacArthur for the loan of an aircraft to accomplish this design, but the scheme itself appears to be Chief Abbot Takashina's own beautiful conception. If he had pulled it off, it would have been the talk of the town for generations to come. However, the general's office first checked with the Civil Information and Education Section because religion was under its jurisdiction. A memorandum dated March 3 from section chief Lieutenant Colonel Nugent to Colonel Bunker advised that the request be denied and the following reply sent:

Although your intention of utilizing the Flower Festival as an occasion for propagation of peace is commendable, it will be impossible to place United

States aircraft at your disposal for the purpose stated in your petition. It is sincerely hoped, however, that your efforts to inspire a desire of peace in the hearts of all Japanese of the Buddhist faith will be successful, and that you may continue in future to exert the spiritual influence at your disposal for this worthy objective.

The reply diplomatically endorsed the spirit of the plan, while denying the request for an American aircraft. But CI&E had other reasons for the denial, as noted at the end of the memo:

> CIE would oppose granting of Abbot Takashina's request even if this were possible, in view of the factional struggles within the Sodo Sect. It is suspected Abbot Takashina, a principal figure in the disputes, hoped that cooperation of SCAP in his Flower Festival stunt would enhance his prestige and undo his opposition.

As might be expected, CI&E had a firm grasp on the realities of Japan. MacArthur signed the memo, "O.K. MacA."

The next letter was another ambitious plan to promote peace that caused perplexity at GHQ. The writer was Nakahama Kiyoshi, a resident of Tokyo, who claimed to be the grandson of John Mung. Mung, originally the fisherman Nakahama Manjirō of Tosa, was rescued at sea by an American whaling vessel at the age of fourteen in 1841, near the end of the Edo period. Through the kindness of the American captain, he was educated in Fairhaven, Massachusetts. After his return to Japan a decade later, he employed his current knowledge of the United States and his language ability as a translator and interpreter during the opening of Japan to the West. According to the grandson's letter, dated December 28, 1949, his aim was to carry out the wishes of his grandfather and his father and establish a "Fairhaven Society" to contribute to human development and world peace through U.S.–Japanese friendship. It will be difficult to raise funds for the new society, the letter stated, so Nakahama had developed a plan to mount an exhibit that would earn money, and he was hoping for MacArthur's support and encouragement. The plan was presented as follows, in English:

Application for Permission of the Loan of the Films, Still Pictures, & Other Articles Showing the Power of Atomic Bomb, the Strength of Armed Forces of the United States of America.

Purpose: To enlighten the Japanese public in the formidable power of this weapon in future warfare and to give the people a firmer conviction that a closer cooperation with America is an unshakable necessity for Japan's future prosperity and safety.

Reasons: The announcement made some time ago by the American Government to the effect that an atomic bomb is also completed by Soviet Russia struck our people with astonishment and apprehension, shaking our people's trust in the military strength of America to a certain degree. A divided trust may give rise to the anti-Democratic movement and may cause the possibility of exaggerating and over-estimating the real strength of Soviet Russia. To show the Japanese public how America stands today in modern military matters will minimize the general apprehension brought about by Russian claim of having completed an atomic bomb.

Program: To conduct a visual exhibit of the power of American atomic bomb, of American Land, Sea and Air Forces, and of the newest inventions in the military field, by means of films, pictures, and other visual forms, all over Japan. An exhibition trip to all major cities and even to small towns may be conducted, using department stores, shrines, temples, auditoriums, schools, and factories as places of exhibition.

Articles desired for Loaning: Films, pictures, and other visual articles fit for visual educational purposes, being naturally only those that the American military authorities are willing to loan for such publicity use. Descriptive of explanatory notes will also be helpful.

After reading this letter, MacArthur wrote on the top of it "To Col. Nugent to handle directly. MacA." In a reply to Nakahama, dated January 9, 1950, Nugent wrote, "Careful consideration of the proposed display . . . has forced the conclusion that it would be inadvisable." The following reasons were given:

It is difficult to believe that many of your countrymen are seriously alarmed over the ability of the Soviet Union to set off an atomic explosion. And nowhere in the world, surely, is there less need than in Japan to arrange a special display of American military might to convince skeptics that the United States is not without the strength to meet the challenge of any aggressor. Moreover, such a display would seem inappropriate in a country which has renounced war and wants to concentrate on peaceful pursuits.

It was fine to be pro-American, but GHQ probably felt that this proposal was going too far, and perhaps also concluded that forcefully reminding the Japanese people of the atomic destruction of Hiroshima and Nagasaki was not necessarily in the interest of the United States. This was shortly before the beginning of the Korean War, and in his New Year's message MacArthur had begun to emphasize the need for Japan to have the right to self-defense. But, for the most part, Janus was still displaying his peaceful face and concealing the face of war.

NUMEROUS PROPOSALS ON THE KOREAN WAR

But the stream of history flows rapidly. At dawn on June 25, 1950, the North Korean army crossed the 38th parallel and attacked the South. It is said that when MacArthur heard the news, he instantly became ten years younger. Aide-de-camp Bunker compared the general to a fire horse that gets excited by the smell of fire and becomes several times stronger than normal.[4] Janus now turned his warrior face to the fore.

It was natural for the Japanese to offer a variety of advice to the fighting general. In a letter in English dated July 20, the right-wing leader and former "Class A" war crime suspect Kodama Yoshio argued that an Asian army could better fight an Asian enemy, and he offered his services.

July 20, 1950

General of the Army, Douglas MacArthur,
Supreme Commander for the Allied Powers,
General Headquarters, Dai Ichi Bldg.,
Tokyo.

Your Excellency:

Please allow me the liberty of stating my frank opinion concerning the Korean Incident. Leaving aside all arguments, I am of the conviction that the defense of South Korea from the communist invasion is in itself a preliminary skirmish to the ultimate communist infiltration of the Japanese homelands. In other words, the result of this conflict to the Japanese is a matter of either life or death. The sacrifices of the American troops keeps mounting with the passing of days but the present situation does not even allow the Japanese to wave their flag in expression of gratitude to the troops leaving Japan for the front.

We are aware that the communists are actively scattering anti-war and anti-American handbills and leaflets on our streets but we are equally aware of the conspicuous absence of posters and leaflets expressing our gratitude and cheering your actions.

Your Excellency, from my long experience on the continent I firmly believe that the defensive warfare cannot be terminated in a short period with an army of fifty or even a hundred thousand troops and no matter how many aircrafts may be used. My reason for this conclusion is that this is a war between men and mud. Whether the enemy may be North Koreans or Chinese Communists they are merely inexhaustible mud flung on the outside world by the mighty steam shovel of the USSR.

My conclusion is simple. The ones who ably understand the orientals are the orientals themselves and the ones who can successfully oppose an oriental must himself be an oriental. Of course, it seems impossible for the present Japanese to immediately take the field in cooperation with your troops because of international complications but for a Japanese to become a member of the United States Forces and cooperate in that manner is comprehensible.

My conscience does not allow me to stand akimbo and observe the present situation from the sidelines as an outsider and see Americans sacrificed when the question involves the very life or death of the Japanese.

My past is that of a nationalist and militarist and the proper authorities in your Headquarters are familiar with my record of three years in Sugamo Prison as an A class war crimes suspect. I wish to frankly state and with the strongest conviction that the country and people who gave the strongest opposition to the United States in World War II, are today, the firmest and strongest of friends.

Your Excellency, I wish to request your approval of sending me and my numerous trusted friends to South Korea immediately as members of your troops in order to cooperate with your men on the field.

And if our blood should flow and if we are killed on the field of battle alongside your men I believe that it could be sufficiently proved that the existence of the nationalists of the past were never a threat to the United States.

I remain,
Your obedient servant,
[signed] Y. Kodama

It is a measure of how quickly the Cold War transformed the atmosphere surrounding the occupation that Kodama, a little over a year after being released from prison (the charges against him, as well as those against future prime minister Kishi Nobusuke and seventeen others, were dropped on the grounds of insufficient evidence immediately after the first round of war crimes trials ended in December 1948) could propose returning to active duty, at the side of his former enemy, under the mantle of anticommunism.

Other former military leaders were of a like mind. The former military attaché to the Japanese embassy in Washington, Itami Matsuo, a retired lieutenant general who boasted a personal acquaintance with MacArthur but had never received a reply to the many letters he had written since the occupation began, sent the following note, handwritten in English:

July 28, 1950

My dear General,

I shall be exceedingly pleased, if you kindly give me the chance of talking with you quite confidentially in haste, in order to tell you my own humble views about the plan of war operation in Corea, of which I believe myself that this plan might be the most effective and easily practicable way under the actual situation in Corea.

Yours sincerely
M. Itami
366 Ikejiri, Setagaya, Tokyo
Tel. Setagaya 721.

Photo 11.2   *General MacArthur leads an inspection tour of the beachhead at Inchon, Korea, soon after the Marines stormed the enemy-held port on September 15, 1950. Accompanying MacArthur are Seventh Fleet commander Vice Adm. Arthur D. Struble (left), and First Marine Division commander Maj. Gen. O. P. Smith (right).* Source: *U.S. Army*

There is no evidence that MacArthur paid any attention to these proposals, but people kept on sending letters with ideas and suggestions. The following letter, proposing a million-strong "volunteer defense force," was sent by a member of the Lower House of the Diet. It is a long letter, typewritten in English, which I would like to reproduce in detail because it offers a representative conservative perspective on communism.

28 July 1950
General of the Army Douglas MacArthur
Supreme Commander for the Allied Forces
General Headquarters
Tokyo, Japan

Dear sir:
The Korean crisis, with its grave implications on the future of the United Nations and of Japan, emboldens me directly to address this appeal to you.

On 18 July, 1950, I was prompted by the same reason to submit the same suggestion to Maj-Gen. William Marquat, whom I have had the pleasure of meeting on several occasions connected with our domestic problems. My proposal calls for immediate preparations for the organiza-tion of a Volunteer Defense Force consisting of Japanese servicemen under American control for the stabilization of Japan and, whenever needed, for giving aid to the U.S. and U.N. forces engaged in the struggle against Communism.

My conviction in the urgency of this need and strong desire to reach with it all the highest levels of General Headquarters which might be interested in the matter lead me to quote the following pertinent paragraphs from my let-ter to General Marquat:

The United States occupation of Japan is a unique phenomenon with-out parallel in the history of the world. Nowhere else and at no other time has there been such a practice of occupation policies based upon such sym-pathy and consideration toward the conquered people, based upon the high ideals and traditions of Democracy and the precepts of free institutions. In this fact is rooted the very great admiration, respect and feeling of trust that have been sprung among the Japanese people toward General MacArthur.

Now war has broken out in neighboring Korea. American troops in Japan are being called upon to fight—at the sacrifice of their lives—in Korea to re-sist the Red invasion. For us to watch these events, perforce as onlookers, with folded arms, is no easy experience.

The problems of Korea has a direct bearing on Japan. The two countries are separated only by a narrow strip of sea. Their intercourse dates back in history for over ten centuries. For a period of 40 years the Korean people were under Japanese administration. There are many Japanese who are thoroughly familiar with all things Korean, including the natural geographical features of this country and the manners and habits of its people. The Japanese and the Korean peoples both speak a common language.

In the present circumstances it is my feeling that it would do well for the United States to make every possible use of this Japanese familiarity with Korean problems. If authority and permission were to be given I would be among the first to volunteer my services for the organization of a Japanese Volunteer Force, under U.S.–U.N. direction, which could participate in the current war effort against the aggressors. It is my conviction that such a military force in such a joint effort would ultimately prove a worthwhile undertaking and a valuable asset to the United States and the other United Nations.

It may well be said that, while Japan remains an occupied country, any proposition such as this one, coming from a Japanese citizen, is inappropriate, even impertinent. Be it so, may I be so bold as to urge my conviction of the great desirability of preparing the foundations for a Japanese Volunteer Force for, at least, the maintenance of order in Japan and to serve in case of need as an insurance against Communist violence in this country.

The Korean Communist disturbance is a neighborhood fire which threatens to spread to the Japanese homeland almost at any time. Communist insurrection in Japan must be stopped at any cost.

It is certainly ironic to suggest that Japan's colonial occupation of Korea gave the Japanese a superior knowledge of Korean geography, customs, and manners, but there is a certain resonance with Kodama's assertion that Asians are better than Westerners at fighting other Asians. The letter elaborates on how easily developments in Korea might spread to Japan, emphasizing the internal threat of communist insurrection.

That Japanese Communists are vigilantly preparing for such insurrection is all too clear to everyone. The Communist movement in Japan has forged ahead into our government departments, our police forces, our universities

*and colleges and even forming cells in schools of lower grade: and the move-
ment as a whole is conducting its affairs surreptitiously underground. At the
opportune moment, at a given signal, the Reds are prepared to emerge in their
open force to commit chaos, sabotage and civil war. It is against this known
peril that I advocate the organization, with no loss of time, of a Volunteer
Force for protection of the Japanese. The existence of such a force in Japan,
under American management, would give the United States a free hand to
carry on its struggle against the Communists in Korea, wherever else similar
trouble might occur in Asia.*

*I know that this proposal will provoke both approval and violent oppo-
sition in the United States. Opponents to the proposition inevitably will
cite the danger of reviving a Japanese army with all the aggressive, ultra-
nationalistic evil features of the pre-war and wartime Japanese military establishment in attendance. This would be akin to debating the quality of
water when one's house is on fire. Moreover, the fear, I am convinced, is
groundless.*

The letter continues, but it is worth pausing to note that the date
is July 28, 1950. In his open letter to Prime Minister Yoshida dated
July 8, MacArthur had already ordered the establishment of a national police reserve force of 75,000 and an increase in the size of the
coast guard by 8,000. The directive of course did not establish a
Japanese armed force to fight in Korea; as MacArthur later testified
before the Senate Joint Armed Services and Foreign Relations Committee, it was a "lightly armed police force" to maintain internal order after American armed forces were sent to the front. Unsatisfied
by these moves, the writer of the letter suggests the formation of a
much larger volunteer defense force, rooted in the patriotism of the
Japanese people.

*The proposed Volunteer Defense Force for maintenance of order in Japan
would have no room in any part of its organization for those elements of the
former Japanese military establishment who actively organized and waged
war against the Allies in World War II. This type of men are, to this day, responsible to the Japanese people as war criminals and, furthermore, they are
opportunists ready to serve any cause for personal gain. But there are others
who were once members of the Japanese army-navy whose integrity, honesty*

and patriotism as well as a genuine leaning toward the ideals of the Free nations may stand them and the rest of us in good stead in the present hour of danger. On the other hand, unless the Japanese of this brand are properly orientated, there is the constant danger that the Communists, taking advantage of the economic adversity affecting nearly all these men, will seek by all means to draw them into the Red camp.

I propose that the Volunteer Force be a civilian organization consisting of civilians ready to serve their country in a patriotic cause with direction exercised by the United States Army. I believe that its effects would be maximized if the force were organized and maintained "as friend rather than a servant." I believe that it would be best to seek the nucleus of the proposed force among elements of the existing Volunteer Fire Brigades, which function in all parts of Japan as a voluntary unit serving a public cause without pay. I believe that it would be possible eventually to form a Volunteer Force of one-million men and I believe that this could be accomplished within a period of no more than two months if proper steps were taken.

One of the reasons why I advocate earliest possible organization of the proposed Volunteer Force is that, under its system, intelligence would become greatly improved. It would become feasible by making use of its system for the United States as well as the Japanese government to know in advance and prepare for any perils of insurrection.

The force would serve as a military organization for the defense of Japan in the event of a crisis. Barring such a crisis the force would maintain vigilance over our essential public installations and assure their safe operation. It would in addition serve, again under American direction, any useful purposes for the preservation of domestic stability in Japan.

The above is an outline of the proposal, which I feel to be an urgent need at the present moment. I beg that you find time to give this matter your personal consideration and, according to your own judgment, to pass on the matter to the officers of the appropriate departments of General Headquarters.

I would be most happy if you could find time to grant me an opportunity so that I may call upon you in person and discuss further aspects of this matter in detail.

Respectfully yours,
[signed] Koichi Seko
House of Representatives
Tokyo

Sekō Kōichi was a veteran member of the Diet who was first elected from the second district of Wakayama in 1932. As the parliamentary vice minister of home affairs during the first Yoshida cabinet in 1946, he became famous for uncovering hoarded goods as de facto chairman of a committee dealing with the problems of hoarding. When the Democratic Liberal Party was formed in 1948, he refused to participate and aligned himself with the New Liberal Party. At the time this letter was written, he was a member of the Kōsei Club. He had studied in Berlin before the war, and it could be that he wrote this letter in English by himself, or he could have had a good translator.

It was not only conservative members of the Diet who proposed a volunteer force to prevent a communist insurrection. The following was another such proposal, neatly handwritten in English with pen and ink, with a surprising degree of self-confidence for a young man.

N. Kojima
5, 4-chome, Oji,
Kita-ku, Tokyo
6 Jan. 1950 [1951]

Dear General,

I am one of the students of Tokyo University. I am feeling I can not refrain from writing you, the virtual leader of Japan, what I think the best answer to the problem of rearmament of our country. Since your New Year Message to Japanese people showed crystal clear, your deep concern over the matter, I feel it is my duty, as a citizen living in a world of democracy, to make at least a far cry to you regarding the matter. I sincerely hope you will take time to read my opinion.

The day has gone, seems to me, when each nations have their own military power. The countries behind the iron and bamboo curtains under the leadership of Stalin are now organizing an international troop consisting of volunteers to be sent to the battle grounds of Korea. While the free nations still can not reach a conclusion about their power of defence.

The U.N. is the only hope in these dark day which may establish a world of justice and peace. But as revealed in Korean troubles, unless it has a great police power strong enough that an aggressor do not dare to start their evil *plans. What is the most strong factor which is preventing the formation of a powerful world police force? The shortage of man-power.*

Looking back to the situation in Japan. If she again be armed with her own army that will not only give a good excuse to the red army for invading Japan but also will destroy our economy for her poor economy simply can not support such a big well equipped army again. If the U.S. troops left, the result would be the same unless it is made clear not the U.S. but U.N. troops are stationed to keep Japan safe.

Unlike Diet member Sekō, who proposed an independent reserve force for Japan, this university student suggests that sending a Japanese volunteer force to the United Nations will strengthen it and also contribute to the defense of Japan. His attributing the UN's weakness as a police force to insufficient manpower was perhaps ill-informed. At any rate, he continued with detailed plans:

Here is my proposal or you might say to solve these dilemmas. Japan can send some 1,000,000 young energic men to the U.N. to make the police power. The figure is not exaggerating. If you consider the numbers of young men who applied for the Police Reserve (actually an army).

But what the poor Japan can contribute to the U.N. is only man-power. Arms should be supplied from the U.N. I believe this can at least solve several tough problems facing Japan.

First, it is unnecessary to change our precious new constitution renouncing war because those are strictly volunteers to serve in the U.N. police force. They will not fight for Japan but for the world.

Second, Chinese or Russian army will hesitate to cross the Japan Sea because of the severe punishment they may expect from the U.N. police force. Not only Japan but all over the world the red invasion will be checked and the irregually [illegally] taken countries like Korea may eventually be given back.

Third, it can easily solve the most difficult problem of Japan. The over population without resorting to emigration.

Fourth, it may raise the standard of living here by full employment.

I am now praying God to give you the highest divine wisdom which my bring out the everlasting peace on earth.

faithfully yours,
Nakaji Kojima

I will leave the evaluation of this proposal to the reader and only point out that the initial B on this and the previous letter indicates that neither letter reached MacArthur. Even a letter that was written in impressive English had a difficult time getting past aide-de-camp Bunker. There is little doubt that the majority of the proposals addressed to MacArthur met a similar fate.

REGISTER YOUR NAME IN JAPAN, ENCOURAGE FERMENTED SOYBEANS

Such a variety of suggestions were sent in by such a range of people! The letters quoted so far in this chapter came from MacArthur's files, but let me close with several from the abundance of suggestions buried in the GHQ documents at the National Archives II. The first comes from the Government Section file.

February 24, 1950

Dear General MacArthur:

To General MacArthur, who is generous in his tremendous assistance in the reconstruction of Japan, I humbly request you accept the following five requests.

I realize how impolite this note is, but I am sick at the moment and am unable to come to Tokyo. As soon as I recover, I would like to call on you personally.

To rescue Japan from its present situation, I am always deeply hopeful that you will implement these five items.

The Five Items

1. As a citizen of Japan, I offer my gratitude to the United States of America for all the help given us.

2. Please turn the cabinet into a people's cabinet.

3. Please allow photographs of General MacArthur and the emperor to be respectfully posted for the education of the children.

4. For the sake of educating the people of Japan, I request that the general move his family registry to Japan.

5. To protect the people of Japan, I request that the young men of Japan be trained primarily through education without weapons.

End

Nakamura Kuwazō [seal]
3355 Futae-chō, Amakusa-gun,
Kumamoto Prefecture

Although written with impressive calligraphy, the letter is more emotional than most proposals or petitions, and it must have been received with some perplexity. One can't help smiling at the suggestions to post the general's photograph alongside that of the emperor and to move the general's family registry to Japan. The writer had no way of knowing that there is no family registration in the United States, but the Japanese approach of embracing a foreign ruler is once again evident in this letter.

The next letter, from the Economic and Scientific Section files, is a proposal from Yamazaki Hyakuji, a sixty-year-old professor of agriculture at Utsunomiya University.

December 1949

Your Excellency General MacArthur:
 I. Gratitude as a citizen of the world [omitted]
 II. Gratitude as a Japanese
  1. I sent you a letter, dated March 15 of this year.
  2. In it I emphasized the following points:
   (a) Fermented soybeans [itohiki nattō] are the cheese and butter of the Japanese people.
   (b) To maintain and enhance the people's health, everyone in the country should be encouraged to eat fermented soybeans.
   (c) For the above purpose, great increases in soybean production and import are necessary.
   (d) I sincerely request Your Excellency's consideration.
  3. Since the fall fermented soybeans have been appearing in abundance in the storefronts of Kantō, Tōhoku, and Hokkaidō. They have been spreading rapidly in the Tōkai, Kansai, Chūgoku, Shikoku, Kyūshū, and Hokuriku areas.

*4. I believe this to be the result of Your Excellency's consideration. My
heart is overflowing with gratitude.*

Thank you very much; thank you very much. . . .

This is all by way of preface to the main thrust of the letter, "III.
Japanese national character and communism," which begins with the
writer's life story and a historical explanation of the origins of Japanese feudalism, leading to his thesis that "it is most effective to educate the entire Japanese population based on the scientific truth that
'Communism is a utopian society that is impossible to achieve.' I am
practicing this conviction." He makes the interesting observation
that Japanese have a tendency to admire dissidents as heroes and
that "if being under military occupation can be considered a form of
feudalism, to resist and riot against it raises the 'danger of being seen
as heroic and gallant.' Isn't this what Japanese communists are aim-
ing at?" he asks. "I fear it a great deal." Then, like many others who
wrote to MacArthur, he states his primary concern at the end, almost
as an afterthought.

Postscript
*1. To have you fully understand my thoughts, I would like you to read my
manuscript, "The Path of the Japanese People," with the alternate title, "The
Cultural and Global Mission of the Japanese People."*
2. No publisher is willing to print it, so the manuscript is not a book as yet.

It is perhaps not surprising that he had not found a publisher, but the
writer could not have been more serious. Unfortunately, his letter did
not receive the honor of getting into MacArthur's files, as it was di-
verted to the Economic and Scientific Section. One can detect the
glimmer of hope that the supreme commander would read his manuscript, which would impress a potential publisher, but that was not in
the realm of possibility.

Another writer submitted his manuscript, "The Building of a True
Japan and Its Mission," to MacArthur, via Colonel Wheeler in March
1946, and then wrote again three months later, in tortured English, to
inquire as to whether the general had read the book. Having concluded

that it was not likely to happen, he politely included a three-yen stamp and asked that the manuscript be returned.

The stronger a person's belief that MacArthur would read his book, the deeper the agony when his hopes were dashed. Aide-de-camp Wheeler's heartless response dated August 13 stated simply that the manuscript had been misplaced and could not be found.

12

FAVORS TO ASK

YOUR EXCELLENCY IS THE ONLY ONE I CAN TURN TO

 As the absolute ruler of occupied Japan, MacArthur towered above the Japanese people, but there was also a feeling of closeness toward him that gave people hope that the letters they sent him would be read. It seemed only natural for people to write the general asking him to grant a request, mediate a dispute, or even help them obtain a job.

These requests, even more than the other kinds of letters, reflect with great specificity the social conditions of the time and thus represent a unique kind of historical testimony. Moreover, MacArthur served as a sounding board, bringing the writers' personality, intelligence, abilities, and prejudices into clear definition. It is worth noting again that these voices are not passing cries of despair born of the crisis of defeat and occupation, but rather a consistent bass line that can still be heard today. Let us take a look at the characteristics of the Japanese people apparent in these letters.

The first is from a group of people in Hyōgo Prefecture who wanted MacArthur to order a reluctant candidate to run in the election for the national Diet. The letter, written on ceremonial paper in flowing calligraphy, was personally presented to GHQ by a representative of the group. (An English translation, handwritten in pen, was attached, but what follows is a translation from the original Japanese.)[1]

March 5, 1947

Petition

By order of the General Headquarters of the Allied forces, our nation's new constitution is to be promulgated this coming May 3. New members of national and regional legislatures are to be elected before the enforcement of the new constitution, and a democratic Japan will begin anew. All of our people should reverently offer thanks and gratitude, redeem ourselves, and contribute to world peace.

For this important general election, we want to nominate Watanabe Taizō (833 Asaka, Nunugi-mura, Hikami-gun, Hyōgo Prefecture) to run as our candidate for the national Diet, but he has declined for the reasons listed below. We feel that we will not be able to exercise our voting rights in a meaningful manner. As a representative of those who support him, I hereby appeal to you and explain the situation.

Reasons for Declining his Candidacy

1. He worries that he is not qualified for the position due to age, physical health, and education.

2. He feels the existing political parties have forgotten their mission for a defeated Japan. They are only interested in party politics and political advantage, and they engage in political mudslinging, leading the country into confusion and panic, thus alienating the people from politics.

3. He fears that without the support of General Headquarters and without allies in the political parties, as a Diet member he would not be able to participate in parliamentary politics, and he would merely be filling the seat in the Diet.

Citing the above concerns, he refuses to accept the candidacy, but in our locality, people consider his qualifications to be sufficient and would have him as village head or prefectural assembly member; but we hope to have him become a Diet member so that he can make great contributions to world peace. However, he refuses to accept our recommendation, so the only way left is to rely on General Headquarters to order him to run for office and help us fulfill our hopes. We hereby make an appeal regarding this situation.

Satō Shigeki [seal]
Representative of the Supporters
Hikami-gun, Hyōgo Prefecture

The English version actually read, "We hereby appeal . . . to our most honorable Supreme Commander for the Allied Powers," meaning the request was directed to MacArthur himself. According to a memo dated March 7, Colonel Bunker met with the representative and explained that even the supreme commander could not take this kind of action. He suggested that other forms of pressure might be more effective.

The idea that MacArthur should order someone to run in the election so that his supporters can "exercise [their] voting rights in a meaningful manner" is rather amusing, despite the high seriousness of the letter. The tragicomic truth was that these people did not have the least understanding of what democracy or free elections were all about. If we ask MacArthur, somehow it will all work out—that was the spirit of the time, as well as a manifestation of the national tendency to depend on authority figures. Bunker's recommendation apparently did nothing to change the man's mind because he was not a candidate in the April election.

The next letter to MacArthur also concerns an election, the second election for the House of Councilors, which was held three years later on June 4, 1950. The writer had run from the national constituency and failed to win election. The letter begins as follows:[2]

June 1950

To the Only Person in the World I Trust,
Your Excellency General MacArthur:
   There is no one in Japan other than Your Excellency to whom I can appeal about this sad incident. May I please be favored with your attention.
   I am reporting to you about election interference by one of the major Japanese newspapers, the Mainichi shimbun *(of Tokyo), which ignored the election bulletin and printed an erroneous article contrary to the truth. For the sake of unbiased public opinion, I implore Your Excellency to deal strictly with this incident.*
   (1) The Mainichi shimbun *report interfering with the election.*
   On May 27, 1950, an article under the headline "Campaign Broadcasts" in the Mainichi shimbun *said, "Campaign broadcasts by candidates for the House of Councilors are nothing more than pitiful begging, 'Please may I have*

your sympathy,' which is unbearable to listen to." It was in the form of a letter to the editor. This is a malicious slander and totally contrary to the speech I broadcast two days previous on May 25.

In my speech I said, "Among the many candidates, none have policies that get to the gist of politics. I felt deeply that unless I ran, Japan would not be saved, so on the filing deadline I forced myself out of my sickbed and resolutely announced my candidacy. The critical point in today's politics is to distribute American aid to occupied areas to medium and small businesses and save the economy from shortages of capital and the murderous recession. (Dr. Welsh is of the same opinion.) The next is a total reorganization of finance and with new revenue of 300 billion [yen] to carry out a large tax cut. We must save the people from the pitiful situation of suicide and family suicide." I presented this grand platform and received good response from intellectuals.

Besides, I have been a member of the board of directors of the Gakudō Society [formed around the statesman Ozaki Yukio, whose pseudonym was Gakudō] for many years and have been invited to speak at many places as Ozaki Yukio's representative. Ozaki's philosophy was absolutely opposed to the approach of "please may I have your sympathy" in campaign speeches, so why would I say such a thing! (The recording from the broadcast company should make this clear.) Contrary to the truth, the newspaper had slandered me, so that very day by special delivery I sent a request addressed to the editor in chief for the retraction of their article.

(2) Request for retraction ignored.

The Mainichi shimbun ignored my request to rescind their erroneous article, and they never ran a correction.

(3) Moreover, they ignored the election bulletin.

The Mainichi shimbun not only ignored the above request for retraction, but on the day before election, June 3, in a front-page column called "Yoroku" written by the editorial staff they said, "Old Man Ozaki's only protégé was the late Tagawa Daikichirō," and nullified my public announcement in election bulletins, radio broadcasts, and election advertising that "I have been a member of the board of directors of Gakudō Society for many years and have been invited to speak at many meetings as Ozaki Yukio's representative." They have totally denied the fact that I am an important person under Ozaki Yukio's banner and completely ignored my name and position. With a cow-

ardly, dishonest article they obstructed my election and consequently I was defeated. The widespread dishonesty and arrogance of the large newspapers is more than despicable, and for the sake of social justice they absolutely cannot be ignored.

Your Excellency, noble General MacArthur who cherishes benevolence and justice, I look to you to deal strictly with this strange and sinful newspaper that turns its back on the respected mission and responsibility of the press, unfairly deceives the people, and misleads the world. At the same time, I beg that you order the Mainichi shimbun to print this letter as is in their newspaper for three days.

Takano Seihachirō
Chairman, Financial Research Society
Candidate for House of Councilors
Nationwide Constituency

The writer used lined manuscript paper from *Shin shimei* (New mission), the organ of the Gakudō Society. The characters are neatly written in pen, but his excited state is evident in places where the meaning is not clear or erroneous verb endings are used. More to the point, the complaint does not make sense because the anonymous letter to the editor printed in the *Mainichi* criticized the low quality of the campaign but did not mention Takano Seihachirō by name. So it cannot be argued that the article was singling out Takano's broadcast. The claim that the *Mainichi shimbun* interfered with the election and caused his defeat by publishing an anonymous letter and not rescinding it is simply false.

The *Mainichi* column mentioned here discussed the greatness of Ozaki Yukio, who was visiting the United States at the time, and mentions Tagawa Daikichirō as his only protégé, ignoring the self-appointed "important person under Ozaki Yukio's banner." According to the election results, Takano came in 299th among 311 candidates in the nationwide constituency. He received 6,350 votes, about 1 percent of the top candidate's total. It was a crushing defeat. Perhaps he needed to vent his anger at the humiliating loss. Making the *Mainichi shimbun* his scapegoat and taking his appeal to MacArthur was a complicated way of achieving catharsis, but it was understandable.

Besides, he was the type of person who would claim to have "the god of politics," Ozaki Gakudō, as mentor and in the same letter state that he and Dr. Edward C. Welsh, chief of the Antitrust and Cartels Division in the Economic and Scientific Section of GHQ, shared the same opinion on the Japanese economy. Perhaps no one but MacArthur would suffice as the outlet for his frustrations.

PLEASE SETTLE OUR DISPUTES

The next petition requests MacArthur to intervene in a village dispute.[3]

December 10, 1949
The Honorable General MacArthur

Petition

As citizens of the nation of Japan, we must respect democracy and work toward the early development of a cultured Japan. As described in the enclosed document, the branches of the trees at our village shrine have spread over our fields during the past several decades, causing great loss and hindering the harvest of our crops. However, taxes and quotas were not decreased accordingly. It was felt that if we cut the branches of the trees we could increase our harvests and pay the taxes and meet our quotas, so we inquired at the prefectural government office regarding permission to do the cutting. Following their directions, we submitted an application for permission to do the cutting dated May 29, 1949. The prefecture promptly issued the permission, and accordingly we carried out the cutting. The village head and the representative of the shrine congregation raised objections, saying that our application was inadequately prepared. They in turn received permission to keep the trees, and they called several meetings of the village council to argue that our action was unlawful and should be punished. Ultimately they held a general meeting of the villagers and decided to use village funds to pay for legal action. As a result we became criminals in the eyes of the villagers, so we went to the prefectural office again to explain our situation, and the decision was that our application and the permission had been filed first and were valid. As we investigate and think about this incident, if our documents were not in order, the village head should have directed us to correct them. Instead he aroused the district head and the representative of the shrine congregation and blew up the situation. In exploring the reason for this, [we found that] his objective was to make the representative of this petition, agricultural land commissioner Tsuchiya, resign his important post. So he, village head M [hereafter only initials will be used], aroused district head T and village councilor/shrine congregation representative K, and the three conspired that if the villagers were stirred up, we would have to apologize. We have heard that the plan was to add the condition of resigning the post of agricultural land commissioner. These three men had previously taken advantage of their public offices and secretly spent 3,400 yen from the shrine budget. It is clear from the council meeting minutes that the three made unlawful plans to conceal their deed. It is assumed that there were other similar criminal activities. We believe that if their activities were legally judged, they would fall under Articles 95 (section 2), 230, and 231 of the Criminal Code, and under Articles 1, 2, and 3 of Imperial Ordinance no. 1 of 1947. From this perspective, the villagers probably know that men like this who harbor political conspiracies are not fit to hold public office. We hope to have somewhat better people for the future cultural development of our village. It is obvious from past experience that having these present men as leaders will bring harm to our village in the future. This is a terrible situation, and we humbly petition you to thoroughly investigate and take proper measures to purge them from public office.

Tsuchiya Yūsaku
Petition Representative
128 Ōaza Hatori, Fukuori-mura
Abe-gun, Shizuoka Prefecture
[followed by twelve other names and seals]

This petition was not asking MacArthur to mediate the arguments within the village; rather, one side was looking to bring his dominant power into play to overpower its opponent. The authority of the supreme commander was too powerful to play the role of a dispassionate judge, but like a strong magnet he drew everyone to want him on their side. "Democracy" and "cultural Japan" were the catchwords of the time, and the supreme commander embodied those symbols, so having him on your side made victory certain.

But of course MacArthur did not get involved in such mundane matters. This letter was buried in the files of the Economic and Scientific Section, so it probably was routed directly to the section and never got to MacArthur's desk. We do not know the outcome of the dispute, but I am sure that GHQ made no attempt to intervene.

The next letter reports on a dispute of a different kind. It concerns an internal conflict within the publishing world, which because of its scale had the potential to influence the direction of postwar Japanese culture. The letter is from Kimura Ki, a writer known for his colorful, active involvement in the fields of history, culture, and criticism from the 1920s until the 1980s. The letter is in English, typewritten on four pages.[4]

Your Excellency General MacArthur;

I am a writer of Japanese nationality. Soon after Your Excellency's arrival in Tokyo I presented to your perusal my humble opinion that no democratization of Japan could be hoped for unless a drastic renovation is carried out in her publishing world. In January this year I wrote a short history of your Excellency which appeared in "the King", the most popular magazine in Japan. I again boldly took the liberty of presenting to you a copy of the magazine together with a picture post-card. The repeated audacity I was guilty of may have left my humble name in an obscure corner of your Excellency's memory. Recently an English version of my little work entitled "Historical Sketches of General MacArthur" appeared in series in the Youth's Companion, *an English weekly for students. Let me have again the honour of presenting the English version under separate cover. Should Your Excellency spare just a few minutes to its reading, the author would deem it a great favour.*

I have not been able to locate Kimura's previous letter on the reform of the publishing industry, but the nine-page "Biography of General MacArthur" appearing in the January 1946 issue of *King* is a balanced profile of the general, despite his admission that "General MacArthur was my favorite." (The Government Section of GHQ had the article translated, so MacArthur, who is said to have been extremely sensitive to the evaluation of others, must have read it.) Kimura was unique in Japan in the length of his connection with MacArthur.[5] For example, as a war correspondent in 1942, he reported on the state of MacArthur's residence after he fled from Manila to Bataan, and Kimura became the leading media expert on MacArthur in Japan during the war.

The main thrust of his letter follows:

Your Excellency, allow me to put again to your judgment my humble opin-ion on the present deplorable situation of the publishing world of Japan. In the pre-war days Japan boasted more than 2,000 publishers, large and small, and in quantity and variety of her publications Japan stood unrivalled in the world, as the statistics clearly shows. During the China Incidents, as we used to call it, our Bureaucrats in concert with our Militarists ordered a reorgani-zation of the press world to be put in force, and in consequence the number of the publishers was reduced to 300. Against the publishers who would not cooperate with the Government in the prosecution of the war, paper supply was stopped and some of them were put out of existence. All the publications, as might be supposed, were made use of by the military clique as the means of their propaganda. The central organ of publications activities was neither more nor less than the Japan Publishers Society, so that if there is any that is to be accused in the press circles of Japan on the charge of war-crimes, it must be the Japan Publishers Society.

As the matter of fact, however, immediately after the cessation of hostili-ties, this society simply changed its name into the Japan Publishers Associa-tion, and assuming all the functions its predecessor was provided with, it in-sists on holding sway of the publishing world. Strange to say, this association, having succeeded to the property of the Society amounting to some seven mil-lion yen has still on its managing staff a few old members, who in conspiracy with some outsiders belonging to the school of Radicalists have caused "the Press War-Criminal Court" to be opened. Declaring that they are backed by the G.H.Q., they have tried leading publishers and condemned them.

These handful of persons, to all intents and purposes, are a gang, and all the publications, placed under their despotic control are destined somewhat to turn red.

Your Excellency, I have not the remotest intention of painting too gloomy a picture of the real situation. Honestly speaking, it gives me the shudders to think of the future of this country.

A journalist's ability is judged by how well he can simplify a compli-cated set of facts. Explaining the internal conflicts in Japan's postwar publishing world would probably require a doctoral dissertation. But here, in his appeal to MacArthur, Kimura describes the danger that the publishing controls put in place by the militarists during the war may now be exercised by leftist leaders. This is brilliant, an argument that would immediately get the attention of a champion anticommunist like MacArthur. Kimura makes his own position quite clear by labeling as gangsters those who control the Japan Publishers Association. On the other hand, he had no intention of addressing the issue of the publishers' war responsibilities, for had he done so, his own literary activities during the war would have been called into question. Immediately after Germany's surrender, for example, Kimura, who was then a part-time employee of the Navy Ministry, published an article entitled "A Proposal for Punishing America" in the periodical *Senden* (Propaganda) on June 15, 1945. Kimura listed fifteen proposals in an effort to fan Japan's fighting spirit, including the following: "Item 9: The main anti-Japan instigators should be punished severely—Grew, Nimitz, MacArthur, etc. Especially, Grew should receive the death sentence."[6]

THE SAME BIRD SINGS A DIFFERENT SONG

There is a saying that goes, Birds change with the seasons. When the birds change, the songs change. Lyrics like "severe punishment for MacArthur" were for wartime songs, and it is perhaps natural that after the war songs of praise for MacArthur would be sung. However, in Japan, the times may have changed but the birds remained the same. Many simply started singing a different song. Kimura was not the only one; many other writers did likewise, and publishers were no different. Given that reality, it was difficult to address the issue of wartime collaboration.

It is true that the Japan Publishers Association established an internal disciplinary committee and began to denounce "war criminal publishers." The effort was supported by R. H. Berkov, the first chief of the CI&E press division. The committee members, not all of whom were "radicals" as Kimura claims, included men of considerable standing such as Suehiro Gentarō, Tatsuno Takashi, and Yamakawa Hitoshi.[7] The Japan Publishers Association was formed on October 10, 1945, and at a special general meeting on January 24 of the following year, it announced the names of seven publishers as "war criminals." Included in the list were Kōdansha, Ōbunsha, Shufunotomo-Sha, and Ienohikari Kyōkai. The disciplinary committee was created by resolution of the general meeting, and it variously directed the seven publishers to discontinue magazine publishing, limit business activities, liquidate the company (in the case of Ōbunsha), or replace chief executives. However, these directives had no legal authority, so the publishers failed to comply with the orders. It was only when they were enforced through the allocation of paper, which was in extremely short supply, that the disciplinary measures had any effect. The publishers association had inherited from its predecessor the authority to allocate paper among the publishers. Thus while the point of contention for Japanese publishers immediately after surrender was officially the pursuit of war criminals, in actual practice it came down to the allocation of paper. Kimura's letter addresses this very issue:

On October 27th, last year [1945] the directive from the G.H.Q. deprived the Japan Publishers Association of its right of paper control and told the Japanese Government to be responsible for this business. At the issue of this directive, we thought the tyranny of the Association would be put an end to, but contrary to our expectation, the Ministry of Commerce, under the pretext that it had no organ within its capacity to take the control of paper, entrusted the Association with the function of making original plans for deciding the paper quota to be allowed for each of the publishers. The government authorities concerned had an office for this work installed in the Association's headquarters and made the Association pay the salaries of the clerks working in the office. It is quite clear from these circumstances that the Japan Publishers Association is invested with the actual power of controlling paper allocation, so that it naturally follows that the Association wields authority over the publishers just as did the militarists over the nation before and during the war.

Your Excellency, such being the case, the directive issued on October 27th last year has been left unobserved, for which deplorable state of things the Ministry of Commerce and Industry must be accused of their failure in performing their duty.

To take an instance of the tyranny exercised by the Association, the Making Original Plan for Deciding Paper Allocation Committee planned for allowing no paper quota for the four big publishers, the Shufunotomo, the Kodansha, the Obunsha and the Ienohikarisha, and the Ministry of Commerce and Industry failed to fulfill their promise that they would keep sharp eyes on the Committee so as not to let them do any foul play, for the authorities who submitted the original plan to the deliberation of the Paper Rationing Committee temporarily put in charge of the duties, were careless in the choice of the personnel of the Committee.

According to the G.H.Q. directive the Committee should be composed of fifteen persons of whom five were to represent the government, another five, publishers, and remaining five were to be picked from among the learned and experienced persons. Nearly half of the Committee thus formed have proved to be Communists and those who have sympathy with Communism. These Radicalists, working in close affiliation have succeeded in inducing the Committee into the decision that against the foregoing four publishers paper allocation would be "suspended", which decision means practically the stoppage of paper supply.

Here again, the situation was more complicated than Kimura implied. The power to allocate paper passed from the Japan Publishers Association to the Cabinet Information Bureau, and with the abolition of the bureau was moved to the Ministry of Commerce and Industry. The name, Committee for the Allocation of Paper to Newspapers and Publishers, remained unchanged throughout. The publishers association formed an internal Paper Policy Committee to advise and monitor the official allocation committee. The publishers association had clerical staff who were experienced in paper allocation from the days of the prewar Japan Publishers Society. For this reason, when the authority to allocate paper passed to the Ministry of Commerce and Industry, it engaged some of these people as "temporary unpaid staff" and entrusted them with developing a plan for allocating paper. This Kimura describes as follows: "The government authorities . . . made the Association pay the salaries of the clerks working in the office," a clever exposition that accomplishes the journalist's job of simplifying the situation.

The publishers association took the further step of obtaining outside evaluation of the allocation plan from a Cultural Committee made up of fourteen scholars and cultural leaders. The ministry's allocation committee took into consideration the original allocation plan and the opinions of the Cultural Committee and then issued a final plan. It was not simply a rubber stamp of the publishers association, as Kimura implied.

As to the selection of members of the allocation committee, which was reorganized in March, considerable influence was exercised by Tarō Tsukahara, a leftist *kibei nisei* (a second-generation Japanese American educated in Japan) from the CI&E Section at GHQ (he later transferred to the Government Section and worked closely with deputy chief Kades). There were other leftists on the committee, including Fujikawa Satoru (from the publishing division of the Jiji news agency), who had been in charge of the influential Kōza series on Japanese capitalism while he was at Iwanami Shoten; and Fujioka Junkichi (from Shōkō Shoin), who was chairman of the publishers association's paper policy committee. But Kimura's allegation that "nearly half of the Committee thus formed have proved to be Communists and those who have sympathy with Communism" was misleading. Kimura was likely appealing to MacArthur's anticommunism, but this characterization seems malicious. The Cultural Committee concurred in the suspension of paper allocation for twelve periodicals published by Kōdansha and three other publishers. Kimura could not, of course, accept this decision, since it meant no paper allocation for Kōdansha's *King*, "the most popular magazine in Japan," in which his "Biography of General MacArthur" appeared. He very conveniently closed his eyes to the fact that *King* and the other magazines had joined the militarists in fanning the people's will to fight during the war. While the letter appears full of agony, it is actually a very clever piece of work. It closes as follows:

This injustice that the Committee have dealt to the four publishers has angered Mr. McEvoy, Manager of the Tokyo Branch of the Literary [Readers] Digest. He has brought this case before the G.H.Q. authorities, if I am not misinformed.

In view of the fact that the magazine "King" which has the largest circulation of the kind in Japan, "the Ienohikari," the foremost magazine for agrarian communities, the topmost ladies' magazines, "the Shufunotomo" and the "Fujinkurabu," the most popular magazine for middle grade school boys and girls are being issued from the four publishers, the stoppage of paper supply to them means that eighty per cent of the magazine readers in Japan will be deprived of their favourite reading materials.

Your Excellency, if permitted, I should like to ask a big favor of you, that is, the Ministry of Commerce should be reminded by the GHQ of the responsibility placed upon them by the directive issued on October 27 last year in connection with the paper rationing for publications.

In conclusion let me tell a bit about insignificant myself. I was offered the chairmanship of the Council of the Japan Free Publications [Publishers] Association which was formed in April this year by publishers who have made up their mind to wage a crusade against the bolshevization of the Japanese publishing world.

In case Your Excellency should have doubt about my character, please refer to Major Tilton in your office and Navy Captain Stone in the Liaison Office, whose acquaintance I have had the honour of striking up.

Yours humble servant,
[signed] Ki Kimura

The Free Publishers Association was formed by twenty-two publishers who were disturbed by the radicalization of the Japan Publishers Association, including the publishers ostracized as war criminals—Ōbunsha, Kōdansha, Shufunotomo-Sha, Ienohikari Kyōkai, and others. Their adopted slogan was "Correct Leftist Leanings and Revive Free Enterprise." Kimura undoubtedly assumed the post of chairman with high aspirations. His letter has no date, but the decision to suspend the allocation of paper to the four publishers was announced May 23, 1946, and he must have responded to the crisis with his direct appeal to MacArthur. The immediate effect of the letter is not known, but allocation was only suspended once, and subsequent developments indicate that the Free Publishers Association prevailed, as many publishers switched over from the Japan Publishers Association. The Free Publishers Association continued to pressure GHQ on a variety of issues of concern to the publishing industry, and it gradually emerged as the mainstream voice of the industry, while the Japan Publishers Association fell into decline.

HOMELAND AND FRIENDSHIP DO NOT MATTER

The next letter is a request to be allowed into the American armed forces.[8]

February 3, 1950
The Honorable General MacArthur
   I humbly make my request in haste.
   I served as a corporal medic in the Japanese army during the war.
   Since the war, I have been working at the family business.

Now, my request at this time is that, as the U.S.–Soviet relationship is deteriorating, please hire me as a soldier or even a janitor in your army.
Your Excellency I would like to contribute even a small amount to world peace.
Please accept my request. I will be eagerly awaiting your reply.
My educational background is written on the back. [omitted]

S. T.

The postwar economic recovery was slow. It was a time of unemployment and jobs were difficult to come by. The situation was especially difficult for those repatriated from overseas and former members of the military. Naturally, many thought of appealing to MacArthur for a job. But in this case, a former army medic who, according to his résumé, had left Waseda Higher Engineering School during his first year because of illness, was willing to leave his family business, join the American forces, and fight the Soviets. This was not an ordinary request for a job because it raised issues of loyalty. The United States may have been occupying Japan at the time, but it remained a foreign country and a former enemy. One cannot enter a foreign military without forfeiting one's own citizenship. It is surprising that this person does not seem to be in the least aware of this fact. It is easy to say it is "for world peace," but did he realize that he would have to be crossing national borders?

There were others who actively tried to embrace MacArthur as their new sovereign. A number of former *kamikaze* pilots volunteered for the U.S. military "for the sake of peace" and to "annihilate communism." The next letter, a direct appeal to MacArthur from the town of Sōsha in Okayama Prefecture, is a request to join the American forces to destroy the ambition of "a certain victorious nation" (i.e., the Soviet Union) to conquer the world. It is undated, but it was received at ATIS on June 13, 1947. The letter read in part:[9]

We desire peace from our heart. The huge enterprise of everlasting peace for mankind requires great sacrifice. For the sake of establishing peace, I constantly hope to utilize my knowledge of airplane operation to join the American military and destroy the ambitions of Country X, thus becoming a stepping-stone for peace. What do I care about the safety of my single life!!

This is the reason I hereby send this letter to my beloved General MacArthur and sincerely request acceptance into his military.

T. S.

The following appeal to MacArthur suggested that "most of the Japanese harbor animosity toward the occupation forces," and that, as a "countermeasure, Japanese should be hired as detectives," with the writer himself volunteering for the job. The letter, undated but stamped May 8, 1947, reads as follows:[10]

Pardon me for dispensing with preliminaries.

The thoughts, language, and behavior of the Japanese, certainly, are better understood by a Japanese who has lived side by side from birth than by the occupation forces. Only a Japanese would understand animosity toward the occupation forces and violations of orders. The occupation forces hire many Japanese, but because they are true Japanese, they will absolutely not speak of things detrimental to the Japanese or Japan. You must hire detectives and develop your policies on the basis of having a true picture of the Japanese. Of course, you must use people who will pledge allegiance to the United States. If you are going to hire detectives, please hire me first. Among my relatives and friends there are former members of the army and navy, people who harbor animosity toward the occupation forces, one who killed an Allied POW and is still free, and those who violate various orders, etc. If these people are skillfully interviewed, hitherto unknown facts may also become clear. If occupation policy calls for the investigation of black marketing, there are big operators, illegal brokers, and shady companies around me.

If you will hire me as a detective, I am willing to renounce the country in which I was born, my home and everything. And no matter what my friends may say, for the occupation forces' sake, I am not afraid to sell Japan and the Japanese for my work, so I beg you to please hire me. [The rest of the letter is omitted.]

A. B.

A. B. is the code name this person gave himself. His real name and address in Tokyo were on the envelope. What an expression of allegiance to a blue-eyed master!

There were a number of similar offers. For example, a woman from Fukushima Prefecture wrote, "Since I am competent in English, in preparation for the next war, please let me be an American spy. Although it is peacetime, one never knows what is in people's hearts. I urge you to please use me as your hired hand."

TO AMERICA, TO AMERICA

Of course, those offering themselves and their hearts to the United States were a small minority. But many, old and young alike, had hopes of actually going to America to study and see the world. Let me start with a letter from a young girl:

To General Douglas MacArthur:
   The beautiful fall with its clear skies is coming to a close. As the fall passes, Japan is a country in disorder, having lost the war. To make Japan better, we must be earnest, and have good-hearted, kind hope, or Japan will become even worse. We have to build a peaceful and cultured nation. We boys and girls must learn from Professor Yukawa who received the Nobel Prize. We must not lose heart just because we lost the war. We must not be lazy.
   If the United States does not bring us food, what will happen to Japan? We will have to die gradually. We must pray for happiness.
   We must go, one after the other, to foreign countries to study and do research. My home is so poor that I can hardly go to school, but to rebuild this home, studying must come first.
   I want to go to America to study and return to Japan as a fine person. I want to die having done something to benefit my country. I want to go to America, join hands, and study in harmony. Please let me go. I beseech you.
   I am ashamed to say that my home is poor and we lead a very hard life. But to become a great person, one must not break down.
   I have many other hopes, but I will end my letter here. I will study English well!!
   I am thirteen years old. My name is Shimada Umeka. Good-bye.

From Ume

Despite the childish writing and faltering logic, sweet is the best word to describe this letter. The postmark is not clear, but the date seems to be December 7, 1949.[11] Although few children had the confidence to send a letter like this, going to the United States to study and building Japan as a peaceful and cultured nation was the unfulfilled dream of many children during those years.

And it was not only the children. Many adults also saw the United States as the wellspring of culture and the source of the cure that would bring Japan back to life. The following is an ostentatious document, written in the archaic *sōrōbun* style.[12]

May 16, 1947
Supreme Commander for the Allied Powers
The Honorable General MacArthur

Regarding Petition for Permission for Travel to the US
Applicant for Travel: Tomiko Takagi

You are well aware of the grievous situation of confusion and deadlock in all quarters of postwar Japan, especially the dullness of the culture of daily life and the impoverishment of apparel in particular.

The above-mentioned person has been involved for many years in making and teaching domestic handicrafts, and in research and popularization of practical and artistic knitting. It is also well established that she is a prominent leader in the field.

Accordingly, she would like to realize her long-held desire to travel to the United States (her preference is this fall around November) and personally observe and research in detail the above subjects in an advanced country. After her return, it is her desire to educate young women, and also to introduce and promote the superior apparel culture of the United States through the news media and magazines (including our magazine). Thus, she will raise the standards of our sunken and shriveled life culture and also contribute to the rebuilding of a cultured Japan.

It is my hope that you will give special consideration regarding the permission for her to travel. I hereby petition on her behalf.

Ōshima Shūichi [seal], President,
Shufu to Seikatsu Sha, Family Magazine
9, 1-chōme, Nishi-Kanda
Chiyoda-ku, Tokyo

Today, Japanese designers are among the leaders in international fashion, and one is struck by how quickly the "rebuilding of a cultured

Japan" was accomplished. The following letter, from a leading Japanese woman, is a final example of these requests to go to the United States to study.[13]

August 9, 1949
Supreme Commander for the Allied Powers
The Honorable General MacArthur

I offer my gratitude to Your Excellency for your diligence in performing your duties during the hot season.

I am one of the first Japanese women to be elected to the Diet.

At 5:00 P.M. on May 20, 1946, we women members of the Lower House of the Diet were invited to see Your Excellency, and I can still clearly recall your image when we heard your kind words. I always tell my countrymen that Japan being occupied by the United States instead of China or the Soviet Union is the silver lining in a dark cloud. Please forgive me for expressing myself honestly as a politician. I have never considered my personal gain or benefit, and my mind is filled with thoughts on how the people of the world can live happily in peace. I believe it is the duty of politicians to guarantee the people's livelihood and provide for their happiness.

True peace means discarding all weapons and relying on religion, does it not? I hope that world peace will be maintained through Christianity. I also believe in Christianity. Women love peace instinctively. Japanese women also detest cruel war and love peace, but until we were occupied by your country we did not have the right to speak, so we had no choice but to blindly follow the tyranny of the men.

Japanese letters of that era, especially women's letters, have long introductions. This one is typical. She finally came to the point: "For Japan to win the current ideological war, I believe that only the power of women's love can counter brutal communism." Therefore, it was necessary to build training centers in the cities and rural areas to develop leaders for women. The letter continues:

For this purpose, I would like to visit your country to observe what might be instructive. To rebuild Japan, we must look to the advanced American culture for guidance.

Photo 12.1   Women were given the right to vote for the first time in the first postwar general election, held April 10, 1946. Thirty-nine women were elected to the Diet, symbolizing a revolutionary change in the status of women. Source: Kyōdō News Service

I have relatives in America, so I am aware of America's many virtues. My niece (the daughter of my younger sister) manages a hotel in Fresno, California. Prisoners of war repatriated from the Soviet Union have told me about conditions there. I do not want a single Japanese to become a member of the Communist Party that supports the cowardly and inhumane Soviet Union. Please help rescue Japan from the brutal Communist Party.

For the past half year, I have been inquiring of the staff at the Ministry of Foreign Affairs and General Headquarters about my desire to visit your country, but I have been told that I cannot submit an application for permission to visit the United States because I cannot speak English fluently and because I do not have an invitation. A group of Diet members is going to make an observation trip to your country, but not a single woman member is participating. In this manner, I regret to say, Japan still does not recognize women.

I read in the July 30 Niigata nippō a report that your public affairs office had announced that it is "planning to send Japanese leaders from various fields to the United States. It was announced that a committee had been es-

tablished to select members for a study tour of the United States." I beg that with Your Excellency's generous consideration, you accept my presumptuous request and allow me to travel to the United States.
I pray for Your Excellency's health.

Respectfully,
Nomura Misu

Thirty-nine women were elected for the first time ever to the Lower House of the Diet in the first postwar general election. For whatever reasons, most quickly faded from the public stage. The level of savvy the writer exhibits in this letter is impressive, but it is clear that it did not have the power to move MacArthur.

The final letter of this chapter is also a petition from a politician. The writer is Hatoyama Ichirō, who was purged from public office in 1946 shortly before he was able to form a cabinet as leader of the Liberal Party. The original was in English, which is reproduced here:[14]

November 27, 1950
General Douglas MacArthur
General Headquarters
Supreme Commander for the Allied Powers
Tokyo, Japan

Dear General MacArthur:
On May 3, 1946, four and one half years ago, shortly after the beginning of the occupation of Japan I was purged by SCAP prohibiting me from holding any political office in Japan. At the time of my purge I knew there was some misunderstanding but felt that time and investigation would clear me.

I am strongly of the opinion that my complete investigation will show that I have always been a very strong liberal who advocated against the war and at the same time jeopardized my security in Japan when the militarists were at the height of their power. Then too, I have always been one of strong opposition to the Communists aims in the Far East. As a result, those connected with the Communist Party have fought me bitterly and are very happy over the fact that I still remain on the purge list.

Now I respectfully submit to you my humble request that I be depurged from my present status for the following reasons:

1. Reference should be made to my previous appeals.

2. Prime Minister Yoshida, not only my fellow member in the Liberal Party but also my personal friend, needs my help in the present political picture. It is my strong belief that Mr. Yoshida is better acquainted with the present situation of Japan both internally and externally than any other we have in Japan. Having been the Prime Minister in Japan during these several years and with his valuable experience I feel that the Japanese politicians should cooperate to the fullest extent so that he may have their full support in the negotiation of the coming peace treaty with the Allied Powers, headed by the United States.

3. I shall have the opportunity to do everything in my power to assist and help Mr. Yoshida during this crucial period in obtaining and maintaining full support from the Japanese people.

There is no real need to make a detailed comparison between the self-serving picture of a "liberal" that Hatoyama paints and the tracks he left across prewar Japanese politics. Suffice it to say that he was an influential politician who was especially well-known for leading a crackdown on academic freedom at Kyoto University in 1933 while he was serving as minister of education. If he thought that claiming to be a champion of anticommunism would absolve him of responsibility for his prewar activities, that was wishful thinking. Above all, Yoshida had absolutely no need of assistance from Hatoyama. And what was Hatoyama planning to do if he was depurged? The letter continues:

4. In the event my purge should be lifted it is my intention with approval of Mr. Yoshida to lecture through-out Japan on the question of the principles of democracy (of which my background and acts show that I have always been a strong proponent) and to assist him in any other way he thinks feasible. Further it is hoped that I may have the opportunity of making a study-tour of the United States to see and learn further about democracy in order to assist in reconstruction of Japan on the policy of democratic principles as illustrated by the way of life in the United States. As you may be aware my father, who was educated in the United States, taught me to respect and love America where everyone has equal opportunity.

5. It is my understanding that there are some individuals in Japan, particularly those of communistic philosophy, who have by their devious and insidious outlets have caused to spread the false rumor that a lifting of the purge against me would cause a political chaos in Japan. They know that this is not true. On the contrary they would rather keep me out of the political scene in order to attempt to discredit and more easily attack Mr. Yoshida and the Liberal Party as they feel a lifting of the purge against me would give strength and support to the Prime Minister.

6. In conclusion I wish to state that my only desire is to aid in making Japan a peaceful and democratic country which in turn would help bring about peace and understanding in this one world of our.

Therefore I again respectfully make my earnest appeal for my depurging and pledge you that I will do my utmost towards accomplishing my aims as set out above.

Very truly yours,
[signed] Ichiro HATOYAMA

The letter was written in English, which might help explain its lack of persuasiveness, but even so, the whole document is lacking in force. Negotiations on the peace treaty were progressing rapidly, and Yoshida—to whom Hatoyama thought he had temporarily delegated political power—was about to reap the credit and the glory. At such a time, it is understandable that Hatoyama would regret his continuing purge from public office, but this letter lacks the force to convey that feeling. For him to say that he would be careful to not get in Yoshida's way if he was depurged is a timid attitude for a former president of the leading party. When he gets around to saying he would like a chance to tour the United States to study democracy, he is in the same boat as the thirteen-year-old girl and the woman Diet member. Am I being too critical of Hatoyama? I do not think so. We may feel sympathy for the weakness of the Japanese that is evident in letters to MacArthur from both ordinary citizens and political leaders, but that does not mean we should withhold a critical eye. In any case, Hatoyama was not depurged, but he managed a political comeback after the occupation ended and served two years as prime minister during the mid-1950s.

FERVENT REQUESTS

GET WORD TO MY HUSBAND, A WAR CRIMINAL ON DEATH ROW

元帥

The Honorable Commander MacArthur

Excuse me for dispensing with preliminaries. Please forgive my impoliteness in sending you a poorly written letter without warning.

I do not know where to begin. I am trying to be calm, and though I doubt whether you will listen to my private request, I have decided to write to you.

I appeal to Your Excellency, Commander MacArthur. It is nothing more than this, so I will turn directly to the subject. I am the wife of Tachibana Masao, who is in Prison Camp One on Luzon in the Philippines, waiting to be executed, and my request concerns nothing else. I want to get word to him before he leaves this earth, because he still does not know whether his child is a boy or a girl. He has not heard that his son was born on January 1 last year. I wrote to him shortly after New Year's Day this year, but it seems the letter has not reached him. The baby has been named Norio, and I wish more than anything I could show him our child, but there is nothing I can do, so I request at least that:

Your Excellency, Commander MacArthur, by your mercy, please inform him before he is executed that Norio was born and will be raised as his heir. Please consider this as a gift to Tachibana Masao, who will fall like a cherry blossom. No matter how much I have thought about it, nothing can be done, so I have decided to appeal to you.

I firmly believe that my husband will leave this world in peace, and to fall in the Philippines where his comrades lay buried must be his true desire.

When he hears this news, he will be happy and die fulfilled, and I too will have no regrets. So please give your consideration to this, one woman's most important request.

Please accept my apologies for my disorganized writing.

Tachibana Mitsuko

Among the thousands of letters to MacArthur, this appeal[1] from the wife of a war criminal stands out for its sad content, and the writer's emotion pierces the heart of the reader. Since it is from an ordinary person who is not adept at letter writing, the language is awkward and there are many mistaken characters, but that only increases the sense of desperation that the letter conveys.

According to the unofficial records of the military tribunal in the Philippines, Tachibana Masao was a warrant officer attached to the Manila division of the military police. He was arraigned for "murder and the sanctioning [of crimes by the Japanese military] against the people of the Manila area during law enforcement activities."[2] Whether the proceedings of military tribunals held immediately after the war in many parts of southeast Asia were legally fair or not is still debated today, but this is not the place to examine a specific verdict. Moreover, Tachibana's wife is not pleading for his life in her letter, she is only asking that her husband be given a parting gift of the knowledge that a son had been born. Her husband's execution was pending, yet her letter does not appear distraught on this account. She writes that her husband will be satisfied with the news of his son, and he will fall like a cherry blossom, so therefore "I too will have no regrets." This is admirably gallant, the spirit of Japanese women that was cultivated during the war. I was surprised to discover that this spirit continued into the postwar period.

The postmark on this letter reads, "Nuno Post Office, Kōchi Prefecture, April 6, 1946." It seems that it took some time at the ATIS, for a synopsis of the letter didn't reach MacArthur until after May 9. MacArthur's short signature appears at the top of the synopsis, and his written note says, "To C/S [Chief of Staff]. Have this done—MacA." As the commander in chief, MacArthur had the power to reduce a sentence given by a military tribunal under his command, but he never used it. In this case, the letter asked not for a mitigation of the sentence, and to agree to notify a father of his son's name was an expression of a warrior's empathy. Unfortunately, that empathy was in vain— Tachibana Masao had been hanged on April 11. The sadness of this letter deepens even more. It is not known whether MacArthur wrote back to Tachibana Mitsuko after his chief of staff notified him of the misfortune.

The next letter also concerns a husband who was sacrificed to the war, though it carries a quite different nuance.

To General MacArthur, who is like our God:

A lone woman from a farm village makes this appeal to our great General MacArthur.

Since the defeat, we are democratically improving our lives daily in compliance with the Potsdam Declaration.

In our village too, as called for in the Potsdam Declaration, our brothers and husbands are now returning to their beloved homes. At a time when parents, siblings, wives, and children are full of joy at reuniting with their men and are grateful for the general's benevolence, I alone have been dealt a very sad fate.

It concerns my husband. He left six long years ago and fought on Bougainville Island, where the whole company died in battle. Only four survivors escaped to the jungle, where they were captured by the Allied forces. In October 1945, he was turned over to the Japanese army for repatriation under the Potsdam Declaration, but in December his case was submitted to Japanese court martial, and upon his arrival in Japan he was sent to prison. In April, I was notified that my husband was ill and I traveled to distant Nagasaki to visit him. When I saw my husband, I could not believe that this was the same man. Please understand how sad I felt at that time.

Of course, the guilty must be punished. If he had stolen government property, punishment would be unavoidable. But general, do you know that today, after the military cliques have been disbanded, desertion is a crime punishable by twelve years [imprisonment]? I fervently request that he be declared innocent and returned home. The crime was fabricated by the bosses of the militarists who are now on trial as criminals. Please eliminate this kind of crime from present-day Japan. Otherwise, I am afraid Japanese imperialism and militarism will persist forever.

The reason is that, until now, Japanese were trained to be soldiers from the time of their birth. They were taught that the military is a strict place, and because it is strict, to run away meant the death penalty. Because that foundation for militarism still survives, I think there are many wives with the same sad fate as mine throughout Japan. I hear that in the same Nagasaki Prison where my husband is, there are about a hundred men, held for the same crime of desertion. With my meager strength, I would have liked to make a national movement about this problem and appeal to the great general with public opinion, but I decided to write to you first.

I hope that with the great general's power the present minister of justice, who is blind to the situation, will be quickly purged. Only then can a farm village become truly democratic.

From a Sad Woman

There is no name on the letter, but the return address on the envelope reads Katahira Fumi from the village of Gunzan in Kagoshima Prefecture, and the date of receipt at ATIS was May 9, 1946. I found this letter in the Alfred Hussey Files at the University of Michigan. Hussey was a lawyer who became a commander in the U.S. Navy and later served as chief of the governmental powers division of the Government Section, GHQ. A member of the group that drafted the Japanese constitution, he did original research on the history of the emperor system and was interested in the Japanese imperial army, so it probably became part of his job to look into "desertion under fire," which carried over into the postwar era as a violation of military law.

This woman's tone is severe, asking, "General, do you know?" Her husband had survived the long war and made it back to his homeland after an absence of six years, only to be imprisoned for desertion. She wanted to start a national movement to win the release of her husband as well as the many other Japanese who were imprisoned for the same crime throughout Japan. This attitude reflected a woman's feelings for her husband, but it was also supported by her convictions about democracy. If the first letter in this chapter exhibits the integrity of the traditional woman, we can see in the second the determination of the new woman of the postwar era.

A LETTER FROM A MOTHER

The next letter is from a mother worrying about her child's safety, a universal sentiment that transcends time.[3]

November 18
To General MacArthur

The autumn coolness increases by the day, and you must be extremely busy.

All of the people respect General MacArthur for personally leading a peaceful Japan during these three months since the surrender.

One example is the consideration you've shown in the demobilization of Japanese forces within and outside of Japan, for which I am most grateful.

My son is still with the Manchurian corps (along the Soviet border), but we do not know what unit he belongs to, and besides, we do not know whether he is alive or dead, so I worry about him day and night. Recently a few soldiers, including the son of a friend, escaped and returned home. According to him, Russia is using Japanese soldiers as laborers to expand military installations, but once the construction is complete the soldiers will be shot because repatriating them would mean revealing classified information. Russia's excuse is that they are using Japanese labor in place of collecting reparations, but I feel that the duty to pay reparations should be borne by the solidarity of all the people, with their blood and sweat. They have struggled a great deal in Manchuria for food, clothing, and fuel, but on top of that, to be treated like slaves and then to be shot . . . there is no suffering worse than this for a mother.

If my son was killed in battle, fighting bravely, at least it would be some comfort and allow me to face society. But for a parent to hear that he may be treated like an animal and face an undignified death makes me feel that I would go through anything to save him. As it says in an old poem:

> *More than his life a warrior cherishes his name,*
> *For there is no other way but the way itself.*

The Japanese people value their country and the honor of their family. At the appropriate time, one falls bravely like a beautiful cherry blossom. But to face an improper death must be worse than death itself for my son.

Photo 13.1   A fishing boat arrives in the port of Hakata, Kyūshū, jammed with repatriating Japanese on October 18, 1945. The port was also crowded with Chinese and Koreans seeking to return to their homelands. Some 6.5 million Japanese were stranded overseas at the end of the war, including 3 million civilians; it took years for many to make their way home, and tens of thousands of refugees died en route. Source: *Mainichi Shimbunsha*

    The situation has come to this pass, and I have no choice but to rely on the general's power. Please save the soldiers in Manchuria. Whether I am awake or asleep my heart aches with this problem. Please forgive me for my many difficult requests. I wait eagerly for the general's early action.

    As the cold season is approaching, I pray to God that you will take care of yourself.

Sincerely,
From a Mother

As you can see, there is no name on this letter. The envelope only says, "From a mother, Kure City, November 18," but the English synopsis done by ATIS gives the year as 1945. The letter was written shortly after the war, and the people were not told until much later of the true condition of the Japanese soldiers who surrendered to the advancing Soviet army in Manchuria, many of whom did indeed die in captivity. The reports of those who escaped and made it home only increased people's apprehension and doubt, so it was natural that a concerned mother would petition MacArthur to save her son.

The mother's distinction between an honorable death in combat and the undignified death of a prisoner of war reflects an interesting aesthetics of death. Once again MacArthur is told of the beauty of falling like a cherry blossom and treated to the ancient poem that reminds us, "More than his life, a warrior cherishes his name."

FROM THE ABYSS OF ILLNESS AND POVERTY

These letters have raised concerns about family members, and many people turned to MacArthur for help. Among them was a theology student studying in the United States whose wife in Japan was critically ill with tuberculosis, and he asked for assistance in bringing her to the United States for surgery. On the top of this letter is the note, "File no answer," with the initials S. H., which probably meant Colonel Sydney Huff. It was probably left to the discretion of MacArthur's adjutants whether to pass personal requests on to the commander, so many of the Japanese letters did not reach MacArthur. It has also been pointed out that MacArthur initialed the documents he read less frequently toward the end of the occupation.[4] The date of the theology student's letter is November 30, 1950, after the onset of the Korean War, so the fighting general likely had more pressing issues on his mind.

As one might expect, there were some letters asking for help in fighting the writer's own illness. The next letter is an example. The writer, a young boy, insists that his illness can only be cured by advanced American medical technology, and he goes on to describe his plans on how he would repay for the help if he recovers. People's dreams are timeless, but here they also reflect the spirit of the postwar era.[5]

General Douglas MacArthur

Dear General MacArthur:

I believe that you are a great, firm, and kind person like God. Please accept this gift as a present to your family. I have a special favor to ask you. Around the summer of 1947, I suddenly lost hearing in my right ear. I can still hear with my left ear, but a famous doctor has said that it also will gradually lose its hearing. His diagnosis is incurable otosclerosis. In the March 1947 issue of the monthly Readers Digest [Japanese edition], there is an article, "And the Deaf Shall Hear," about the ear surgeon Dr. Julius Lempert of New York. I have been to all the doctors in Japan but cannot be cured. I am convinced that Dr. Julius Lempert's surgical method will cure me, so I want to see him. I would like your permission to go to the United States. A short period would do, but please let me go. Whether I will have a bright world or the dark world of the deaf depends on you. I face the greatest problem of my whole life now. This is a cry like burning fire. I want to go as soon as possible. If allowed to go to the United States and if my ears are cured, I will give my life to working for the happiness of the people of the world. If I were allowed to have American citizenship, I could live strongly with grand hopes and ideals. I have heard that at present there are huge undeveloped areas in America. I will cultivate a huge piece of land and grow a lot of wheat, and deliver it willingly. I will pray from my heart for people's happiness. I swear that I will complete the development. I will consider this a way of repaying for the restoration of my hearing, and I will work with all my might. If American citizenship cannot be granted, I will work my hardest for the reconstruction of Japan.

In any case, there is no hope unless my hearing is restored. I want to go to America and have my ears completely taken care of. I want to go quickly while I can still hear. I lost my mother ten years ago in 1939, and for the past ten years a nanny raised me in our farmhouse. My father whom I relied on also passed away last November. I am determined to prevail over all hardship and suffering. I do not have to worry about a family. In the whole world I have only you who can allow my trip to the United States. How happy I would be if you gave me permission. Please allow me to go. I pray to God every day. I vow to be a great person. Please save my life. Please give me a definite reply of yes or no. I shall be waiting.

Good-bye,
M. I. (18 years old)
Written on the night of April 15 [1947]

This young man seems to have truly believed that MacArthur was the only person in the world who could grant his request. He does not mention anything about travel costs and medical expenses, but his point that "I do not have to worry about a family" probably did not mean that there were no monetary worries. He probably thought of permission to go to the United States as a trump card that would solve all his problems. The letter indicates that he believed the almighty MacArthur would make everything possible.

The writer of the next letter reports that his father has passed away, leaving just the household estate, and inheritance taxes have been assessed. But the writer cannot afford them, so he appeals to His Excellency, the general to please do something to help. It is a fascinating piece of writing.[6]

December 23, 1949, The Birthday of the Crown Prince
The Honorable General MacArthur

Petition

Dear Sir:

This year too has only a few days left. Merry Christmas is just around the corner. I convey my sincere gratitude to Your Excellency the General for your devotion to military affairs day and night. The day for the peace treaty is also approaching. As I have written some time ago, my one of a kind obstinate father passed away at the age of seventy-seven. The poor man had most of his farmland taken away because of liberation [land reform], with compensation that amounted to giving it away. He was left in a pathetic situation with a few inferior paddies to farm, so he is probably happier dead than alive. Because of escalating prices, nothing can be done with the large estate and the big old house he left, so things have been left to rot, and finally the roof of the warehouse collapsed. A big hole has been left, people talk about it looking like it was hit by a bomb, and I feel resentment.

There is a heavy inheritance tax even on this wretched house, since my father died. I received notices on December 5 and 15 to appear at the Ibaraki Tax Office, and according to their assessment, the tax amounts to 128,288 yen. In my present situation I am having difficulty paying the fee for my rations of staple food, so how could I ever pay such a large sum? They said I should sell my house and timberland, but there is not much of the latter, and besides, most of it is designated as wind barrier, and I am not free to cut the timber. If I sold the house, I would be homeless the next day.

In postwar Japan, morality has fallen to the ground. Greedy officials and bureaucrats are engaged in rapacious exploitation. The ordinary people are in a wretched state. The city halls become larger and grander, nearly swarming with officials, while the citizens become more and more emaciated. This is not democracy but "theftocracy" [the two words are homonyms in Japanese]. We often recall the happiness of the great Meiji and Taishō eras and lament our present misfortune. Please help this pitiable family. My frail wife takes to bed often from overwork, and my mother is too old to be of any use. I have no children, and when I think of the future tears fall endlessly. Is there anything so miserable? Yet in this house of poverty, there is the national treasure of national treasures, unique in all of Japan. I hope Your Excellency the General will present it to the imperial family to commemorate the coming peace conference. It is my wish that our two countries will continue their peaceful relationship as long as heaven and earth last and reap the fruit of coexistence and coprosperity. Finally I pray for Your Excellency the General's lasting military fortune and good health. May I please have your consideration.

Sincerely yours,
Yamamoto Sadae
4035 Ōaza Saidera,
Suita City, Osaka Prefecture

This writer is making an appeal about his truly pathetic situation, but there is something of an air of diffidence in the letter. Could this be called black humor? He pleads, "Please help this pitiable family," but he does not say what he wants to have done. Maybe this is an indirect approach peculiar to the Japanese—to assume that if he describes the difficulty he is in, MacArthur will take the necessary steps to help.

But more amazing, after describing this dire situation, he reveals the existence of a national treasure in his household. Even if he was serious, there is no explanation of what the treasure was, and he did not actually give it to MacArthur. There is a certain casualness here that is not seen in ordinary letters. The writer clearly finds the two-tiered rule of MacArthur and the emperor to be perfectly natural. In the end, perhaps he did not expect any help from MacArthur but was writing the letter to obtain a cathartic release of his accumulated frustration.

The next letter, from a young girl in Kyoto, is a desperate appeal about the poverty of her family and a request to MacArthur to do something to help.[7]

April 1, 1947

Dear General MacArthur,

I was thinking everyday about whom I could turn to, when I saw an article about the general in the Asahi shimbun, *and I thought I should ask the general, so I am writing this letter. We learned from our teacher that Japan was defeated and the people have the obligation of paying reparations through taxes, so I am thinking that when I grow up I too will work hard. Recently the tax bill came, and it is so very high that the grownups are all crying. I thought that Japan had become a democratic country, but in the same line of work, those who do more business pay lower taxes and those who eke out a meager living pay higher taxes. In my family, my mother was often sick, and she was staying with relatives in the country during the war when she was killed in a bomb attack. My father is also frail, but he works as a plasterer and supports my older sister, my brother, and me. The recent tax bill was so high that even if he sold some tools and kimono it would not cover the taxes, so he went to the tax office for a consultation. They told him that once set, the tax bill cannot be changed.*

My father says that unless he sells my older sister to pay the taxes, the tax office will confiscate his tools, and he is also worried about next year's taxes. These days he is saying strange things.

I overheard my father and many other people saying that they should set fire to the tax office.

Dear General MacArthur, the people really resent those former military leaders who forced us into war and still make us suffer.

I request fairer taxes before my father and others burn down the tax office.

I was supposed to go to work after I finished elementary school, but now I have to go three more years [because compulsory education was increased to nine years], so I feel sorry for my father.

General MacArthur, please tell the tax officers to let us pay the taxes in installments. I cannot tell you my real name because my father talked about burning down the tax office, and I am afraid he may be taken off to jail.

General MacArthur, please help.

Mitsuji Yoshiko

As she wrote in the letter, the name is a pseudonym. Decades later, the letter still leaves the reader with a sense of hopelessness for the author and her family.

OH VENERABLE APOSTLE OF GOD, PLEASE SAVE MY POLITICAL LIFE

The next letter, written in 1949, is an appeal to MacArthur from a writer, Oda Toshiyo, who was purged from public office for advocating militarism and ultranationalism in his writings before and during the war. Oda calls himself a poet and his letter conveys a unique fervor, but he stands out among the many people who wrote to MacArthur in the degree to which he prostrates himself before the new authority.

Petition
Your Excellency General MacArthur,
   I have the honor of respectfully submitting a letter to Your Excellency General MacArthur, supreme commander for the Allied powers, whom I respect beyond all others.
   I am a poor citizen of defeated Japan. I am also the unknown starving poet, with the pen name Nishimura Tsuru, who sent you three poems in March 1947 out of sheer gratitude for the benevolence you bestowed like the sun's rays on the people of a defeated nation. This fall, when crisis is threatening East Asia and Your Excellency is absorbed with military and political matters, I, that same poor poet, apologize from the bottom of my heart for the rudeness of having to write to you again to petition to be depurged.
   Your Excellency the General, whom I admire!
   The reason why I believe that I have no choice but to bother you again is not because I seek to live in idleness, desire benefit or the return of my honor. It is only because I want to repay even one ten-thousandth of the benevolence of Your Excellency who is the parent of my life and the lives of all my beloved people of Japan. Because I myself and all the people waged the abhorrent Pacific War, which we cannot forget even in our dreams, we have received God's admonition and punishment through the destiny of defeat. At the time we were determined that "death" was the only fate that awaited us. But Your Excellency, your officers and soldiers, and the people of your country gave all of

us—ah, what glory!—"life," liberation, and true religion instead of the "death" we anticipated. I was simply moved to tears. I had nothing but remorse and sorrow for my ignorance and immorality. The deep emotion I felt at the time has not faded a bit since then, and a great fire of gratitude still burns in my heart.

The benevolent occupation policies that Your Excellency, Your Excellency's subordinates, and the people of your country extended to our defeated people—to praise them as a miracle of the 20th century would still be insufficient praise for this great human accomplishment I admire so much. Your Excellency the General, whom I revere. . . .

In the near future, I plan to submit a letter to Your Excellency detailing all the incidents of my entire life from birth to the present as well as the changes in my ideology; it is now being translated. It will soon be in your hands, and when it receives the honor of your perusal, it will become clear that at all times the one thing that I constantly prayed for was that the wretched Japanese people suffering from poverty and oppression would be liberated quickly.

The ideal Japanese society that I envisioned was precisely what Your Excellency applied to Japan and still is implementing through your occupation policies. The liberation of farmers, the liberation of laborers, the liberation of women—Oh God, behold this! The innumerable chains he has loosed! The faces of the people beaming with happiness and filled with hope, the faces, the faces, the faces!

Oh, who could loose the many ugly chains? None other than the former enemy commander, General MacArthur.

When I think of this glory, I can only praise Our Lord Christ's love and glory. Oh, venerable apostle of God, Your Excellency General MacArthur, I published three books before and during the war that led to the judgment that I was a supporter of militarism at the recent Japan purge committee (first screening).

The three books were *Konoe shin taisei no zenbō* (The total picture of Konoe's new order), *Yokusan undō to Konoe kō* (Prince Konoe and the movement to assist the throne), and *Dengeki saishō Tōjō Hideki* (Hideki Tōjō, the lightning prime minister). In a letter to Prime Minister Yoshida asking to be depurged, Oda insisted that "the three books were mostly made up of clippings from newspapers of the time, and I should really not be called the author." I was able to read the second of the three books, and it does incorporate quite a few of Konoe's talks and announcements, but overall it appears to be the writer's work. The book spares no hyperbole in its praise for Konoe's effort to organize the Japanese people into a "new order" in the name of "assistance to imperial rule," in the wake of signing the Tripartite Pact with Nazi Germany and Italy. The text boldly declares that "storms of incendiary upheaval—East and West, the world is now a live stage for heroes. Germany's Führer Hitler, Italy's Prime Minister Mussolini, and Japan's Prince Konoe, each a hero equal to today's world, in total sympathy with each other, bound together by their great plans, they march on one path toward the creation of a new world order." No wonder he could not avoid being purged.

Relatively few writers and scholars—268—were purged solely for their literary activity. Among them were the writers Yamaoka Sōhachi, Hino Ashihei, and Ozaki Shirō. The arguments they made in their appeals to be depurged provide a fascinating insight into their individual assessment of their war responsibility.[8] Let us see what Oda had to say:

> At that time, the reason that I could not help but go ahead with the stupidity of publishing these books was that I was in the depths of poverty with a family of four households and fourteen members to keep from starvation. Moreover, it was nothing but my last resort as an emergency mode of self-defense to escape the bonds of repeated arrest and detention by the greedy and cruel police with their illegal accusations. Besides, like all Japanese at the time, I was swept up by the persistent propaganda of the military and the government that said, "We must escape the destiny of having the two rich countries, the United States and England, take the lives of the eighty million people of the small, weak country Japan and annihilate us, etc., etc."

Many of those who were purged gave the excuse that they engaged in their literary activity in order to make a living, but this implied that the need to put bread on the table justified anything that was written. It goes without saying that a writer's responsibility should extend to examining the role that his publications play. Oda provided a detailed explanation for his claim that he wrote in "self-defense" in a separate letter. He argued that he had no choice but to convert and cooperate with national policy in order to escape the legal harassment he was subjected to because of his public activities. This is not grounds for depurging, however, because the purge directive targeted the contents of publications, not the circumstances that led to their production. Nor does his third point—that he was taken in by the propaganda of the military and government—relieve him of responsibility for actively fanning the flames of militarism through his own propaganda.

For example, Oda published a book during the war called *Seisen dōyōshū—Nippon banzai* (Nursery rhymes for the holy war: Japan banzai!), which was published by the Teikoku Kyōikukai, or the Imperial Education Association. Perhaps because it was a children's book, this book was not included in the justification for his purge order, but it begins with the following words:

> An unbroken line from the time of the gods,
> His Majesty the Emperor.
> Land of the rising sun Japan,
> Land of the gods that shines on the world.

It concludes as follows:

> Behold, behold, we'll smash America.
> Till we raise our flag over
> The enemy's capital Washington,
> No matter the hardship,
> We won't give up till victory is ours.

IF I HAD ONLY SEEN AMERICA

Of course once the war was over, no amount of remorse could undo being a tool of militarism to this extent. The petition bemoans this very fact. Oda goes on to lament that if he had only seen America once before the war, he would not have made this mistake:

Now we Japanese have come to understand how the logic of such propaganda maintained the power of the military and how it was based on shallow reasoning. However, no matter what the reason, I confess I feel grief beyond words over my lack of discretion and dignity. If I had traveled in the United States for even a month before the war and seen for myself a little of the humanitarian American character, I am sure I would not have published such stupid books no matter how much I and all the members of my family had been persecuted or even physically mutilated. I can't help thinking that, if it had only occurred to me at the time to plan a trip to America, even if it meant being poor or becoming a beggar, could I not have found a way to gather the funds necessary for a tour of America? It is crying over spilled milk, but even with a short visit of a month or two, could I not have had the capacity of understanding the character of your fellow citizens?

It is quite doubtful that a tour of the United States would have been the miracle drug to inoculate Oda from the ideological influence of militarism. However, the logic behind this letter is to lament the failure to travel to the States in the past as a way of glorifying the American victor as the embodiment of righteousness today. In sidling up to the new ruler, the writer

Photo 13.2   The facade of the Japan Instant Construction Co., Inc., in the Tameike district of downtown Tokyo was painted by Oda Toshiyo with a message of support for MacArthur's presidential candidacy in the spring of 1948. The message evolved over time, until it contained what amounted to a political platform of its own: "We ask for everlasting world peace. We will endeavor to protect world democracy. We will strive for elevation of world humanity. We will cooperate with the American people. We hope for new life through our efforts. We will strive to collect new and progressive cultures. God will protect those who always honor love and truth." Source: U.S. Army

Photo 13.3   Oda Toshiyo campaigns in support of MacArthur's presidential candidacy on the streets of Tokyo. The poster describes MacArthur as "the best-qualified person to protect democracy and mankind form [sic] the ruffian who disturb the peace of the world." This photograph appeared in Time *magazine, April 19, 1948.*
Source: *Bettman-Corbis/PPS*

of this letter found it necessary to engage in this kind of convoluted logic because he was begging MacArthur to release him from the chagrin of being purged. His appeal is almost pathetic. It continues:

Your Most Revered Excellency General MacArthur:

If the rule is that a person purged for publishing an undesirable book absolutely cannot be pardoned no matter what the reason, even if at present he may be burning with a desire to serve the welfare of mankind in the future, then I am prepared to consider it inevitable and humbly accept your measures.

But, but . . . I believe that Your Excellency as a deeply religious man and the American people of a pious Christian country will generously forgive this pitiful, foolish sinner who knew not how to behave, according to the teachings of Jesus Christ who preached [that one should forgive] "seventy times seven" [sins, Matthew 18:22] and prayed, "Forgive us our trespasses, as we forgive those who trespass against us."

Moreover, I know not of others, but I am firmly and deeply convinced that Your Excellency would not ignore the tears of a sorrowful man who repented and "left his net and followed him" [Matthew 4:20].

Your Excellency the General:

I ask you please to hear the convulsed, wailing plea of a poet, who weeps day and night for the honor of being able to offer my life and my work for righteousness and for the path of God under the same sun and sky as the holy general, Your Excellency, who in this world of chaos and uncertainty tirelessly seeks righteousness as though he thirsted and hungered for it. At a time of crisis for the peoples of this world, please allow me to work, even an insignificant amount, as a poor servant in your holy undertaking.

It seems that once a bird experiences the joy of warbling, it will try to sing regardless of the times. Of course, when the times change, the song changes. The new song will have to be a paean to a democracy that bears MacArthur's seal. During the war, this poet had sung, "Destroy America and Britain, the enemies of the world, said our great emperor. . . ." But he points out that the artists Miyamoto Saburō and Fujita Tsuguji also glorified the war with their paintings, but they avoided being purged. He argues that he should be released from the purge too and be allowed to sing the song of the new era. He concludes as follows:

The artist who did the ugly war painting of the meeting between generals Yamashita and Percival, and even the artist who portrayed the battle of Attu have been given special favor since they have not been purged. If you can also accept me, the poor poet Oda Toshiyo, under the warm umbrella of your benevolence, although I am forty-four years of age and my contribution may be paper thin, I promise to give my all for world humanism and for the advancement of democracy in Japan.

I beg of you again and again.

In closing, I pray for the health of Your Excellency and your wife.

Respectfully yours,
Oda Toshiyo

What kind of person was Oda Toshiyo? In 1948, when conservatives in the Republican Party tried to persuade MacArthur to run for president, the general made it clear he was interested. At that time, someone painted the side of a building in the center of Tokyo with a message in English, which read: "Pray For General MacArthur's Success In The Presidential Election," and in a downtown district, he stood on the street with a megaphone and delivered a speech in support of the general's candidacy. That person was Oda Toshiyo, identified as chairman of the Association for Promotion of Eternal World Peace. In the general election of January 1949, Oda ran for office as an independent candidate from the first district of Tokyo, but on January 14, just before the election, his purge from public office was announced and he was automatically disqualified.

A massive amount of material, constituting a "statement" and "evidence [of innocence]"—both of which were mimeographed—was submitted on May 7, 1949, along with Oda's petition to be depurged. I happened to obtain a copy thirty years later in a rare book sale. Naturally the petition must have been sent to MacArthur directly, but I have not been able to locate it at the MacArthur Memorial or among the documents of the Government Section of GHQ. The purge from public office was conducted by categories, and once a decision was made, it was extremely difficult for an individual to be depurged. It is likely that this letter, despite its flood of emotion, did not achieve its goal. However, it remains for us a marvelous window into the world of a writer fully entwined with his time.

14

FAREWELL

 There is an end to all things. As easily as the Japanese adapted to the abnormal state of being occupied, the honeymoon between the rulers and the ruled could not go on indefinitely. Even those who welcomed MacArthur as their savior in the misery of defeat and asked him, in all seriousness, "General, please remain in this country forever and ever," naturally began to feel some discomfort about these sentiments once the country proceeded down the road to recovery. Although there were many who grew accustomed to being occupied and came to accept it as a natural state of affairs, in time that harmony was disrupted, and discordant sounds began to be heard.

More than anything else, this resulted from the fundamentally unsustainable nature of a military occupation, the control of a country by a foreign army. Another factor was the spread of the Cold War into Asia via the Chinese revolution. At the beginning of 1949, four years into the occupation, as it became clear that the Chinese communists were moving to victory, the United States suddenly made a rightward turn in its occupation policy. The shift was expressed in the slogan "from reform to reconstruction," and it ushered in an economic retrenchment that led to the mass dismissal of workers. The creaking sounds of the aging occupation became louder.

Yet, as we have seen, throughout 1949 and even into 1950 letters expressing trust and respect for MacArthur continued to arrive at GHQ. The occupation policies may have shifted, but the Japanese people's support for MacArthur in general remained strong. That being said, the number of letters did not compare with the deluge that came immediately after the war, and some were openly hostile toward MacArthur.

For example, after MacArthur delivered his annual New Year's message on January 1, 1950, a fierce, biting response was received. MacArthur had described Japan as one of the few places on earth completely at peace and, with his customary rhetorical flourish, asserted that "the ideal of human freedom, vigorously taking root in Japanese hearts" meant that "the myth of an unbridgeable gulf between the ways of the East and the ways of the West has been thoroughly exploded." He also noted that it was the noble support of the American people that enabled Japan to take strides toward economic self-sufficiency.[1]

All of the fruits of the occupation that MacArthur rhapsodized were mocked at length in the letter. Naturally, it is not signed, but the entire letter was written in blood, and the intensity of the writer's feelings is tangible. Unfortunately, I have not been able to locate the original letter; only the following English summary, prepared by ATIS, remains in the Government Section files.[2]

GENERAL HEADQUARTERS
SUPREME COMMANDER FOR THE ALLIED POWERS
MILITARY INTELLIGENCE SECTION. GENERAL STAFF
ALLIED TRANSLATOR AND INTERPRETER SECTION

NOTE: Translation directed by Commander-in-Chief
Received ATIS: 10 Jan 50
DIGEST OF LETTER

TO: General MacARTHUR
FROM: (No name)
TOKYO To [Tokyo Metropolis]
DATE: (No date)

The writer sends a four-page letter written in blood criticizing Occupation policies.

Refuting the Supreme Commander's New Year's message lauding JAPAN as one of the few peaceful nations on earth, he asks if General MacARTHUR can understand the feelings of the Japanese people who had to greet a fifth New Year under the shackles of occupation. He asks if Gen-

eral MacARTHUR is aware of how many soldiers under his command are guilty of misdeeds. Stating that the Japanese cannot utter a single word of protest against confiscation of their houses, acts of violence upon their wives and daughters, a five-year sentence for displaying a single wall bulletin, et cetera, he inquires if this is a democracy and if the General thinks that the Japanese are enjoying freedom under such conditions.

He avers that the gulf between the East and West has been bridged only in that the conquerors have resorted to violence in order to have intimate relations with Japanese women. He accuses the General of being bent on destroying Japan's admirable traits of loyalty and filial piety, asserting that revision of the civil law has served only to increase crimes and to demoralize the public.

It is clear that the man is a rightist, and he is criticizing MacArthur's occupation from a nationalist standpoint. His vehement attack continues across a wide spectrum of charges, with a reckless rage. Economic reform amounts to inciting unnecessary competition among industrialists. American aid isn't enough to compensate for the violence perpetrated against Japanese women. And if MacArthur is so enamored of the Japanese constitution, why doesn't he tell Truman to use it as a guide in revising the American Constitution? He then sarcastically dismisses MacArthur's hope of making Japan "the Switzerland of the East" by asking whether there are any foreign military bases in Switzerland. The ATIS summary continues:

He denounces as equivocation the United States' contention that the American troops are stationed in JAPAN to prevent this country from falling into the hands of the Communist Party, and he asserts that the presence of these troops will contribute only to extending the Communist influence. No Japanese but street girls, he states, want American military forces to stay in JAPAN.

He states that it was fortunate for the UNITED STATES that the Japanese people's strong feeling about the atrocities wrought on HIROSHIMA and NAGASAKI have been superseded by their fury against Stalin's outrageous behavior.

Pointing out that American policy toward CHINA failed because of the notoriously bad conduct of her [American] troops which enraged Chinese

*youths, he warns that the General and his subordinates are about to repeat
the same blunder by staying longer than necessary in JAPAN. He states that
the General probably has never heard any Japanese speak unpleasantly or
maliciously of the UNITED STATES, just as the Japanese military commanders failed to detect the deep-rooted anti-Japanese sentiment among the
indigenous people of MANCHURIA and CHINA.*

*In concluding his vehement attack, he asserts that steps for the early con-
clusion of a peace treaty should be taken, with stipulations to cover the complete withdrawal of American troops from Japanese territories (with the possible exception of OKINAWA) and the entrusting of Japanese patriots who
once fought so bravely against the Americans with the defense of JAPAN.*

While recognizing that this English summary may differ from the
original Japanese, I nevertheless included it here because of the sentiment that fills the letter. This feeling flowed like a stream in the dark
depths of Japanese hearts under occupation, and it rarely showed itself
on the surface. This kind of intensely nationalistic argument is more
fundamental than the anti-American, pro-Soviet ideology of the left,
and it is also more mature (and nuanced, as demonstrated by the exception granted U.S. troops on Okinawa) than the raw "hate America"
emotions of the immediate postwar period. Thus it grabs the reader's attention. If MacArthur had read the letter, he might well have remarked,
"The occupation has gone on too long."

However, the Korean War started soon after this, and the nationalists' antioccupation sentiments faded into the background once again.
Instead, the image of the Americans fighting on the Korea Peninsula to
protect Japan from communist invasion captured the imagination of
many Japanese. Fan letters to MacArthur increased again; there was
even a middle school that sent "comfort packages" to U.N. soldiers at
the front. And this was when the notorious rightist, Kodama Yoshio, appealed to MacArthur to let Japanese forces join the war effort.

On the other hand, after the Korean War started, louder voices criticizing the occupation were heard from members of the Japan Communist Party and their sympathizers, who were facing increasing pressure
from MacArthur. The occupation's suppression of the Communist Party
had taken various forms since May of the previous year. A series of mys-
terious incidents involving the communist-controlled national railway

union took place during the summer of 1949 (including a runaway train that killed ten people and a cargo train derailment); although it was not conclusively proved that the union or the Communist Party were responsible, these incidents were used to the fullest to discredit the party. The Yoshida government even considered riding the tide and outlawing the Communist Party around that time. Just before the Korean War began, MacArthur purged from public office all twenty-four members of the party's central committee and seventeen top editors of *Akahata*, the party newspaper. The confrontation between the communists and the occupation forces had come to a head.

"GOOD-BYE, GENERAL MACARTHUR"

However, opponents of the occupation remained a small minority. The majority, although aware of the creaking sounds coming from the aging occupation, still aligned themselves with it and continued to respect the general, who was now fighting in Korea. Thus, in the confined universe of occupied Japan in which MacArthur served as the axis, it came as a total surprise to the Japanese for him to disappear suddenly one day in the spring of 1951, as a result of being dismissed from command by President Truman on the grounds of insubordination in his conduct of the war in Korea.

MacArthur's hasty departure rocked Japan, but there are few letters expressing these feelings. Those that exist are kept at the MacArthur Memorial, and oddly there are no letters from individuals written in Japanese. There were only five days between MacArthur's dismissal on April 11 and his departure on the morning of April 16, so certainly this is part of the reason for the small number of letters. (Not knowing his address, few people would have even considered sending a letter to the United States; and even if they had, MacArthur no longer had the services of GHQ translators.) Then too the shock may have been so severe that people could not think about writing letters. MacArthur represented that kind of towering presence to the Japanese. When the news of his dismissal was announced, some expressed their feelings by going to his quarters at the American embassy and kneeling on the ground in front of the outer gate.

The Japanese began to awaken to the fact that there was someone in this world more powerful than MacArthur. There had been little awareness that MacArthur's statements and actions as commander in the field had repeatedly infringed on the prerogatives and authority of the commander in chief, President Truman. Through the dismissal, many Japanese learned for the first time about the "supremacy of the civil over the military" so prominent in the U.S. Constitution. Nonetheless, when faced with the sudden departure of their Great Father—so called by the writer of "Tensei jingo" (Vox populi, vox dei), the popular column in the *Asahi shimbun*—even those who had earlier written letters to MacArthur without hesitation suddenly lost their ability to express themselves.

Among the small number of letters of farewell kept at the MacArthur Memorial, those written by individuals and not from the government or organizations are all in English. Maybe it is risky to try to fathom the feelings of the Japanese at that time from just a few letters, but there must have been countless people who shared the feelings expressed by the following letter:

4, Dobo-cho, Mita
Shiba, Minato-ku, Tokyo
April 14, 1951

Dear General Macarthur,

I am so sorry to hear that you suddenly leave our country. I miss you very much. I'm sure every one of us Japanese feel as if there is no light in our way; for we, Japanese, have walked with you every day, since you made the first step in Japan in 1945.

Now, I cannot express my immense gratitude for you. Thank you so much, dear General Macarthur!

Even if you leave Japan, we never forget your kind instructions. We will follow the way you clearly showed us during the past 5 years, and work for the eternal peace in the world.

Will you please pray for our country although you come back home.

May God bless thee and protect thy family forever and ever!

Yours sincerely,
Kazuko Horiki

To the Japanese, the figure of the departing general symbolized the span of five years and eight months since the war ended, a period of tumultuous change. One era had ended, but it was still uncertain who would lead the nation through the next period. Naturally, there was great sadness. While expressing the grief of parting, remorse, and confusion, the letter also conveys a determination to overcome these feelings and strive to lead the best life possible. The feeling that this was the only way to repay MacArthur for his kindness was shared by many Japanese at the time.

The following letter came from someone who was quite well-informed. It begins in a similar vein of regret over the departure but goes on to express hope for MacArthur's future.

Photo 14.1 *Japanese citizens lined the streets leading to Haneda airport to bid General MacArthur farewell on April 16, 1951. Newspapers put their numbers at over 200,000; the general himself would later set the figure at 2 million, many of whom, he said, wept openly as they waved good-bye.* Source: *U.S. Army*

Photo 14.2   "With deepest regret," old and young Japanese bid farewell to Douglas MacArthur. Source: U.S. Army

THE AMERICA-JAPAN CULTURAL SOCIETY
No. 17, 3-chome, Shintomicho, Chuoku
Tokyo, April 14, 1951.

General of the Army Douglas MacArthur,
The American Embassy, Tokyo.

Dear General MacArthur:
   Your sudden departure from Tokyo makes us very sad, and the entire Japanese people are weeping in their hearts.
   For the last six years, you have given your life and soul to save the Japanese nation and to upbuild a new democracy. By your noble character and lofty ideals, you have won the hearts of eighty-three millions of my people to yourself and to your country. For centuries to come our people will remember you as our true friend and benefactor, and the savior of our country.
   President Truman has committed the greatest blunder in the American history. Its effect on Japan and Eastern Asia will be very disastrous. He has

shaken the Japanese confidence in the United States, and helped to advance the Kremlin's interests. He has stabbed on the back the most gallant hero and farsighted statesman, and has crucified him on the cross. I know that the sense of justice of the American people as well as of the Japanese people will never tolerate such ingratitude and injustice. It is a pity that he became a catspaw of No. 10 Downing Street!

My dear General: While I feel so sad at your leaving, I have consolation when I realize that you have a larger mission at home. I know that millions of Americans are anxiously awaiting your return to perform a larger task to save your country and the whole world. Then, the Japanese people will have more confidence in the United States as a champion of liberty and freedom against the Communist aggressors.

Please accept a humble gift which my wife and myself wish to present to you and Mrs. MacArthur as token of our gratitude.

With highest regard, I am
Most respectfully yours,
[signed]
JIUJI C. KASAI, President
The America-Japan Cultural Society.

The writer of this letter had studied at Harvard University and was elected to the Diet before and after the war. He regularly offered advice to MacArthur and sent him fruits of the season. Although it is understandable that he would have wanted MacArthur to become president to erase the humiliation of his dismissal, the fact that he considered this even remotely possible reflects the limited vision of those who were considered knowledgeable about the United States at the time. Undoubtedly, his affection for MacArthur clouded his judgment.

This same affection was evident in a letter from Prime Minister Yoshida Shigeru. Yoshida had served as prime minister during almost two-thirds of MacArthur's tenure, including a critical period from May 1946 to May 1947 during which the new constitution was adopted. Following a succession of coalition governments, Yoshida returned to office in October 1948, consolidating the power of the conservative Democratic Liberal Party (later the Liberal Democratic Party), and he remained prime minister for the duration of the occupation and beyond, until December 1954. Yoshida and MacArthur carried on a voluminous correspondence during these years, mostly of an official nature.[3] A rare personal note was struck in the following letter, which was sent after MacArthur's departure was announced.[4]

April 14, 1951
General of the Army Douglas MacArthur,
American Embassy,
Tokyo.

My dear General,
   Words fail me to tell you how shocked and how grieved I am at your precipitous departure from our shores.
   In this personal note it would be superfluous of me to duplicate the resolutions and testimonials of appreciation and thanks which are being sent to you from both Houses of the Diet and many other quarters, and which constitute a spontaneous tribute of the nation to the monumental task you have accomplished as Supreme Commander for the Allied Powers in remoulding and revitalizing our country. All Japanese from the Emperor to the man on the street regret your going.
   Allow me to assure you that the memory of the intimate contact I have been privileged to enjoy during these past years will remain for me an inexhaustible source of pleasure and inspiration.
   I wish bon voyage to you, Mrs. MacArthur and Master Arthur. May God bless you all with health, happiness and prosperity wherever you may be.

Yours sincerely,
[signed]
Shigeru Yoshida

Tens of thousands of Japanese lined the streets leading to the airport on April 16 to witness the general's last moments on Japanese soil. Their sentiments were captured in posters, written in English, displayed among the crowds: "With deepest regret." "Good-bye Gen MacArthur. We still love you." A postcard sent to MacArthur on April 14 by special delivery captured the mood succinctly. It was neatly written with pen in English.

Dear General MacArthur,

Thank you for your great achievements in Japan and Asia. I will remem-
ber you forever. And I wish your good health.

Yours sincerely,
A Japanese.

Did the Japanese find a place for MacArthur in their memory forever? The Yoshida government passed a cabinet resolution designat-
ing MacArthur a "lifetime state guest," and a plan to build a General
MacArthur Memorial was initiated in Tokyo, with prominent figures
of society as its organizers. A campaign to raise funds to build a statue
commemorating his achievements was also begun. All of these efforts
were aborted when MacArthur, in testifying before the Senate on
May 5, described the Japanese as being "like a boy of twelve" in terms
of the cultural and political maturity of Japan's society and government.[5] The statement was seen in Japan as a stunning slap in the
face, an insult that made any further thought of commemorating the
general unimaginable.

If the Japanese at that time had truly believed in MacArthur as
their "Great Father," they might not have been disappointed at being
called twelve-year-olds. But I believe the statement made many realize the depth of their dependence on MacArthur, and this awareness
was embarrassing. There was also a measure of chagrin over having snuggled up to the occupation too readily. This is the reason
the Japanese tried their best to forget MacArthur after he left, which
is indeed what happened. The occupation itself came to an end
on April 28, 1952, a year after MacArthur departed, and the Japanese set themselves to the task of reclaiming the postwar recovery
as their own, albeit under the continuing aegis of their American
ally.

Today, most people in Japan still know MacArthur's name, and he
is still credited with benevolent, even wise, leadership during the occupation years, though the intense adulation of the man has passed
from the Japanese consciousness. But the actual meaning of remem-
bering MacArthur lies in carefully evaluating the reforms he carried
out during the occupation and placing him within the context of

history. As the Canadian scholar E. H. Norman maintained, history is to a nation what memory is to an individual. To understand MacArthur's place in Japan's collective memory, it is essential to hear the voices of the people of that time, recorded in the vast correspondence addressed to the general during the years he ruled Japan.

NOTES

INTRODUCTION

1. Except where noted otherwise, all letters contained in this volume were originally in Japanese. This letter is in the Letters from the Japanese file, in the G-II (Military Intelligence Section) files of the GHQ/SCAP documents (Record Group 331) in the National Archives II. The original Japanese letter is reproduced in Sodei Rinjirō, *Makkāsā no nisen-nichi* (Tokyo: Chūō Kōronsha, 1974), 113–14.

2. Shūkan Shinchō Editorial Department, ed., *Makkāsā no Nihon* (Tokyo: Shinchōsha, 1970), 2:54.

3. Douglas MacArthur, *Reminiscences* (New York: McGraw-Hill, 1964), 281–82.

4. Personal interview.

5. The handwritten report is stored at the MacArthur Memorial, Bureau of Archives. See also GHQ, Far East Command, General Staff, Military Intelligence Section, "ATIS: Letters to SCAP" (January 22, 1950), which includes an analysis of the content of letters received in December 1949, in the MacArthur Memorial archives.

6. Conversations with University of Kansas Professor Emeritus Grant K. Goodman, a former lieutenant in the ATIS.

7. Record Group 10, Boxes 172–74.

8. Sodei Rinjirō, *Makkāsā no nisen-nichi* (Tokyo: Chūō Kōronsha, 1974).

9. Sodei Rinjirō, *Haikei Makkāsā gensui-sama: Senryōka no Nihonjin no tegami* (Tokyo: Ōtsuki Shoten, 1985).

CHAPTER 1

1. This letter is in the Private Correspondence file in the MacArthur Memorial archives.

2. U.S. Congress, Senate, Committee on Armed Services and the Committee on Foreign Relations, *Hearings to Conduct an Inquiry into the Military Situation in the Far East*

and the Facts Surrounding the Relief of General of the Army Douglas MacArthur from His Assignments in that Area, 82d Cong., 1st sess., 1951, pt. 1, 310.

3. This letter is in the Letters from the Japanese file, in the G-II files of the GHQ/SCAP documents in the National Archives II.

4. This letter is in the G-II files in the National Archives II.

CHAPTER 2

1. This letter is in the Letters from the Japanese file in the MacArthur Memorial archives. The original is in English, reproduced here verbatim.

2. John Gunther, *The Riddle of MacArthur* (New York: Harper & Row, 1950), 92.

3. Fuse Kanji, *Aru bengoshi no shōgai—Fuse Tatsuji* (Tokyo: Iwanami Shinsho, 1963).

4. Fuse, 91.

5. Fuse, 94.

6. Fuse, 93.

7. Fuse, 92.

8. Fuse, 92.

9. Kida Minoru, *Jinsei repōto* (Tokyo: Kumoi Shoten, 1957), 139.

10. Fuse, 94.

11. Gunther, *Riddle of MacArthur*, 8.

12. This letter is in the Letters from the Japanese file in the MacArthur Memorial archives. The original is in English, reproduced here verbatim.

13. Takahashi Hiroshi and Suzuki Kunihiko, *Tennōke no hisshitachi* (Tokyo: Gendaishi Shuppankai, 1981), 191.

14. This letter is in the Letters from the Japanese file in the MacArthur Memorial archives.

CHAPTER 3

1. This letter is in the MacArthur Memorial archives. The original is in English, re-produced here verbatim.

2. Rapes and assaults on Japanese women were by no means uncommon, especially early in the occupation, but these incidents were not reported in the Japanese press.

3. *Nippon Times*, October 17, 1945.

4. Letters of this sort have been published elsewhere (e.g., in Shūkan Shinchō Editorial Department, eds., *Makkāsā no Nihon*, 2 vols. [Tokyo: Shinchōsha, 1970]), but here I am limiting my selection to what I read at the National Archives II. The rest of the letters in this chapter were found in the Letters from the Japanese file, in the G-II files of the GHQ/SCAP documents.

5. The economic sanctions imposed on Japan in Asia by the American, British, Chinese, and Dutch governments in the years preceding the outbreak of the war.

6. Robert B. Textor, *Failure in Japan* (New York: John Day, 1951), 340.

CHAPTER 4

1. U.S. Department of State, *Foreign Relations of the United States, 1946*, 8:395–97.
2. *Tokyo shimbun*, October 31, 1983, report on an essay, "Saving Japan's Imperial Institution" by Ray A. Moore.
3. Takeda Kiyoko, *Tennō-sei no sōkoku* (Tokyo: Iwanami Shoten, 1978).
4. Yamauchi Tōru, *Jūshintachi no Sugamo* (Tokyo: Korube Shuppansha, 1984).
5. Kume Masao, "Nihon Beishūron—Nikaidō hōdan (4)," *Sekai shunjū*, February 1950.
6. Takeuchi Yoshimi, "Kenryoku to geijutsu," in *Gendai Nihon bungaku taikei* (Tokyo: Chikuma Shobō, 1971), 78: 343.

CHAPTER 5

1. I have chosen to use only initials here because criticism of the emperor and the emperor system remains controversial, and critics sometimes become targets of harassment by extreme nationalists.

CHAPTER 6

1. The letter is in the MacArthur Memorial archives. It was not part of the Letters from the Japanese file but buried within General Correspondence. It is reproduced here verbatim.
2. This letter is in the G-II files at the National Archives II.
3. This letter is in the MacArthur Memorial archives.
4. This letter is in the MacArthur Memorial archives.

CHAPTER 7

1. This letter and the others in this chapter are in the archives at the MacArthur Memorial.
2. See *Makkāsā: Kiroku—Sengo Nihon no genten*, ed. Sodei Rinjirō and Fukushima Jūrō (Tokyo: Nippon Hōsō Shuppan Kyōkai, 1982), 201.

CHAPTER 8

1. This letter, along with most of those in this chapter, is archived at the MacArthur Memorial.

2. Color photos of both sides of the fan are included in *Senryōka no jidai,* ed. Sodei Rinjirō, vol. 9 of *Shōwa Nihonshi* (Tokyo: Akatsuki Kyōiku Tosho, 1977), 8–9.

3. The follow-up to Yoshimoto's letters is also archived at the MacArthur Memorial.

CHAPTER 9

1. This letter is in the G-II, GHQ/SCAP files at the National Archives II.

2. William J. Sebald, *With MacArthur in Japan* (New York: Norton, 1965), 113.

3. *Asahi shimbun,* October 22, 1949.

4. This letter is in the National Diet Library microfilms of Government Section files at the National Archives II.

5. See his note in *Nihon gaikōshi jiten* (Tokyo: Ministry of Foreign Affairs, 1979), 12.

6. The following letters are in the National Diet Library microfilms of the CI&E files, unless otherwise noted.

7. This letter is in the G-II files at the National Archives II.

8. This letter is in the MacArthur Memorial archives.

9. This letter is in the National Diet Library microfilms of Government Section files at the National Archives II.

10. This letter is in the Letters from the Japanese file in the MacArthur Memorial archives.

11. A letter from Hatoyama to MacArthur, requesting his depurging, appears in Chapter 12.

12. This letter is in the G-II Letters from the Japanese file at the National Archives II.

CHAPTER 10

1. The letters included in this chapter are in the G-II files at the National Archives II.

2. See Katayori Mitsugu, "Katō Etsurō ron," in *Katō Etsurō manga shō* (Tokyo: private edition, 1960).

CHAPTER 11

1. Occupation of Japan Project, Oral History Collection, Columbia University, New York. Used with permission of Faubion Bowers.

2. Personal interview.

3. Unless otherwise noted, the letters quoted in this chapter are in the MacArthur Memorial archives.

4. Personal interview.

CHAPTER 12

1. This letter is in the MacArthur Memorial archives.
2. This letter is in the National Diet Library microfilms of Government Section files in the National Archives II.
3. This letter is in the Economic and Scientific Section files in the National Archives II.
4. This letter is in the MacArthur Memorial archives.
5. For details, see the entry for Kimura Ki in "Makkāsā hyakka jiten" in *Makkāsā: Kiroku—Sengo Nihon no genten,* ed. Sodei Rinjirō and Fukushima Jūrō (Tokyo: Nippon Hōsō Shuppan Kyōkai, 1982), 162–63.
6. See Ōya Sōichi, *Ichi oku shūjin* (Tokyo: Kaname Shobo, 1952).
7. Suehiro was a professor of labor law at Tokyo University, Tatsuno was a professor of French literature also at Tokyo University, and Yamakawa was a leading theoretician in the Japan Socialist Party. For more details, see Miyamori Masao, *Hitotsu no shuppan bunkakai shiwa—Haisen chokugo no jidai* (Tokyo: Chūō University Press, 1970).
8. This letter is in the Government Section files in the National Archives II.
9. This letter is in the G-II files in the National Archives II.
10. This letter is in the G-II files in the National Archives II.
11. This letter is in the CI&E Section files in the National Archives II.
12. This letter is in the MacArthur Memorial archives.
13. This letter is in the CI&E Section files in the National Archives II.
14. This letter is in the MacArthur Memorial archives.

CHAPTER 13

1. This letter is in the MacArthur Memorial archives.
2. See *Hitō sen to sono sensō saiban: Sangeki no kiroku,* ed. Saka Kuniyasu (Tokyo: Tōchō-sha, 1967).
3. This letter is in the G-II files in the National Archives II.
4. Interview with Edward J. Boone Jr., former archivist at the MacArthur Memorial.
5. This letter is in the MacArthur Memorial archives. Only the initials of the person's name have been used.
6. This letter is in the Economic and Scientific Section files in the National Archives II.
7. This letter is in the G-II files in the National Archives II.
8. Regarding these three writers, see Tsurumi Shunsuke, "Tsuihō sareta hitobito no iibun," *Shisō no kagaku,* August 1966.

CHAPTER 14

1. "General MacArthur's New Year Message," *Nippon Times,* January 1, 1950, 1.

2. This letter is in the microfilm records in the National Diet Library.

3. The entire Yoshida–MacArthur correspondence, as well as letters exchanged by other occupation-era prime ministers and MacArthur, has been compiled in English and Japanese translation in *Yoshida Shigeru–Makkāsā ōfuku shokanshū (1945–1951)* (Correspondence between General MacArthur, Prime Minister Yoshida, and Other High Japanese Officials [1945–1951]), trans. and ed. Sodei Rinjirō (Tokyo: Hōsei Daigaku Shuppankyoku, 2000).

4. *Yoshida Shigeru–Makkāsā ōfuku shokanshū*, pt. 3, 221.

5. U. S. Congress, Senate, Committee on Armed Services and the Committee on Foreign Relations, *Hearings to Conduct an Inquiry into the Military Situation in the Far East and the Facts Surrounding the Relief of General of the Army Douglas MacArthur from His Assignments in that Area*, 82d Cong., 1st sess., 1951, pt. 1, 312.

ABOUT THE AUTHOR

Sodei Rinjirō is professor emeritus at Hōsei University in Tokyo. Born in 1932 in rural Miyagi Prefecture in northern Japan, he holds master's degrees in political science from Waseda University in Tokyo and from UCLA, where he studied for six years in the early 1960s. After returning to Japan he worked as a freelance writer and lecturer in American politics. His writing came to focus on the American occupation of Japan, culminating in 1974 in his major work, a biography of MacArthur, which won two national book awards and brought him a tenured professorship at Hōsei, one of Japan's major universities. Sodei is considered Japan's leading scholar of MacArthur, and he has published several additional studies of MacArthur and the occupation. He retired from Hōsei in 1999 and lives in Tokyo with his wife, Takako.

Asian Voices
Series Editor: Mark Selden

Tales of Tibet: Sky Burials, Prayer Wheels, and Wind Horses
    edited and translated by Herbert Batt, foreword by Tsering Shakya
Comfort Woman: A Filipina's Story of Prostitution and Slavery under the Japanese Military
    by Maria Rosa Henson, introduction by Yuki Tanaka
Growing up Untouchable in India: A Dalit Autobiography
    by Vasant Moon, translated by Gail Omvedt, introduction by Eleanor Zelliot
Japan's Past, Japan's Future: One Historian's Odyssey
    by Ienaga Saburō, translated and introduced by Richard H. Minear
Unbroken Spirits: Nineteen Years in South Korea's Gulag
    by Suh Sung, translated by Jean Inglis, foreword by James Palais
Bitter Flowers, Sweet Flowers: East Timor, Indonesia, and the World Community
    edited by Richard Tanter, Mark Selden, and Stephen R. Shalom
Voicing Concerns: Contemporary Chinese Critical Inquiry
    edited by Gloria Davies, conclusion by Geremie Barmé

Forthcoming Titles
Hong Kong Diary: Years of Transition
    by Josephine M. T. Khu
Responsibility, Reciprocity, and Resistance: Moral Politics in a Chinese Village
    by Hok Bun Ku
Rowing the Eternal Sea: The Life of a Minamata Fisherman
    by Keibo Oiwa, narrated by Masato Ogata, translated by Karen Colligan-Taylor
Red Is Not the Only Color: A Collection of Contemporary Chinese Fiction on Love and Sex between Women
    edited by Patricia Sieber